The Defense Procurement Mess

THE DEFENSE PROCUREMENT MESS

WILLIAM H. GREGORY

A Twentieth Century Fund Essay

Lexington Books

D.C. Heath and Company • Lexington, Massachusetts • Toronto

The Twentieth Century Fund is a research foundation undertaking timely analyses of economic, political, and social issues. Not-for-profit and non-partisan, the Fund was founded in 1919 and endowed by Edward A. Filene.

BOARD OF TRUSTEES OF THE TWENTIETH CENTURY FUND

Morris B. Abram
H. Brandt Ayers
Peter A. A. Berle
José A. Cabranes
Joseph A. Califano, Jr.
Alexander Morgan Capron
Edward E. David, Jr.
Brewster C. Denny, *Chairman*
Charles V. Hamilton
August Heckscher, Emeritus
Matina S. Horner
James A. Leach

Georges-Henri Martin, Emeritus
Lawrence K. Miller, Emeritus
P. Michael Pitfield
Don K. Price, Emeritus
Richard Ravitch
Arthur M. Schlesinger, Jr., Emeritus
Albert Shanker
Harvey I. Sloane, M.D.
Theodore C. Sorensen
James Tobin, Emeritus
David B. Truman, Emeritus
Shirley Williams

Marcia Bystryn, *Acting Director*

Library of Congress Cataloging-in-Publication Data

Gregory, William H.
　The defense procurement mess / William H. Gregory.
　p.　　cm.
　"A Twentieth century fund essay."
　Bibliography: p.
　Includes index.
　ISBN 0-669-20807-8 (alk. paper)
　1. United States--Armed Forces--Procurement. I. Title.
UC263.G74 1989
355.6'212'0973--dc19　　　　　　　　　　　　　　88-30400

Copyright © 1989 by The Twentieth Century Fund

All rights reserved. No part of this publication may be reproduced or transmitted in any form or by any means, electronic or mechanical, including photocopy, recording, or any information storage or retrieval system, without permission in writing from the publisher.

Published simultaneously in Canada
Printed in the United States of America
International Standard Book Number: 0-669-20807-8
Library of Congress Catalog Card Number: 88-30400

The paper used in this publication meets the minimum requirements of American National Standard for Information Sciences—Permanence of Paper for Printed Library Materials, ANSI Z39.48-1984.

∞

89 90 91 92　8 7 6 5 4 3 2 1

To a battered cadre of skilled military and civilian program managers and a vanishing nucleus of acquisition specialists deep in the corridors of the Pentagon, at bases in the field, or in factories. Their shared experience has made this book possible and their perseverance in the face of adversity over the last three decades kept the military buying system functioning.

Table of Contents

Foreword
by Marcia Bystryn ix

Preface xi

Acknowledgments xv

1. The Roots of the Problem   1
2. Requirements: Where the Process Begins   19
3. Doling Out the Money   33
4. Congress Stirs the Pot   49
5. Contracts and Specifications: The Paper Mill   65
6. Provisioning: A Fount of Horror Stories   87
7. Making the Pentagon More Businesslike   105
8. Uncertainty: Technical and Financial   129
9. Evading the System   155
10. Fraud Revisited: Criminalization in Acquisition   171
11. Where Do We Go from Here?   191

Selected Bibliography 211

Index 213

About the Author 221

Foreword

Marcia Bystryn, Acting Director
The Twentieth Century Fund

DEFENSE contractors have always borne an onus. The reputation of the sutlers who supplied goods—often of poor quality—to troops fighting in the Mexican War and Civil War could be described, at best, as unsavory. And the "merchants of death" of World War I were succeeded by the "profiteers" of World War II. Since then, a series of procurement scandals have rocked the Defense Department, the most recent resulting in Congressional charges of "waste, fraud, and abuse" in the nation's weapons-acquisition system that will be investigated in the early months of 1989.

Certainly the system needs improvement, and Congress periodically obliges by creating regulations designed to constrain the operations of the Pentagon and its suppliers. But have these reforms improved America's weapons-acquisition system? William H. Gregory, who was editor-in-chief of *Aviation Week and Space Technology* for almost three decades, argues persuasively in the following pages that they have not. In fact it is overmanagement—by both the Pentagon and Congress—and the consequent lengthening of the weapons-development cycle that constitute the real problem.

Gregory believes that the Defense Department and Congress are simply too far from the scene—too often lacking either the engineering or industrial management talent necessary for the kind of detailed decisions they are making. More importantly though, the overmanagement they have mandated deflects the acquisition system from its basic objective. And that objective is getting equipment to American forces in the field as quickly and as cheaply as possible—equipment that works and whose technology is superior to a potential enemy's.

Clearly Gregory is swimming against the tide. For much of the public—horrified by $1,000 Allen wrenchs and $600 ashtrays—the answer is more regulation and oversight. That is the conventional wisdom, but all too often the conventional wisdom is simply conventional, not wisdom. Thus, the Fund commissioned Gregory to write this book, which we believe furthers our understanding of this complex yet critical issue. We are grateful to him for it.

Preface

AMERICA'S weapons-acquisition system is in deep trouble. The problem is all the worse because its ills have been misunderstood, if not deliberately distorted. Those who understand the system and can best suggest how to deal with its problems are too far down in the ranks to be heard or are drowned out by the noise of scandal, horror story, and (especially) misdirected reform that is intensifying the trouble.

Scandals are distracting attention from deeper-seated ills. The worst of these are overmanagement, by both Pentagon and Congress, and the consequent lengthening of the weapons-development cycle. Excess paperwork and interminable delays in getting hardware to the field are costing the taxpayer billions. The scandals have centered on nickel-and-dime situations by comparison. Often, at root, scandals are simply reasonable arguments over who owes what to whom under the ambiguous terms of today's copious regulations and complex contracts, or they concern judgment calls as to how much infallibility should be expected of engineers and manufacturers in producing defense equipment.

This is not to gloss over technical fumbling or sloppy accounting by the defense industry or government. But, by and large, neither military managers nor defense contractors are crooks. Of course, neither are they Boy Scouts. Contractors will do what they think they must to win contracts. If that extends to hiring a consultant to poach documents or intelligence from the government, that's no surprise. If that extends to overselling the merits of a technical approach or kidding legislators on costs, that is no surprise either.

Such roughhousing does not arise in a vacuum. Defense contracting was a here today–gone tomorrow business, or a sideline, until after World War II. As a by-product of the cold war and of attempts to reform the contracting system, defense contractors grew into giant companies with giant private investment. Their armies of workers became an economic constituency and an income stream for communities. Their fortunes made or broke political careers. Then, repeated reform mandated more and more competition for lifeblood contracts. Desperation for new business drove contractor operations, and just one manifestation was the way companies threw money around Washington to court politicians and influence the awarding of contracts.

Reform of the weapons-acquisition system has produced precious little by way of improvement. Rather, incessant finger pointing, second guessing, scandal brandishing, regulation writing, and general viewing with alarm have produced an atmosphere of distrust—hardly conducive to getting the job done. The patriotism that once distinguished the defense business from all others has been submerged. Now it is a matter of government managers, smarting under congressional jibes, and contractors, sorely wounded by their tarring for malfunctions of the acquisition system itself, playing a game of who can extract the last penny from the other. While contractors are accused of overcharging, the government is by no means immune from interpreting contracts to its own advantage—and using the threat of prosecution to win out in negotiations.

Acquisition's troubles are not a product of the Reagan administration alone, although the caliber of some of its Pentagon appointees aggravated existing strains. Nor did acquisition's problems stem solely from Jimmy Carter's tenure, or Gerald Ford's or Richard Nixon's. They are a truly bipartisan effort evolving over the four decades since World War II. Hence there are no quick fixes.

Regulation has been the solution of choice in the past. Good regulation helps good managers, but weapons-acquisition regulation has been pursuing an impossible dream: legislating perfection. Driven essentially by Congress, regulation and reform in the Pentagon have pushed paperwork and procedure to prevent every possible mistake. But this has not worked. It could not. No regulation can create good management or top-notch people. No regulation exists that someone can't get around if motives are base enough or desperation powerful enough. With $150 billion or more sluicing out of the Pentagon every year for hardware, software, technical advice, and study, there obviously will be those whose greed for a share crosses ethical boundaries.

Inflamed by the prospect of covetousness, Congress and the Pentagon have called for more auditors and more audits. Audits are essential to any business, but they have become a cult in government. Audits, horror stories, prosecutions—sometimes merited, sometimes not—have shifted the focus of acquisition from research and manufacture to police work.

While no politician or civil servant wants to be seen as loose with the dollar, the unfortunate consequence is that the original objective of weapons acquisition is becoming lost in scandal noise. That objective is to get equipment to American forces in the field as quickly and as cheaply as possible—equipment that works and whose technology is superior to a potential enemy's. Disasters can come in any of those categories, but the most worrisome has been in the "quickly" department. Overmanagement has grossly stretched out the time necessary to develop weapons and has, in the process, driven up their costs.

Management failures do indeed occur in forging this country's military weapons. After all, the term SNAFU entered the language from the services after World War II. But the bigger disaster has been a failure of management policy. Overmanagement, over-regulation, over-oversight, all have crowded out the small, effective project-management teams that could get the job done fast and at reasonable cost. Instead, cumbersome acquisition processes effectively mask a program's going awry until the disaster is truly a stupendous one.

What follows is a deeper look at a process with real problems that are insidiously eating away at the defense-acquisition system's innards while politicians and reformers tilt away at scandals—real or otherwise—whose significance is not what appears on the surface. Public confidence in the acquisition system has plummeted as a result and the dangers to national security are multifarious. Citizens will not willingly continue to support a wasteful defense effort. Worse, the nation's military research and development base may be overmanaged and overreformed into impotence, so that weaponry's technical edge cannot be maintained even if the taxpayers are willing to shell out for it.

Acknowledgments

I would like to express my appreciation to the Twentieth Century Fund for supporting the research and writing of this book. It was an opportunity to pull together my thinking on and to further explore a subject that has, over the past thirty years, been the focus of my work. I would especially like to thank Ron Chernow and Roger Kimball, program officers at the Fund, who guided me through the research phase, and Pamela Gilfond, senior editor at the Fund, whose enthusiasm and craftsmanship improved the manuscript immeasurably.

1

The Roots of the Problem

How the American military buys its equipment is the subject of public derision. In the minds of much of the citizenry, the Pentagon procurement system is scandalous and the defense industry is manned by fast-buck artists, incompetents, or deranged Dr. Stranageloves who, when they lack weapons of mass destruction to tinker with, design $600 hammers or $5,000 coffeepots. The perception of the average taxpayer is that his military hardware money is being tossed around by profligate generals or admirals seduced by greedy, unconscionable contractors; instead of more bang for the buck, military procurement goes either for shoddy equipment or high-tech extravagances that don't work in the field.

Naturally, the perception of the military and the contractors is different. Both believe their service to their country has been traduced by the press and by some in Congress. To the generals and the admirals, and to the contractors, the media are acting irresponsibly if not disloyally with their refrain of waste, fraud, and abuse. Both the military and the defense industry complain that Congress itself has caused some of the situations it has pilloried in hearings and press handouts. Legislation—a vast oversupply of legislation in the military's view—has complicated regulations that govern military procurement and introduced further contradictions or vagueness.

Even more resentment stems from what the defense procurement apparatus calls congressional micromanagement. What this means is that Congress, rather than sticking to its roles of policy review and guarding the gates of the Treasury, has immersed itself in the details of weapons selection and program management. Further, complaints have been voiced that congressional votes on weapons spending too often come down to logrolling over how much money and how many jobs go to whose district, rather than to the merits of programs.

Nor is there harmony in the military-industrial complex. In some instances, top-level policymakers in the Pentagon and working-level managers in the field are convinced they have been let down badly by contractors who quote ridiculous prices in catalogues or who take advantage of the government in sales of spare parts. As a consequence, rightly or wrongly, there have been efforts to nail companies to the wall. For its part, industry mutters that even the purportedly friendly-to-business Reagan administration has made it the scapegoat for the failings of the government's own procurement system or its managers.

Truth to greater or lesser degree lies in all of these perceptions. But posturing over waste, fraud, and abuse has made these evils out to be more substantive than they are. Jacques Gansler, a former Defense Department official later with the Analytic Sciences Corporation, put it this way at a Senate subcommittee hearing: "We're arguing about nickels and dimes while the billions go marching quietly out the door."

What he was getting at was the denouement of one of the classic policy fiascoes of the twentieth century. The nation's system for buying hundreds of billions of dollars worth of military equipment is in deep trouble, but not because of waste, fraud, and abuse. What has happened is that, to guard against waste, fraud, and abuse, the government has spent millions over the past two decades to root out relative pennies. While the government, as custodian of the public purse, cannot ignore blatant misuse of funds, the harsh reality is that it would be cheaper to pay greater attention to efficiency in defense acquisition than to crime.

Thus, ironically, one of the basic causes of the acquisition system's illness is the prescriptions of a regiment of doctors who set out to cure what was merely a nasty cold. Only the experience of a relative handful of veteran military and civil servants, along with a tested industrial cadre, has been able to keep it functioning as well as it does. They are fighting an overwhelming burden of paperwork, bureaucratic layers, and second-guessing, and their ranks are diminishing through retirement or disenchantment. In this mire of paperwork and regulation, in the rabbit warren of the Pentagon and the hearing rooms of Congress, the program manager has been submerged and the time it takes to develop and field new hardware has stretched out grotesquely.

Eclipsed program managers are not the root cause of the acquisition mess, but rather a symptom and symbol of the fact that the government does not trust its own people or those in industry to carry out the job. The mischief that this lack of confidence has bred is awesome. Military program managers, who ought to have working responsibility, are in one niche; contracting officers, usually civilians who monitor compliance, are in another. Both are second-guessed by auditors. Higher ranking military and civilians in various commands and in the Pentagon, sensitive to public outrage, have steadily encroached on the daily management of programs—usually to the detriment of the programs. Congress has moved in on the Pentagon, its staffers making program decisions and its body politic writing more legislation that, while aimed at fixing the system, more often adds encumbrances. Industry, at the tail of this comet, gets a mixed policy message.

Most of the public indignation over fumbling in acquisition has put the blame on incompetence in the military and venality on the part of contractors. In a massive apparatus like military buying there is both. Yet such easy blame misses other basic and intractable causes.

Generations of overmanagement by higher and higher levels of government—that is, micromanagement—is a primary cause of the defense procurement mess. Another basic cause is overregulation and overspecification (often in response to past problems), which have created massive paperwork requirements in military contracting, costing the taxpayer from 25 percent to more than half of the price of producing weapons themselves.

In addition, in terms of funding, the Pentagon and Congress swing from ignoring entrenched but irrelevant hardware to vacillating on equipment of critical importance. One man's priority is always another man's waste, but Congress and the Pentagon cannot seem to get together on which is which. Unstable funding itself wastes money, as long-range military budget planning becomes a fiction.

Adversarial relationships further poison the process. Auditors from one defense agency are auditing. Program managers from another command are managing. All through the layers of the

Pentagon, people are supervising. Do they coordinate with each other? Contractors, who are at the end of the chain, doubt it. At a higher, more vital level, the Pentagon and Congress, which once understood each other in the nation's interest, are now hostile camps. In their jousting, acquisition efficiency suffers.

Overstaffing, which stifles effective program management, contributes to the problem. A commercial airline, for example, might assign a couple of people to buy a new airplane, providing them support from their finance and engineering departments. The government, in contrast, assigns multiple committees with dozens or hundreds of people to accomplish the same thing. To some extent it has to, just to comply with regulations. These regulations have turned defense contractors into de facto government agencies. Attention to paperwork procedures and fine print has tended to supersede concern over the technical and performance objectives of weapons under development. Form is supplanting substance.

Complicating the problem is that government policymakers get caught up in shibboleths of reform: commonality, prototyping, competition, clever but complex contracting methods. All have their points, but none is a cure to the ailments of military buying, and all, in effect, ignore the fact that people, not methodologies, manage programs.

In addition, as the terms of contracts have become exceedingly complex, misunderstandings have lead to cries of fraud—whether or not it exists. Government managers accuse contractors of taking advantage of hairsplitting terminology to weasel out of compliance or to demand another contract to finish what the government thought was required in the first one. Contractors complain that one arm of the government interprets contracts one way, another in a different way. Much of what is called fraud and collusion is really haggling over what the contract says. Add to this the fact that contractors, the military, or both mesmerize themselves with overly optimistic cost estimates for developing weapons. Then comes the notorious overrun. Following the overrun comes political outrage and, lately, criminal investigation. The whistle-blower and the grand jury have replaced teamwork in government-contractor relations.

The McNamara Revolution

The toils began to wind around the acquisition system thirty years ago when President Dwight D. Eisenhower centralized military authority in the relatively new Department of Defense—in hindsight a dubious blessing. Then, in the Kennedy administration, Robert Strange McNamara brought to the Pentagon a business school management mentality, an array of bright ideas, and a group of eager whiz kids to fix the problem-filled procurement system. Since then, a succession of soothsayers has tried to fix the fixes. After all this tinkering, a system that once designed an aircraft, missile, ship, or tank and got it into production in three to five years now takes ten to fifteen years—or more—to do the same thing. As an air force general, Gerald L. Prather, put it, "The Russians can steal our technology faster than we can get it into the field."

In theory, McNamara's premise was right. That was to try to get the disciplines of the commercial marketplace into defense buying. But the theory went awry in practice. As might be expected in government, paperwork, regulations, and review are the means to change. The result was a slowdown in decisionmaking—the antithesis of how successful private business operates. Further, when the numbers in McNamara's promises began to go wrong, Congress lost confidence in him. The loss of confidence then extended to the whole military apparatus, and it has persisted. Understandably, as a result, Congress has tried to move deeper into program management, complicating the decision-making process and further retarding its pace.

In addition, some of the bright ideas that McNamara's systems analysts brought forth on military equipment design turned sour. One, in particular—the TFX all-purpose fighter and bomber for the air force and the navy—degenerated into a political carnival in Congress and was the genesis of public suspicion about how the Pentagon conceives and buys sophisticated hardware.

Another reason McNamara's theory did not work in practice is that it did not allow for the particular motivation and workings of the bureaucracy. While bloated bureaucrats are figures of fun in the press, the bureaucracy is not stupid or necessarily immobile. If it is attacked by a political appointee or by Congress, it will protect itself the most effective way it can. If that is by inertia, inertia it will be. If it is by adding procedures or regulations, paperwork it will be. If it wants to bury new ideas or new directives, it can do that, too. Although collectively the bureaucracy does not have either the incentive of making lots of money or the "work-or-get-fired" code of the commercial world, it does march to its own selective tune.

One of the most lethal effects of the McNamara revolution was that it debased the function of the program manager. The program manager, civilian or military, was once just that. He ran the project, made the decisions, sold them to a limited hierarchy, and rose or fell with the results. Now the program manager spends the bulk of his time marketing and defending his program in committee and review meetings; the management of the program is diffused into nooks and crannies in the Pentagon and into staff offices in Congress.

D. Brainerd Holmes, former president of Raytheon Co., described how program management used to be. "I was a young guy in my thirties with RCA," he said, running the first billion-dollar electronics development—the design and construction of the Ballistic Missile Early Warning System (BMEWS). "That contract was awarded in late 1957," he told me, "when we were worried about the missile gap, about whether our B-52 bombers could get off the ground, whether Russian missiles would kill our heavy aircraft before they could take off." The solution was to build an early-warning radar antenna the size of a football field on the permafrost of Greenland, followed by another in Alaska. The first had to be built in a hurry because of the presumed Soviet threat, during the Arctic night, in 150 knot winds with temperatures down to minus 40 Fahrenheit. Holmes dealt with an equally young colonel in the Pentagon. They made their decisions and got them signed off by an undersecretary in the Defense Department, who pretty much ran a one-man shop with part-time support from a distinguished academician who served as deputy.

In contrast, today the office of that undersecretary in the Defense Department has become the well-populated staff of the Director of Defense Research and Engineering, which split like an amoeba into new offices, new directors, and larger staffs—mushrooming into an office with branches, principal deputies, deputies to deputies, and aides of other kinds.

When the early-warning radar project was under way, there were none of the formal program reviews at higher and higher levels in the Washington bureaucracy that exist today. Holmes made decisions with his counterpart. They had direct contact with three or four senior air force and defense officials—who got them money and told them to go to it. The result: the project was completed in thirty months and some unused money was turned back to the air force.

The Price of Micromanagement

Why is micromanagement, which has superseded this way of doing business, a bad thing? It removes decisionmaking from the manager on the scene and puts it into the hands of those who cannot possibly know the nitty-gritty ramifications of their choices. Micromanagement is the extension of legitimate and necessary supervision to a self-defeating extreme. In the process, by taking the time for all the review wickets, it drags out the development cycle to the financial detriment of the taxpayer.

In research and development, time translates directly into money. This simple fact is often glossed over or obscured in discussion of military waste, fraud, and abuse. The math is easy. Calculate the aggregate cost of leaving a couple of hundred well-paid engineers on a program a month—or seven to ten years—longer than expected. Multiply that by four hundred or five hundred programs. This contributes significantly to the inexorable cost-climbing.

As Norman R. Augustine, a former army and Department of Defense research and development high-level aide and now head of Martin Marietta, said in a speech a few years ago, hardware or software development takes "slightly over eight years for the median major system—in spite of the fact that many of these systems incorporate technologies with 'half-lives' of less than five years." By his estimate then, actual costs of military systems exceeded estimated costs in constant dollars by an average of 52 percent. Since then, the cycle has no doubt lengthened—with costs continuing to boil over.

A disturbing development has accompanied the bloating of time, paperwork, and bureaucracy in defense procurement—the expansion of the black program. Black is Pentagon jargon for programs classified as secret or higher. While in theory, congressional access to the details of black programs is sharply restricted, an air force acquisition manager estimates that about half of Congress actually has tapped into the black circuit.

Some familiar with the inner workings of black programs say that they are better managed than those conducted in the open. Perhaps shortcutting the ponderous processes of the procurement system has allowed them to finish faster. In the early 1960s, Admiral Bobby R. Inman, with a long career in intelligence, said that in trying to create a perfect acquisition system, reformers turned it from one that took three to five years to field hardware in the early 1960s into one that takes three times longer to do the same job. It is not hard for commanders to figure out that by escaping this system and moving into Inman's black world, projects can run without interference—and possibly faster and better.

Innumerable committees and commissions have analyzed the shortcomings of the military buying system and prescribed reforms—usually pragmatic, limited, and ignored. The latest government body to take such a look is the Packard Commission appointed by President Reagan. Reagan initially resisted the idea, conceived by Representative William L. Dickinson of Alabama, the ranking Republican on the House Armed Services Committee, but gave in when the threat of the waste, fraud, and abuse campaign to his military buildup became too obvious to ignore. By the time the commission, headed by David Packard, former deputy secretary of defense and a founder of Hewlett-Packard, delivered its recommendations, Reagan warmly ordered many of them adopted posthaste. By then, a waste, fraud, and abuse-minded Congress had begun to whittle away at his modernization and expansion of U.S. military forces.

Like its predecessors, the Packard Commission produced good ideas. But despite the commission's recognition that overmanagement is stifling the efficient functioning of the procurement system, it proposed a new office—an acquisition czar in the Pentagon.

That started a new round of bureaucratic fencing over turf in the Defense Department and may do what so many fixes to the system have done before—create more problems than are solved.

This sentiment was expressed in attachments to a letter from Sanford N. McDonnell, now retired chairman of the premier fighter aircraft manufacturer McDonnell Douglas, to Packard when his commission commenced its work.

> Many of today's procurement problems stem from or are exacerbated by yesterday's solutions. . . . There is no way to fail-safe the procurement system . . . many of the cures currently being promulgated to reform spares and overhead pricing are going to be much costlier to the nation than the diseases (if there were any) which stimulated the cures. A former assistant deputy undersecretary of defense estimates that the annual cost of U.S. government personnel added to administer spares pricing reforms will be about $700 million—before considering industry's added costs!

In other words, reforms can cost more than they are worth.

An example of such a situation is the cadre of program and system analysts that McNamara brought into the Defense Department, whose function seems to be to raise issues. While issues must be examined in the beginning, once the hard decisions are made, incessant issue raising simply wastes time and delays the program. Decisions are slow enough in coming, for the legions who can say no in the Pentagon have multiplied and overwhelmed the few who can say yes.

In one such case, Congress had approved development of an advanced version of a short-range attack missile, known as SRAM 2. The air force had, after a competition, what it considered a favorable price for the program from Boeing and was ready to sign up the contractor. Then, from one of the cubicles in the Defense Department, came a request for a study to resolve one official's concern about whether the air force had selected the best warhead. The air force program people then had to spend four or five months redesigning the wheel, as the time limit for the price, terms, and conditions in Boeing's offer drew near. "If Boeing hadn't been willing to extend its original offer," an air force general told me, "we could have lost the whole advantage of the competition we held." In the end, no changes were needed in the warhead.

What about Waste, Fraud, and Abuse?

Have the military and defense contractors merited the kind of oversight and criticism they are getting in the waste, fraud, and abuse campaign? Some in the military think so. Nor have defense contractors been beyond reproach. Foolish things done by contractors in past years include wine, women, and song for congressmen and trips for Pentagon bosses to tropical isles—a drop in the bucket in terms of total costs. Similar activity is routine in the commercial world, but not prudent on the part of companies supported by public money.

Almost forgotten are the payoffs by aerospace companies in the 1970s to overseas government officials in order to win orders (commercial as well as military). Despite protests that such "commissions" were the accepted way to do business in some countries, the revelations laid a foundation for mistrust of defense contractors and the suspicion that defense is synonymous with fraud. In the 1980s, that mistrust led to accusations—and sometimes indictments—of mischarging on contracts or of bribing purchasing agents.

Historically, defense contractors have borne an onus. The sutlers who supported—and overcharged—troops in the Mexican War and in the Civil War left the impression that military suppliers are little better than thieves. Then there is the "merchants of death" epithet for arms manufacture that arose in reaction to the pointless slaughter during World War I's trench warfare. And despite the American industrial-production achievements of World War II, a Senate investigating committee turned up cases of contractor profiteering.

Unless they are involved in military affairs, Americans thus tend to believe that defense is prodigal. Typically, they have been suspicious of military spending and large standing armies. Even during the revolutionary war, the militia had trouble getting its pay and arms, and mistrust of the military exchequer extended throughout the first century and a half of national existence. Congress almost wiped out West Point just before the Mexican War. And as late as the eve of World War II, army recruits were drilling with wooden guns as a result of the parsimony of the nation in spending for the military.

World War II changed all that. Whereas airplanes, tanks, and machine guns were all employed in World War I, they were too embryonic to effectively shorten the mindless trench warfare that dragged on four years in France. But World War II was a war of mobility, a war in which the long reach of the aircraft put entire nations and populations under attack. Like it or not, science and technology became the critical determinants of victory in war. Since then, the cold war, nuclear weapons, eavesdropping, communications and radar jamming, reconnaissance satellites, and a whole range of electronics have intensified the importance of the industrial arsenal.

How the defense acquisition apparatus—which obligates or spends $150 billion or more each fiscal year—has ballooned in the technological explosion that started with World War II is difficult for the outsider to comprehend. Its size challenges the imagination. The navy has leased a high-rise complex across the Potomac River from the Capitol for just its hundreds of headquarters uniformed and civilian forces who buy ships, aircraft, missiles, and electronics. They can't be fitted into the overcrowded Pentagon. Besides its acquisition headquarters in the Washington suburbs, the air force also has centers around the country—as the navy and army both do.

At Wright-Patterson Air Force Base near Dayton, where two major commands share a site near the original Wright bicycle shop, corridor crosses upon corridor lined with cubicles within cubicles. Cryptic letter/number codes identify rows of doors stretching through big brick buildings and little brick buildings filled with the gray metal government-issue furniture that the General Services Administration buys. "What in the name of heaven do all these people DO?" the visitor asks himself as he walks their halls.

Contrary to what a cynical public expects, they are not loafing. Some manage or monitor five thousand or so corporations—from conglomerates to job shops—that supply equipment for two million men and women in uniform. Dealing with these companies, and the volumes of regulations that govern them, involves millions of steps each year, occupying a sizable portion of the Defense Department's one million civilian employees, not to mention military acquisition troops, perhaps 150,000 all told. Others at Wright Field keep track of the detailed record keeping involved in air force support and maintenance. For example, volumes of complex, technical orders regarding equipment have to be cataloged and distributed to operating bases, including emergency changes that have to be made in the field. Aircraft and engine flying hours are tracked to monitor reliability and decisions made on grounding and pursuing fixes. Spare parts, routed through a network of maintenance and supply centers, must be ordered and monitored.

All of the military services—and the Defense Department as well—have installations of this magnitude doing analogous jobs around the world. The sheer paperwork involved in supplying thousands of troops in the field is staggering. About 250,000 civilians are employed throughout the Defense Department and the services just for such maintenance tasks alone.

There are drones on the federal payroll, a grid engraved into their posteriors by infinite hours in contact with the waffle pattern of the standard government-issue chair pad. There also are plenty of dedicated workers, especially in what might be called defense middle management. The best of those work longer hours than their commercial-world counterparts for less money, pursuing principles not fortunes. Unfortunately there is a resentment that permeates large civilian segments of the defense establishment— spawned by the military's insistence that service officers, not civil servants, run programs and departments. Civilians have a response at hand to this second-class-citizen social contract: a stick-to-the-book mentality whose effects range from inertia to nitpicking audits.

Seldom aware of the excruciating detail necessary to running a vast military establishment, the public retains its reserve about big defense (heightened by nervousness over nuclear weapons and nuclear power). It backs large standing forces and weapons research, but with misgivings over the military's voracious appetite for funds. Nuclear weapons, though, left no real choice about what is—by prewar standards—a large military establishment; all this despite vociferous objections from antinuclear groups who have little idea of what the defense would cost if nuclear arms did not exist. Still, because of this dichotomy, accusations of waste, fraud, and abuse fell on fertile ground.

Changing Times, Changing Attitudes

In the early postwar years, soaring on the success of their production victories in World War II, defense contractors basked in an unfamiliar warmth of public respect. Aircraft companies—soon to become the aerospace companies that dominate the defense marketplace—turned loose with unaccustomed amounts of government money, pioneered flight faster than the speed of sound. Eventually, prodded by Soviet Sputniks that led the world into space, they built the Apollo spacecraft, making it possible to put man's first footprints on the moon. They also built the ballistic missiles that are the backbone to U.S. nuclear forces and developed the commercial jet-transport airplane, which revolutionized passenger travel throughout the world. But then something went wrong.

Between the time of the televised lunar landings and the waste, fraud, and abuse hearings in Congress, much of the good feeling evaporated. The public, fed up with the fumbling in Vietnam and the rampant inflation in weapons costs that followed, turned on the military and its supporting industry. But if the public was dissatisfied with what it saw, so too was the military-industrial complex. Military manager and contractor were becoming adversaries, not a team, and they saw their ability to run a program, to get a job done, increasingly constrained by Pentagon and congressional micromanagement.

Defense companies always have marched to different refrains than the rest of business. Defense contractors are not as bottom-line oriented as their commercial brethren. A surprising number of defense company managers may not understand their company's balance sheet—or even want to. They disdain the so-called bean counters, whom they view as accountants with underdeveloped imaginations. The contractors are attuned to technical breakthroughs, the more the better; only dolts carp about the money involved.

Even the financially minded contractors are more revenue than profit driven. The reason is simple. Big contracts with big price tags support big engineering and research groups. Over time, the collective experience of these big teams wins the next multibillion-dollar program, perpetuating the existence of the company. If these programs also happen to turn a profit, so much the better. But a military supplier can stay alive doing little better than breaking even if—a substantial if—it can hold its technical teams together.

An obverse side exists to the coin. If the company loses the next big program, it faces reduction or decimation of its skilled engineering team. In what is a single-customer market, a military producer may have nowhere else to go. Lots has been written about beating swords into plowshares, about converting the defense industry into manufacturing civilian goods. But so different are the disciplines of the two marketplaces that it is probably advisable for a defense company to liquidate and salvage something for its stockholders rather than convert and go bankrupt. Thus, if a company loses a big program, survival is at issue. It is this fact that causes a defense company to shrug off criticism about lavish Washington entertaining, political lobbying, and the like. It is the kind of situation in which a chief executive may not want to know everything his agents are up to.

Competition of this win-or-die kind has led to pricing aberrations. Too many times, contractors, in the throes of trying to win a survival program, have underbid a better qualified and better prepared competitor. They have bought the business, mesmerized by a mix of unfounded optimism and desperation. Self-delusion is rampant in defense contracting: technical mysteries always are assumed to be easier to solve than they turn out to be; programs always are expected to endure long enough so that a contractor can "get well" (that is, recover costs) on later production batches or on spare parts orders; labor and materials always are anticipated to cost less than they really do.

One of the surprising things about defense contracting is how many of the prime suppliers have survived in the forty years since World War II. Some have faded as producers of aircraft, engines, or radios, but have made a living as subcontractors of components manufacturers. Still, the resilience of this handful has masked the overall trend. General James P. Mullins, retired commander of the air force Logistics Command, noted with alarm a few years ago that over the past fifteen years "we lost almost half our defense contractors." Budget cuts in the wake of the Vietnam War started the exodus. These were the smaller companies that supply the precision bits and pieces that make high-technology weapons possible. Some went broke, but even when funding increased again, some of those who survived chose not to return. Clearly, the era of waste, fraud, and abuse has taken some of the appeal out of the defense business.

The industrial side of the military-industrial complex (a name industry snickers at for its naïveté about government-business relations) is appalled at the lack of understanding in top-level defense and congressional circles about how the defense industry functions. Congress is filled with lawyers and committee staff members who rarely have working experience in business, let alone on the shop floor; their comprehension of how any business works, let alone the defense business, often is limited to classroom teachings. Still, industry cannot seem to get across to Congress—and to some in the Defense Department—how it does function.

One of the biggest complaints about the defense industry on Capitol Hill is its failure to generate common positions on anything. Again, there are good reasons for this. Defense companies, depicted as luxuriating in sole-source, long-term government contracts, are in fact so bitterly competitive and individualistic that they cannot reach consensus on their collective best interests. The core of all this is technical competition, which determines survival. Contractors must concentrate on lobbying to get—or maintain—individual programs, not for the common goals of the defense industry.

Changes in both Congress and the Defense Department in the past few decades have contributed to the misunderstandings. In Congress, the old-fashioned, iron-fisted committee chairmen, who knew how the system operated and how to make it perform, are an endangered species. When only the armed services committees ran congressional military oversight, Congress stuck to controlling purse strings and the military made decisions on what weapons it needed. Now there are budget committees, defense appropriation subcommittees, and various other subcommittees all engaged in directing defense. The result of all of this fragmentation is cacophony and confusion in the way Congress deals with defense.

In the Pentagon, the trend in top civilian leadership has been away from those with industrial backgrounds—the unexpected fallout from congressional ethics legislation. Thus the senior Pentagon civilians who oversee acquisition lack an understanding of the military system and how its requirements are industrialized.

Further, a change in government attitude has emerged. The acquisition system has become adversarial. The process increasingly has become committee dealing with committee, government bureaucrat with industry bureaucrat. But are legions of committees, assistant secretaries, congressional staffers, or auditors with a grand jury at hand the way a technically difficult and risky program (such as a space shuttle or a supersonic fighter) should be managed? Perhaps, though some knowledgeable military managers are dismayed over the rupture caused to the kind of teamwork that had been so successful. Adversarial processes may have become a necessary part of our civilization, as it becomes more technically and legally complex. Nonetheless, in the defense arena, the possibility also exists that the excesses of the adversarial process are encouraging the contractor to cover up inevitable problems in the hope they can be fixed before the Pentagon finds out, and inspiring the Pentagon to cover up inevitable problems in the hope that they can be resolved before Congress discovers the truth.

Taking Stock

The military buying system clearly is in trouble. In part, it may be a matter of perceptions. But there is no question that there are very real shortcomings. A 1986 survey by the Boston consulting firm of Arthur D. Little reported that some industry and defense people believe the whole acquisition process is "so cumbersome and often so laden with internal contradictions that it becomes less likely that it will ever function effectively in its present form . . . [that it] is now so fundamentally flawed that it may be beyond repair."

Extensive talks with military and industry managers lead to similarly pessimistic conclusions. Red tape is a familiar epithet in government, but the problem has gone far beyond burdensome paperwork. The defense industry and the military are less able to do the kind of innovative job they must do to keep this country preeminent in military technology. Further, industry has been slow to react to a fundamental shift in military acquisition policy—that is, from performance-at-any-price-equipment to cost-containment. The paper-laden defense industry is on the verge of pricing itself out of the market.

In its zeal to reform the defense acquisition system, the government is making the defense industry like unto itself. Wrapped in a cocoon that begins and ends with the military customer, prisoners of federalese in speech and deed, defense companies face becoming like government bureaus—those that stick around, that is. Even now, in the words of air force brigadier general Kenneth V. Meyer, "the aerospace industry is becoming so rule-bound and regulated that it appears to be neither free nor competitive. . . . Critics and watchers are growing in number while doers are diminishing or, put another way, we have more people concentrating on Caesar's baggage train than on where, when or if he should march on Gaul." Meyer could as easily have said this of the defense industry as a whole.

Because of the increasing regulatory mantle over the acquisition system, the military is having a harder time managing technical development. Good program managers, and their number is legion, have greater trouble running anything because the system discourages decisionmaking. And attracting good people into program management becomes more difficult because of the odium attached to the system.

Critics persist in attacking superficial, short-term problems, not these deep-seated, fundamental ones. But if the long-term problems are not rectified, the taxpayers' willingness to maintain the defense program will erode. The public is willing to pay for a necessary defense, but not for the bureaucratic delays, program management snafus, and misguided congressional meddling that lead to uncontrollable escalation in defense costs.

Did the military and the defense industry, by their failures, bring on the avalanche of oversight and its consequent loss of management control at the working level and the most devastating failure of all—the obscene growth in the length of the development cycle that has launched weapons costs into the stratosphere? I believe that their shortcomings were less damaging than the fixes for them—which added to the problem through the excess oversight and misdirected zeal of those on the fringe of the defense program—and the rule-book inertia of the bureaucracy. No question but that the services and their industrial suppliers have taken a few pratfalls at center stage. While there are good program managers in government and industry, sadly there are also lousy ones. And, as will appear, the good ones are being submerged while none of the remedies seems to be rehabilitating the rest. Still, a line must be drawn between prudent oversight and meddling micromanagement. Despite almost three decades of defense acquisition reform, that boundary has not yet been located.

2

Requirements: Where the Process Begins

THE public has turned a cold eye on the fiascoes—or what are painted as fiascoes—in the workings of the military acquisition system. But little attention is paid as to how the military decides what to buy in the first place—that is, how requirements are laid down. Yet the way the requirement is drawn for a piece of equipment or a complete weapons system can put a program on the right track or produce an embarrassment down the road.

A requirement is a formal description of an operational capability—the ability of equipment to do a job in the field. It is used to determine what specific performance, or what hardware, is needed to solve a particular military problem. Requirements are translated into hardware within the confines of the federal budget; instability in the defense portion of that budget upsets an orderly definition and resolution of military hardware needs.

Requirements are laid down years in advance of when the equipment will be delivered to the combat troops. If technology changes, or a potential enemy revises his battle forces or his strategy and tactics, a valid requirement can become an anachronism. Events have a way of overturning deliberateness and planning. No one has told a potential enemy to stick to the script. Thus, one of the critical problems the military faces is how to write a requirement that will not be prematurely obsolescent.

Two recent studies, one by the presidential blue-ribbon committee on acquisition, the Packard Commission, and one by the Center for Strategic and International Studies, examined the requirements process. The Packard Commission made the point that engineers know only too well: The more time, care, and money invested at the front end of a project, the quicker and cheaper a better and more reliable end product will get into the hands of the field forces.

Both reports noted that the process of integrating grand strategy, national policy, and military requirements leaves something to be desired. No forum exists at the top level to resolve competing demands for weapons; that is, who needs what the worst. The Center for Strategic and International Studies report said that "The thrust of the current process is to concentrate on procurement, management and allocation of resources for individual systems rather than on the overarching rationale and purposes that define the need for and the operational capabilities of those systems" (page 26). In other words, the tail tends to wag the dog. When glittering new technology comes on the scene, there is the temptation to build it for its own sake, not because it is required to meet a national need.

This nation has trouble anyway in making up its mind on what its national objectives are. Former secretary of state Henry Kissinger is fond of saying that his adopted country has no sense of realpolitik. In a recent syndicated newspaper article, he reflected on the ambivalence in the mind of the American electorate: while Americans in and out of government preach about the righteousness of arms control, they cannot accept the consequences—the necessity for a much more expensive conventional military force to balance Soviet strength in troops, tanks, and attack aircraft. So it goes on other strategic and policy issues. No recent U.S. administration has distinguished itself in formulating national strategic policy. For two or three decades, international politics and domestic posturing have shaped strategy rather than the more desirable strategy and national interest shaping political goals.

There is no doubt that integrating national policy and military requirements—that is, attaching more emphasis to the interaction of developer, user, and policymaker during weapons development—would go a long way toward ensuring that the original requirement for a weapons system has not become a dead horse, outmoded by events, evolving strategy, or newer technology. But one of the shortcomings of the requirements process is its rigidity, its codification of the measurements of the hardware program's progress in meeting task and performance goals.

There are reasons that requirements should be rigid and difficult to modify. If the requirement is not clearly drawn or if the rationale of the requirement is fuzzy, a program may wallow. Further, at some point a design must be frozen—a commitment made to shape, size, and performance level. When industrial tooling has been built, when metal has been cut, when thousands of assemblers have been hired, modification becomes disruptive. There is also understandable reluctance by a program's sponsors to tinker with it after winding through the long chain of command to approval. But with this rigidity also comes the tendency to keep pouring funds into a faltering program, rather than searching for alternative solutions.

Who Really Determines the Requirement?

In the final analysis, is it the user in the field or the technologist-turned-salesman in the laboratory who determines military weapons requirements? Or, more to the crux, is it the Office of the Secretary of Defense or Congress, neither of them close enough to the threat to get shot at. By the book, it is the user, but the evolution of a big-ticket weapons system is not so simple. There is interplay among the prospective user, the technology troops, and industry.

The real policy issue is how much new technology is necessary or desirable in new equipment. A favorite quotation I have heard U.S. military commanders attribute to the Russians goes something like, "the best is the enemy of the good enough." Is a field commander better off with existing aircraft or tank technology that is reliable and that his troops or pilots are familiar with, or must he have state-of-the-art technology or, more often, beyond-state-of-the-art technology that is unfamiliar, may not work smoothly at first, and whose reliability is unknown?

Will a new piece of equipment do the job just as effectively with the good enough as with the ultimate? According to the Packard Commission, "all too often, requirements for new weapon systems have been overstated. This has led to overstated specifications, which has led to higher cost equipment. Such so-called goldplating has become deeply embedded in our system today." Simply put, are the benefits in performance or capability of a new weapon (or a particular component in that weapon) worth what design, deployment, and disruption will cost? Is that last mile-an-hour of speed or the last pound in reduced weight worth its marginal cost?

A field commander and his forces are apt to be ambivalent about new technology. Although they like the idea of new equipment that will run circles around what the enemy may have, they also are familiar with the virtues and vices of what they have, they can work around its shortcomings, they are well drilled in how to use and maintain it, and spare parts are more likely to be on the shelves or in the pipeline than they would be for new hardware. They also are suspicious of the new until proven.

On the other side of the issue are the developers, who worry about technology lying undeveloped or sitting on the shelf unused while equipment grows obsolescent in the field. The technologists face the problem of convincing the user of the value of new technology in order to get new technology written into a requirement and to underwrite its development. It may take a good deal of missionary work on their part to accomplish this. The dilemma for the policymaker is to determine where conversion to the faith ends and snake-oil selling begins.

Nominally, requirements are generated by the using commands. In the air force, for example, a requirement may originate in the Tactical Air Command headquartered at Langley Air Force Base, Virginia, which operates the newest stable of air force fighters—the F-16, F-15, and a variety of strike aircraft—to support the army. The source of the requirement may be the Strategic Air Command, which mans the bomber and missile nuclear strike forces; the Training Command, which trains pilots using simple, noncombat aircraft; or the Military Airlift Command, which operates a heavy cargo and passenger airline for the services. These are the users who ultimately have to be sold—not on the need, but on the cost-effectiveness of new technology to meet the need.

The Tactical Air Command and the Strategic Air Command have intelligence staffs that monitor foreign aircraft and missile development as well as what the active forces of potential enemies are up to. They fly exercise missions against simulated enemy forces and conduct war games. If this activity demonstrates an enemy capability that either command cannot deal with using existing forces and equipment, then a new requirement results.

Capability is a term frequently used in the services and it is the basis for strategic and tactical planning. With reference to equipment, capability means the kind of performance the equipment can deliver. In an airplane, that includes how high, how fast, with how much of a load of bombs or ammunition, and for how long it can fly, as well as what it can deliver on a target at what distance. These are not the maximum, just-out-of-the-factory figures but what it can actually do after the rigors of months or years of service.

A commander facing an enemy force analyzes, among other things, its equipment and its performance. He then reaches a conclusion on capabilities—that is, how much damage the enemy force could inflict on his own and how much defensive strength the enemy has. The formal name for the result of this analysis has gone through an evolution of terminology—from required operational capability to statement of need. By the time the service has produced this document, the prospective requirement has gone through considerable massaging.

In the air force, for example, the requirement will have been debated back and forth, formally or otherwise, by the operating command and the research and development organization within the intelligence community, and by the air force headquarters staff within the Pentagon itself. Ideally, the statement of need will be a pristine definition of the basic task the user has in mind, unbiased by any preconceived idea of what particular piece of equipment would fulfill that requirement. If the system works as it should, with the necessary checks and balances, technical alternatives, relative costs, and cost-benefit tradeoffs will grind the nascent requirement to a fine edge. In actuality, however, the user will see an emerging technology or a piece of equipment and say, in effect, "that is just what I need for such and such a job." The requirement then gets written to fit that concept.

If the requirement survives analysis, research, and evaluation within the individual command, it must compete against the requirements generated in other commands for the available pot of budget money. This money must cover not only design, development, and production, but also operation and maintenance in the field. If the requirement survives, it then goes to the next level in the hierarchy—the Office of the Secretary of Defense—where it must pass through the hoops in what is left of the once-powerful Office of Defense Research and Engineering by convincing a new set of players of the need and the validity of this particular hardware solution.

This process is known as concept definition. In the commercial world, the analogous process is the preliminary design phase. Both are aimed at smoking out unknowns—the unexpected problems inherent in a new technology or new product—before full-scale engineering and the expensive process of building tooling for a production line. In the military, it allows time for testing and retesting the validity of the market solution. But the concept definition process also can string out the development cycle and fritter away money if it becomes a bureaucratic ping-pong ball. It also can be used to stall a controversial program that has been thoroughly defined.

Translating Technology into Equipment

The requirement is then turned over to another command for equipment development. Again, using the air force as an example, the requirement would be turned over to the Air Force Systems Command, headquartered at Andrews Air Force Base, near Washington. Both the army and the navy also have systems development commands, created during the McNamara revolution in the Pentagon, but the air force command came first, in the early postwar era.

These systems development commands reflect a profound evolution that was taking place in military hardware. Equipment was no longer just equipment; electronic technology was exploding. Instead of a rifle, with a bolt, a clip, and a few bullets, weapons became complex mechanical and electronic amalgamations, with immense challenges of integration. These new commands also largely separated maintenance and replacement-parts supply from research and development. Eventually, questions arose over whether the divorce led to a dip in reliability and maintainability.

The Air Force Systems Command consists of various centers—called divisions—each devoted to specific technologies. Wright Field in Ohio houses the Aeronautical Systems Division of the Air Force Systems Command. As its name implies, it deals with aircraft, but the boundaries are flexible; it also delves deeply into avionics. The Electronics Systems Division at Hanscom Field in Bedford, Massachusetts, is more concerned with ground-based radar and communications. Centers compete, and a user who wants an electronic system may go to Wright Field rather than Hanscom Field if he thinks his program will be done faster and cheaper there.

A division may be designated the leading center for certain kinds of development. The Electronic Systems Division, for example, was designated the lead center for command and control work for the Strategic Defense Initiative (Star Wars). Each division also does generic research. The Propulsion Laboratory at Wright Field, for example, does generic research on power plants. Perhaps the prime function of a division, though, is to house the managers of programs that rate individual lines in Defense Department budget documents.

A small program (one less than, say, a million dollars), will have a single program manager, period. It might even be one of several programs for which a single manager holds responsibility. Larger programs (in the multi-million-dollar category) may have, in addition to a single manager, either dedicated or ad hoc staff. A billion-dollar program—for example, a full weapons system like the F-16 fighter or the new air force B-1 bomber—will be managed by what is called a System Program Office (SPO); its head is the program director, and it contains a staff of managers for subsystems such as engines, communications, navigation, countermeasures, and the like. It also includes a contracting officer to handle negotiations with the industrial team, and some even have their own public relations officer.

There is no hard and fast rule about what size a program must reach to achieve System Program Office status. Whereas ten or fifteen years ago the SPO was a mighty office, the furor over how military dollars are spent has brought more senior military, Defense Department, and congressional staffers farther into the management realm, and a great deal of the program director's time is now spent briefing these proliferating layers of management.

The McNamara Reforms

Starting in the McNamara era, a structure evolved that provides formal guideposts for program management and scheduling. It includes sophisticated guidelines and techniques for measuring management performance, designed to raise red flags if a program falls off schedule or if development of a critical part is running into unexpected technical difficulties.

Programs are divided into formal phases, though not every program will have all possible phases. These were once called Phase Zero for concept definition and Phases One, Two, and Three for later engineering and production start-up stages. While these stages remain more or less the same, the names were changed to Milestones under a new system fostered by David Packard during his tenure as deputy secretary of defense. More than mere renaming was behind the changes, however. Packard was trying to ensure that everything was in order, that all details were in hand, before development proceeded to the next stage. Milestones were invented as a gate—a way of ensuring against fiasco, a way top Pentagon leadership could block a program from moving into the next phase if technical or financial booby traps were lurking.

Milestone Zero is the threshold at which the secretary of defense or his delegate issues formal approval for a program to proceed—that is, approval of the requirement. Approval is based on a document called the mission need statement that defines mission and threat, alternatives and technology to meet the challenge, availability of hardware under development by allied nations, affordability and funding the service is willing to commit, and a host of others.

Milestone I is the proof of concept phase. The effort here is to demonstrate through models that the technology, or technologies, in the system will do what the sponsors say it will. It requires another document, the system concept paper, that explains why present equipment is inadequate to meet a potential threat.

Milestone II is the point at which the program enters full-scale development and, sometimes, low-rate production. Detailed engineering of the complete system takes place; prototypes of the equipment may be built for testing; metal is cut and assembled for the start of production; so-called hard-tooling (that is, permanent jigs and fixtures and the like) is built and installed; and labor switches from predominantly engineering to predominantly factory blue collar.

Sometimes what are portrayed as embarrassing failures occur during Milestones I or II. But it is in the earlier, lower-cost stages of a program where the failures must happen to avoid far more disastrous surprises later on. An old dictum of development testing is that the worst fate that can befall a program in early phases is a series of random successes. That means testing has not smoked out the inevitable problems. Failures later are grossly expensive, perhaps fatally so. The spectacle of the early Atlas, Titan, and Polaris ballistic missiles exploding on launch pads at Cape Canaveral, or careening wildly after launch was painful to taxpayer and developers alike. But it is far better that those failures came at the start instead of in service, in the field.

Milestone III is the stage at which approval comes for full-rate production and initial deployment. Both Milestones II and III require yet another document, the decision coordinating paper, which covers the possibilities for international cooperation, why a specific alternative was selected (including evaluation of its technical risks and survivability), and logistics considerations.

Reforming the Reforms

In 1986, in the aftermath of the Packard Commission report and the Goldwater-Nichols bill, the Department of Defense reissued the directive governing acquisition. The revised directive, known by its number, 5000.1, requires secretary of defense, rather than service, approval for major programs at Milestone III—again moving decisionmaking to the top. It also adds Milestone IV, a review a year or two after initial deployment of equipment to determine the state of its readiness and support in the field, and Milestone V, another review five or ten years down the line to determine whether modifications are necessary or whether shortcomings are serious enough to require replacement.

The revised directive also created a new committee—the Defense Acquisition Board—to resolve issues and provide guidance. It is headed by the new defense acquisition executive and includes members from the Office of the Secretary of Defense, the Joint Chiefs of Staffs, and the services. Also created were two subsidiary titles—the service acquisition executive (the counterpart, within each service, of the defense acquisition executive) and the program executive officer who reports to him and is assigned responsibility for a block of programs.

Big-money weapons programs are designated either defense acquisition board programs (these are the bigger programs, managed by the Defense Department hierarchy) or component programs (smaller programs, managed within the services), as proposed by the defense acquisition executive and approved by the secretary of defense. The secretary of defense or someone he delegates must approve each milestone review of defense acquisition board programs. In these programs, no more than two management tiers—the new service and program executives—may exist between the program manager at the bottom and the defense acquisition executive at the top. A parallel management structure exists for the component programs at the service level. But component programs are allowed only one management tier—the program executive—between the service acquisition executive at the top and the program manager at the bottom, and the secretary of defense does not need to approve milestone reviews.

Neat as all this sounds, it also reveals why defense weapons development is so constipated. While the directive is supposed to limit the management layers, it also creates at least three new layers in the chain of command: the defense acquisition executive, the service acquisition executive, and the program executives. By segregating acquisition oversight and review under one professional-grade office (the defense acquisition executive, the acquisition czar) it was hoped that amateurs in various rings of the Pentagon would be prevented from mucking around in the process. But those who thought the acquisition executive would bring quick order were mistaken.

Secretary of Defense Caspar Weinberger insisted that he pick his own man as defense acquisition executive. He got his way, and from Bechtel, a construction engineering company he had served, he picked Richard Godwin, who had no deep acquisition experience. After a frustrating year on the job, after failing to establish a charter in the Pentagon for the metes and bounds of his office, Godwin found himself an adviser not a czar. He resigned in late summer 1987. The attempt to put acquisition into expert, experienced hands in the top layers of the Pentagon clearly did not start out very well.

In the early 1970s, the idea emerged that perhaps too many schedule and financial details were burying essential concerns. To make sure that programs got a hard look before proceeding into expensive stages, the program milestone system was created, tied into critical program reviews by the Defense System Acquisition Review Council (DSARC). Each service developed its own subreviews, such as the Air Force System Acquisition Review Council (AFSARC). As a result of the Packard Commission report, DSARC is now the Joint Requirements and Management Board, which not only measures the progress of programs in meeting the terms of requirements but also reexamines original requirements to affirm their continued validity.

In order for programs to pass through these milestones and reviews, program managers must indulge the Pentagon and Congress with an alarming number of briefings. An air force officer, for example, told me it took 240 briefings over two-and-one-half years to win approval for multiyear contracting for the F-16 fighter aircraft. That is an average of 1.8 briefings a week, just for this one aspect of one program. Multiply all the Pentagon's weapons programs and the total of briefings becomes mind-boggling.

Like defense reforms in the past, those of the Packard Commission have met frustration. New directives and new offices are fine, but their impact is dissipated in the sheer mass of existing regulations and the sheer size of the bureaucracy. It will be years before the results become visible, if they ever do.

The Role of the Contractor

Contractors play an informal part in the requirements process and a formal one as the milestones begin. They are a source of much original research, through a cost-sharing system with the Pentagon known as Independent Research and Development. Such research is priced as a negotiated percentage of a contract, in the same fashion that a commercial company builds the cost of product development into its selling prices. Independent research has been criticized because the Pentagon, in effect, is paying for private industrial research. But contractors defend it fiercely as the lifeblood of technical innovation in defense. In fact, independent research is a gray area. At best, it produces innovative ideas and technology that support not only a U.S. military lead but also industry in general. At worst, it generates technology in search of a mission—an illusion that all the country's military problems can be solved with money and equipment, and a reliance on gadgetry at the expense of sound defense policy.

Whatever the final verdict, since World War II, independent research has been the linchpin in this country's reliance on innovation from private industry rather than dependence on government arsenals for defense equipment. But as congressional and Pentagon micromanagement ripples through the acquisition process, as waste, fraud, and abuse becomes a permanent battle cry, this basic premise is changing. The nation is gradually drifting back toward government development of equipment—but through de facto nationalization of industry rather than a return to government arsenals. Government arsenals have a reputation for sluggishness, stodginess, and lack of innovation, though there are exceptions like the navy's missile center at China Lake, California. If this trend continues, free-swinging private industry will be forced into the worst ways of government.

Where We Stand Now

Requirements are in trouble, both as a product of grand strategy and as a procedure for weapons development. In recent years, special commissions have fretted about the shortcomings of political direction, but better strategic thinking seldom turns up. Until the electorate demands strategic ingenuity from its political leaders, the country will muddle along as best it can with the way it initiates its weapons requirements. Those who have to turn requirements into hardware complain, too—in particular about the lack of realism. Yet the military continues to make requirements more demanding, and industry knowingly commits to deliver never-never land because it's the only game in town. Unless contractors court suicide by resisting unrealistic requirements, and only a few have, the game will go on.

The Packard Commission made an important gesture toward realism in fostering the creation of the Joint Requirements Management Board. Because even worse than creating an ill-conceived requirement, or goldplating it with overly elaborate technology, is continuing to live with it blindly, the board's charter allows for challenging a requirement's continuing validity, not merely evaluating whether the weapon under development is meeting the requirement. Unfortunately, though, the results, as a contractor friend of mine summed up, are invisible so far. Inertia is winning. In times past, new boards and acquisition czars might have worked. No more. Both military and industry worry that the grossly overweight system is inching toward immobility. Something in the way of a simple but radical diet is critical.

3

Doling Out the Money

ONCE the requirement for a new military weapons system is approved, somewhere in the process of reaching Milestone Zero, the money has to be found to get it started. A competition for funding begins against the claims of programs already under way, pay raises for personnel, money for training, and new military housing, among others. These exercises start within the individual services and are repeated on up through the Defense Department hierarchy until they reach the secretary of defense, who has the dilemma of resolving the competing claims of each service for funding.

Because of the way federal budgeting works, because of the inherent uncertainty of weapons development, because of the stiff competition for a place in the budget sun, more waste, fraud, and abuse pitfalls are dug. When the program acquires individual identification in the budget, at which point it stands unshielded in the spotlight, estimates must be submitted that will become an annual congressional appropriation with the force of law. Five years hence, perhaps more, the program's financial reputation will rise or fall on these estimates.

Until the time a weapons system goes into full-scale production, it is financed out of a segment of the federal budget called research, development, test and evaluation. In its earliest beginnings, it may not be defined as a specific program at all but lumped into either generalized research efforts, such as aircraft-engine or armored-vehicle technology, or specialized research—a specific kind of engine cycle, for example.

Once a weapons system crosses the $2 million line, or if it falls into a category like aircraft, missiles, ships, or various other kinds of hardware that will be bought in quantity, it becomes a line item in the budget. Then cost estimates, uncertain as they are, become a public commitment. In the struggle for funds lies the pressure for optimistic estimating—optimism that nothing technological will come unzipped in development, optimism that no extra engineering man-hours will be called for, optimism that inflation will stay in check. So it goes on down a lengthy list, extending to the contractor who may be tempted to lowball his bid in a flight of superoptimism or superdesperation to buy the business and then forced to plead for more money down the road. Developers and senior managers who sell the program to the Pentagon or Congress want to believe that estimates are realistic, but experience testifies that often they are not, that often they cannot be.

Cost overruns have become synonymous with waste, fraud, and abuse—not to mention poor management—in the Defense Department and its supporting industry. Yet the term is seldom fully understood by other than the hapless participants. Neither is the term research and development comprehended precisely by outsiders.

Defense Department research and development covers a vast and complex process in defense management and budgeting. Research conjures up the image of scientists in white coats working with test tubes and microscopes in a cluttered laboratory; while what the federal government calls research and development includes some of that, much more is encompassed in the Defense Department's spending under this budget heading. In the president's submission to Congress for fiscal 1987, defense research and development alone accounted for $31.6 billion in estimated outlays.

The reasons for broadening the definition of research and development go back to the Eisenhower administration in the mid-1950s. It was a time when the Soviets had disconcerted the United States with their rapid acquisition of nuclear technology, then alarmed us with intercontinental ballistic missile test firings to show they could deliver those weapons, and finally dismayed us with the launch of the world's first artificial satellite—*Sputnik I*—into outer space. Scientists, engineers, the military, business, and the man in the street all demanded to know what the administration was doing to keep the United States moving in advanced technology.

The solution the administration hit upon was to reclassify, for the budget, all the disparate activities included in the foot-long heading that still stands: research, development, test and evaluation. This covered not only basic research—the white-coated scientist in the laboratory—but also the entire process of bringing an idea from the drawing board into production, including production start-up costs such as tooling. In the case of an airplane or a missile, it also includes flight testing to demonstrate that the vehicle is ready to be built in series production, which involves considerable expense. Once a weapons system enters series production, however, it is funded out of another broad segment of the federal budget: procurement.

Stretching the definition of research and development beyond normal semantics was a political jewel. To appease critics in Congress and the press, it exaggerated the amount of money the administration was spending on basic research. As such clever gavottes end, however, the piper came around for payment. A later generation of critics deplored the vast amount of money going into defense research, claiming that it was out of balance in terms of the overall needs of the nation.

The Cost of Research and Development

Confusion on what the United States is spending on research, narrowly defined as the white-coated scientist kind, still is rampant. See table 3-1 for how the president's defense research and development budget submitted to Congress for fiscal 1987 looked.

Most of us think of basic research when we hear the term *research*. But in the Pentagon, in terms of funding, it is a much more complex business. To Pentagon professionals, funding for basic research is commonly referred to as 6.1 money, in deference to its budget accounting code; it includes money that goes to universities for analytical, nonapplications-type studies; money that goes to industry for applied research; and money that goes to government laboratories. Exploratory development, which is coded 6.2, begins to cross over into the realm of preparation for production. Then comes advanced development, coded 6.3, at which point design and testing of a specific product is well under way. During engineering development, coded 6.4, the transition to production is moving along, with assembly-line tooling in fabrication, with metal

Table 3-1
MILITARY RESEARCH & DEVELOPMENT–FISCAL 1987
IN MILLIONS OF DOLLARS

Basic research	986
Exploratory development	2,599
Advanced development	12,776
Engineering development	11,717
Management and support	2,973
Subtotal, research and development	31,051
Operational systems development	10,879
Total, research, development, test and evaluation	41,930

being cut, or circuit boards being wired. Management and support, coded 6.5, covers overhead, including some of the costs of government-owned laboratories where basic and applied research is conducted.

In addition to the above research and development costs, funding is required for modifications to equipment already in the inventory—that is, operational systems development. Modification fits into the definition of development in the sense that engineering and design are entailed in product improvement. Changes of this kind are far more important than they used to be. Because the costs of a brand-new system—a so-called clean sheet of paper design—have ballooned to such a degree, the military has increasingly turned to modernizing and modifying older hardware to make it last longer. The process is analogous to, but more complex than, dropping a new transmission into the old Chevy to keep it on the road for another year or two.

Because trying to field the perfect weapons system the first time out of the factory door can be enormously expensive, modification to bring equipment into fine tune, to insert advanced technology developed on a more flexible timetable, is now sometimes planned under a technique called preprogrammed product improvement, or P^3I.

The Cost of Procurement

The other—and larger—segment of the defense budget for equipment is procurement. In fiscal 1987, the procurement budget comprised the items listed in table 3-2.

These figures are broad totals from budget summaries and just

Table 3-2
MILITARY PROCUREMENT–FISCAL 1987
IN BILLIONS OF DOLLARS

Army	
Aircraft	3.3
Missiles	2.4
Weapons and tracked vehicles	4.5
Ammunition	2.3
Other	6.1
Total, army	18.6
Navy	
Aircraft	11.3
Weapons (includes missiles)	6.1
Shipbuilding and conversion	11.0
Other	6.5
Marine corps	1.6
Total, navy	36.5
Air force	
Aircraft	19.1
Missiles	9.0
Other	10.9
Total, air force	39.0
Other defense agencies	1.5
Miscellaneous	0.2
Grand total, Department of Defense	95.8

one of several ways the figures are compiled. The Pentagon sends Congress a far more detailed delineation, with row upon row of line items for specific programs. As with all federal budgeting, these figures are not as straightforward as they seem. Not that any flimflam is involved, but the federal budget is just more complex and administered in a more convoluted fashion because of the breadth and timing of large-scale projects.

Budget Authority versus Outlays

All of these figures belong to the category of budget authority requests—that is, the sums the Pentagon hoped that Congress would authorize its agencies to commit—but not necessarily spend—in the fiscal year under consideration. Budget authority is half the loaf. Congress must then, in a second step, pass an appropriations bill, which allows agencies to use their budget authority. Budget authority used to be called new obligational authority and might be understood more easily under that title. It is the new money Congress is being asked to appropriate as opposed to carry-over funding from previous years.

In the case of military buying, budget authority gives the Pentagon legislative permission to go ahead with a program, and may even authorize the full funding necessary over the program's entire life. However—an important however—Congress must follow through with the appropriation in a subsequent bill or bills. Sometimes it doesn't, leaving the Pentagon with authority to start or contract for a program but without the money to pay for it.

When spent, budget appropriations translate into outlays—that is what the Treasury actually issues in checks—for example, to employees, Social Security recipients, or defense contractors. When the budget authority is for meeting the salaries of agency employees, it will be the same or close to outlays. But if funds are obligated for a research-and-development or procurement contract, some money most likely will go for equipment or services to be provided and paid for in subsequent years; thus they will not match outlays. It is this timing difference that adds confusion to the size of the defense hardware budget.

Outlays are a measure of what the federal government is pouring into the economy. The relationship between outlays and taxes received by the government determines whether the government will have to borrow to make ends meet, and, if so, what the size of the now-chronic deficit will be. Outlays have all the shortcomings of estimates. For example, if a contractor falls behind a delivery schedule or if inflation is lower than projected, the government won't be paying what it anticipated. In this instance, a shortfall would occur. In the government's 1985 fiscal year, $92.1 billion in defense outlays came from appropriations and ensuing contracts or other obligations from earlier years. Thus outlays for defense equipment are usually different from estimates for them—sometimes by amounts as sizable as fiscal 1985's $8 billion.

The differences between budget authority and outlays are more substantial. For fiscal 1987, for example, the Pentagon asked for $311.6 billion in budget authority, but planned to spend $274.3

billion in outlays—a difference of roughly $37 billion. Close to one-third of the difference (over $29 billion) between budget authority and outlays had to do with hardware buying—that is, research and development ($41.9 billion requested in budget authority versus an estimated $31.6 billion in outlays) and procurement ($95.8 billion requested in budget authority versus an estimated $76.7 billion in outlays).

Lead times between order and delivery are extensive for equipment like aircraft or, especially, ships. In the commercial world, where an assembly line is up and running, and under favorable conditions, it may take eighteen months after an order is placed to produce a transport-class aircraft. Custom-designed military aircraft are another matter. Technical problems that may have to be solved during development, uncertainties over funding approvals, and cumbersome contracting and review procedures all make for a longer delivery pipeline.

When budget considerations force tradeoffs, military chiefs of staff tend to keep the long-lead items in the budget and drop the ones that can be built back the fastest. Since hardware funding is obligated one year and partly carried over to subsequent years, the savings from the cancellation of a weapons program are more a release from a future liability than a quick fix to meet a single year's budget targets.

Total spending for weapons is awesome in any terms. It is a bit more than 40 percent of annual overall defense outlays. Operations and maintenance consume about 25 percent and people-related costs (such as salaries, pensions, and family housing) roughly the same.

The Budget Game

Pentagon budgeting—just for equipment—is a massive, continuous process dealing with thousands of line items, from bullets and cans of beans costing a few cents (but consolidated to meet the $2 million threshold) to multibillion-dollar capital ships. Five-year budget projections by Defense Department policy and program analysts shape advance planning. Then the Defense Department issues specific fiscal-year targets in a document called the POM (Program Objectives Memorandum), which may or may not conform to the five-year projections. Program managers develop funding requests for their own programs within these guidelines.

Once the individual program budgets are submitted, the process of internal Pentagon budget review gets under way. This peaks in the fall, just as the new federal fiscal year has opened, but only three or four months before the budget for the subsequent year is due for submission to Congress, around the end of January. The process of budgetmaking is similar to that of policymaking, and like sausagemaking, is something that ought not be watched. Some proposed new hardware programs bite the dust in the final surgery of Pentagon budgetmaking; some are brought back for appeal in what in Pentagon jargon is called the reclama process. Others are "adjusted," to put it euphemistically. Production rates may be scaled back to reduce expenses or tradeoffs made between equipment and operations. In the Carter administration, to take one such situation, in order to keep within budget ceilings, the services and the Joint Chiefs of Staff elected to concentrate on equipment modernization to reduce long-term upkeep costs, and cut back on steaming time for ships, flying time for aircraft, and combat-readiness training.

Because budgeting is not an exact science, because weapons costs are not reliably predictable, the executive branch has the option of trying to fix mistakes. If it is running short of funds appropriated by law (as it did in paying for the Vietnam War), it can go to Congress for a supplemental appropriation. It is not unheard of for Congress to be dealing with a budget for the upcoming fiscal year at the same time that it is considering a supplemental request for the current fiscal year.

Such funding uncertainties make it difficult for program managers. This is especially true in cases where Congress is late with budget legislation, as it almost always is. The program manager does not know how much he can obligate for new contracts, and contractors are in a spot as to whether to keep workers on the payroll for an impending job. Programs in stages of fast buildup are left hanging by their thumbs until Congress finally does approve a budget. To add another dash of salt, Congress goes through the dual process—first authorizing funds for programs and then appropriating the money. When Congress fails to finish work on an appropriations bill by the time the new fiscal year begins, a device called a continuing resolution is used to authorize funding at the previous year's level.

To deal with the fact that some programs run into snags and others make rapid progress, the Pentagon can transfer funds for weapons acquisition from one program to another—a step called reprogramming. Reprogramming gives military acquisition managers the flexibility to deal with the unexpected. Naturally, Congress is always suspicious of reprogramming, because the Pentagon can use it to avoid spending on a program it did not want but that Congress pressured it into including in the budget or to spend more on a weapon than Congress was willing to approve. As a result, Congress may tie strings to reprogramming by outright prohibitions or by insisting that the Pentagon come back to Capitol Hill for further approval before it moves any money around.

Another significant player in the budget game is the program element monitor, whose job is to both shepherd his service's program through the budget review process and defend its cost performance (although he has no direct part in its management). A typical situation in which the program element monitor plays an important role is when a program manager has obligated only a fraction of the budget authority well into a budget year. The program element manager will be queried as to whether the program really needed the budgeted amount in the first place. A good program element monitor will coordinate closely enough with the program manager to know whether tough, protracted negotiations with a supplier have delayed commitment of the money, whether the program has encountered a technical snag, or whether something else is amiss. Thus, despite his obscurity to the public, the program element monitor is critical to the survival of a program.

Once a project has moved along the research and development trail through the review wickets in the Pentagon (first in the sponsoring service and then in the Defense Department) to the point where it has become an approved program, it is large enough in dollar terms to rate a separate line item that demands congressional authorization. A typical line-item listing from a fiscal 1987 Pentagon document called Procurement Programs is the navy's Trident II submarine-launched nuclear ballistic missile. Built by Lockheed, it was budgeted for twenty-one missiles for a total of $1,368.9 million (or a calculated unit cost of $65 million). Programs not yet in the assembly-line stage also rate line-item listings. A random example from another Pentagon document, called R,D,T&E Programs (for research, development, test, and evaluation) is the air force's request for $2.1 billion for advanced intercontinental ballistic missile modernization—an amalgamation of work that includes $1.3 billion for a small, single-warhead weapon called Midgetman for launch from mobile carriers.

Unit costs can be computed from these budget figures, though frequently in a wreath of misunderstanding. As with everything else in defense, unit cost is a lot more complicated than it appears on the surface. Though the government deals in total contract costs, unit costs are a useful guideline for comparative pricing of military equipment, and they sometimes serve as targets in bargaining with suppliers.

Because of the way unit cost numbers can be manipulated, double-talk has enshrouded this process. For example, one way of computing the unit cost of a vehicle is the fly-away cost of a military airplane or the drive-away cost of a tank. This is solely the cost of manufacturing the vehicle. It does not include development costs, support costs, and all the rest of the litany of program expenses. This is a perfectly valid way of looking at unit costs, because it is a measure of current manufacturing efficiency, without reflecting what may have been a long and difficult development or design changes to fix shortcomings in the product. In the lobbying and propaganda wars in Washington, combatants sometimes use unit costs calculated one way against unit costs figured another to suit their own purposes.

Another way of computing unit price is through total annual program costs, which are an amalgamation of design costs, test and tooling costs, support-equipment costs, spare-parts costs, and production costs. While manufacturing efficiency is submerged in this method, the cost to the government of fielding the system is portrayed more realistically.

Still another measure favored by policymakers is life-cycle costing—either in terms of a total system or in terms of units. This method adds total program costs from day one and operating costs for a weapon's projected lifetime. But projecting operating costs ten to twenty years into the future is a nebulous sort of guessing game. Still, it is the best measure of the true costs of a weapon—

especially in cases where low operating costs offset expensive development.

Life-cycle costs, unit costs, and such are the nub of so-called tradeoff studies. These tradeoff studies have added another term to the defense lexicon: *cost-effectiveness*. A new weapon should offer increased performance and firepower as well as efficiency; cost-effectiveness is the means for evaluating whether the gains are worth the price.

Tradeoff studies, cost-effectiveness analyses, life-cycle cost estimates, all these are useful guides to decisionmaking in professional hands. But where they come a cropper is when the military or civilian hierarchy in the Pentagon gets up before Congress or the public and begins to toss these numbers around as gospel. What the working troops in the military and industry know are simply best-effort projections become engraved in stone down to the last decimal on the public record. This is exactly what led to the incessant overruns—understandable or otherwise.

Budget requests—both for production and for research and development—have one common peculiarity: All are stated in remarkably precise terms. In Norm Augustine's wonderfully witty look at the military technology world, *Augustine's Laws*, he points out that the more ephemeral the cost estimate, the more precise the digits to which the estimate is carried: "The weaker the data available upon which to base one's position, the greater precision which should be quoted in order to give that data authenticity." The budget estimates cited above for research and development are carried out to as many as seven digits, but, as Augustine points out, the first digits of past program costs have erred on the average by 100 percent.

Precision is more justified in procurement estimates. When equipment has been in production for a length of time (the F-16, for example, which has been in production since the late 1970s), there is a historical cost-record. Assembly-line experience accumulates and a learning curve can be plotted of actual costs against time. As workers become more familiar with a specific system, the work becomes easier and faster. A typical learning curve, therefore, will start at a high initial figure with the first few units produced, then arc steeply down during the initial months of production to flatten as the work force attains its most efficient level in a year or so. A learning curve based on enough factory experience can be an excellent predictor of future assembly-line costs. It has hazards, however. Low production quantities, for instance, do not allow the learning curve to get started. Automation throws in another kind of curve; when automation moves onto the factory floor the learning curve sometimes moves out. A robot does not learn. It does the job at the same rate and the same cost the thousandth time as it did the first.

Even good production-cost estimates, though, can be disrupted by modifications during equipment development. McDonnell Douglas ran into this kind of situation in the early phases of the AH-64 Apache. After it estimated its costs and profit rate, the army insisted that various modifications be incorporated into the helicopter on the production line at the company's expense. While the army held the line on its budgeted costs, McDonnell Douglas's financial statements reflected a lower profit.

Unexpected work force losses also can upset costing. During the Vietnam War, for example, when workers could walk out of one California aircraft plant and instantly find a job at another, learning curves disintegrated. (Feeding in replacements who had to be trained kept the learning curve stubbornly near its starting level.) Further, employee attrition can lead to material shortages, disruptions in delivery schedules, and ballooning costs. Military hardware is prone to these kinds of disruptions when unexpected technical snags snarl production planning. Out-of-station assembly on the plant floor eats dollars—that is when the natural order of assembly-line production is disrupted, when parts are late and the unit has to be pulled aside to await them or opened up again later to accommodate them.

If production-cost estimates sometimes go awry, cost estimates on the development of new military hardware can go farther adrift in a sea of uncertainty. When it becomes a question of inventing something on contract, of developing a piece of equipment that has not been built before—and doing it on a rigid schedule—cost estimating can turn into a fiasco. Much depends on how radical a departure from existing equipment is entailed. Estimating the cost of developing a new computer with conventional chips and architecture, for example, has uncertainty, but the costs of developing and building similar computers are a reasonable guide. Estimating the cost of a computer designed to use an untested, smaller-than-ever-built integrated circuit obviously magnifies the uncertainties.

Trimming the Fat

From all these causes stem the infamous overrun—when the actual costs of a program exceed the estimated budgeted costs. Whether the cause is incompetent management, an unrealistic requirement, a calculated risk to force a significant technical breakthrough, or simply a case where no reliable cost estimate was possible to begin with, the outcome is the same: Actual costs exceed estimates and chagrin follows. Sometimes, to make up the difference, other programs are robbed of funding (through reprogramming) or are terminated. Given the uncertainties inherent in trying to push technology through existing barriers, overruns should be expected. But whether programs in general should routinely exceed estimates is another matter; not all military weapons development pushes technology. Consistent overruns suggest either poor estimating or deliberate unbridled optimism used to sell programs. Neither the military nor industry is prone to level with legislators for fear that the truth would abort programs.

Technical uncertainty is not the only economic trap. Another is that a program will be underfunded to the point where it drags along without generating much return, in effect producing an overrun of another kind. NASA's space shuttle program, for example, was habitually underfunded in the 1970s. The price paid, eventually, for this underfunding played a part in setting the stage for the *Challenger* accident.

Another economic trap is set by the contract-negotiation process. In recent years, the government has used the so-called best and final offer from prospective bidders to make its contract decision. With millions of dollars in revenue at stake, and perhaps the long-term future of a company on the line, bidders get increasingly jittery after scrutinizing their estimated costs the hundredth time and submitting their proposals. At the height of an inevitable raft of rumors, the government then asks for another round of best and final offers. This kind of psychological warfare can go on until the contracting officer is ready to take a set of bids to his superiors and show them how much he has wrung out the competing contractors by his hard-boiled negotiation.

On a nuts-and-bolts type of contract for equipment in production with no surprises left, tough tactics like this can get the lowest reasonable price for the taxpayer. But where there is technical uncertainty, realism in cost estimating is the first casualty. Ratcheting can abet self-delusion of the kind that says maybe the development of the engine or the rocket motor or the fire control radar or the integration of the electronics won't be as difficult or take as long as the bidder thinks. So the contractor begins to shave what started out to be relatively reasonable costs. But there is no way government or industry can estimate the cost of the unknowns that will erupt along the way. Still, contractors believe their own marketing figures, and, commonly enough, the government customer, pressured to be optimistic as well, swallows the puffery.

Estimates were the butt of another of Augustine's laws, which reveals a fundamental problem in contracting—government and otherwise. Based on a study conducted some years ago, Augustine determined that, on average, equipment is delivered in one-third more time than estimated—a pattern that can be traced back to the American Revolution. And this schedule delay is equivalent to cost growth.

When programs do run over costs or when Congress balks at rising budget figures, there comes the matter of trimming the fat. In the Pentagon, the budget-cutting process is seldom so well thought out as the original budgetmaking. Those programs with the best-prepared program element monitors are likely to survive; those in which the program element monitors have not done their homework, or simply happen to be away on leave, are likely to bite the dust. One of the dangers of radical budgetcutting is that the whole, carefully structured process falls into disarray at the last minute, and the country's best interests may be lost in the shuffle.

While flimsy, fuzzy, or fatuous, cost estimates frequently are blamed as the source of grief in acquisition, they are not the real culprit. The real culprit is lack of candor about uncertainty, about what programs in the past gobbled up in the way of extra dollars, about how much they might in the future. Estimating is not a science, not even an art when unproven, exotic technology or high-powered marketing to snare billion-dollar contracts are entailed. Hypocrisy soon envelops projections as the services and their industrial suppliers sell programs, as administrations or Congresses perform sleight of hand to pretend they are holding down deficits or taxes.

Repeated analyses make the same points. Industry, military, defense secretaries, Congress—all must swallow their self-interest and stop kidding each other about the precision of estimates for the development costs of advanced weapons. And Pentagon bosses should be realistic about estimates, allowing margin for error, and use restraint in starting new programs.

Once the Pentagon settles on a budget, as much as it can settle on a budget, it next goes to the Office of Management and Budget, the arm of the White House that puts together all the budgets of the federal agencies for submission, in one enormous package, to Capitol Hill. The numbers from the Pentagon are no surprise to the White House budget crew because their program monitors have been privy to the budget construction process from the beginning. Budget bureau soldiers do not play a decisionmaking role then, but their exposure to the reasoning behind the making of the budget is valuable—though sometimes disruptive—in later stages. Obviously, the jostling over programs is still not over, for the White House budget bureau and Congress are the other two legs of the tripod that determines how much the nation will spend on defense. At this point, national politics begins to intrude in force, where it may override military analysis in budget decisions.

4

Congress Stirs the Pot

IF Pentagon requirements and budgets propose, it is Congress that disposes. Not only does Congress have its budget veto, but it also has taken on multiple other functions in weapons buying. Wielding its oversight and legislative power, Congress has been at the core of the recent metamorphosis in the acquisitions process. Legislation has forced the Pentagon to adopt increasingly complicated regulations that affect military manager and contractor alike. Congressional oversight has spawned greater Pentagon-hierarchy oversight, all directed at the steadily submerging program manager. Congress's loss of confidence in the Defense Department—starting with Defense Secretary McNamara and galvanized by his conduct of the Vietnam War—has done more than anything else to convert Congress's policy and financial review of the defense budget into a crusade for reform and an excuse for mixing into day-to-day detail.

Overshadowed in Congress's crusade for reform, in its determination to reduce waste, fraud, and abuse, has been the original check-and-balance function of the legislature through its control of the purse. Instead, using the leverage it has in parceling out acquisition money, Congress is taking a direct hand in program management. While Congress delves deeper into micromanagement, independent studies show that it is straying from its role as a policymaking board of directors. Thus the legislature is in the awesome position of making decisions on programs and then passing on their merits and their money needs—certainly a distortion of the checks and balances of the three federal branches of government that the founding fathers had in mind.

There was a time when, without sacrificing separate viewpoints and interests, more cooperation existed between Congress and the

Pentagon in budgetmaking and military affairs. Now their adversarial relationship—parallel to that between government and industry—is further destabilizing the budget and management processes. While the making of a defense budget for equipment always has become less formalized as it navigates from the Pentagon into the political sea, the less is becoming profoundly less. And although there have been sporadic attempts by the Pentagon to concentrate purely on budgeting for what the military thinks it needs to carry out its mission—unconstrained by politics, service horse-trading, or the availability of funds—they have not lasted for long.

That word *mission* is almighty to the services. These defined tasks—more than a few to be carried out at all costs—are central to the operation of military organizations. Some missions are fairly specific, such as the seizure by force of a piece of real estate. Some are broad and general in intent, such as the navy's mission to maintain control of those sea lanes of concern to American interests or the army's mission to seize or hold territory. The latter, a military organization's basic purpose in life, is at the pinnacle—the kind of mission laid down by political administrations that determines what the defense establishment is supposed to accomplish for the national interest in the broadest policy sense.

At the beginning of their budgeting cycles, military organizations use the accomplishment of their particular missions in the face of an enemy threat as the basis for drafting their individual budget requests. Reduced to its simplest level, a military organization has no claim to buy a weapons system—no matter how attractive technically or in price—if this equipment does not contribute to the accomplishment of its mission. Ideally, Congress should make its primary budget focus whether the defense budget submitted is best meeting that criterion. But this is not the case.

Just as with requirements, if missions and objectives are not defined cogently to begin with, budgeting can go wrong. If the executive branch has not made its purposes clear, then Congress is handicapped in its attempts to review and reconcile budgets, missions, and objectives. Further, the services periodically go through fits of politicking to enlarge their mission turf, adding to the confusion.

The Packard Commission, which included two former deputy secretaries of defense and one former national security council head, faulted the practice of providing executive-branch guidance to the military through vaguely drawn National Security Decision Directives that, among other things, do not recognize the limits of fiscal resources: "Because of the lack of early Presidential guidance on fiscal limits, defense resource plans are subject to debate and change within the Administration up to the moment the President makes his final decisions before sending his annual budget to Congress" (page 10, "A Quest for Excellence").

The commission's point is all too true. But the problem is even greater. A design-to-cost approach could constrain research and development to the wrong program or the wrong technology at the wrong time. A cost-constrained approach at the inception of a research and development effort will exclude a superficially unpromising idea that later turns out a winner or, worse, produce obsolescent equipment. Further, it is always possible that the least likely contingency in a planning document will be the one to erupt. These are central policy issues in military budgeting and buying because they expose the unpalatable fact that economic efficiency and military effectiveness are not always compatible.

Obviously, in peacetime, in a world of imperfect vision, some kind of weapons acquisition tradeoff has to be made. That tradeoff is what is distilled in the budget that travels from the Pentagon to the White House, in which the military has attempted to cut the cloth to fit the money guidance originally sent by the administration. How well that cloth has been cut, and how well the executive branch has established the pattern for the cutting (through National Security Decision Directives), is what Congress must review.

Uncertain as the initial budget premises are in National Security Decision Directives, the succeeding processes are dogged by even worse instability and confusion. When the budgets of all the federal agencies are aggregated, the process of horse trading begins to accelerate. Now national economic policy, elections, and, by no means least, what military hardware contract will be dropped like manna from heaven in whose congressional district, inject pork-barrel politics into the process.

The "Defense Experts"

Both the White House staff and the Office of Management and Budget have their own defense experts. These experts are far fewer in number than the Pentagon's, but sometimes far more influential in cases where spending is controversial. Sometimes they form a useful bridge between the Pentagon and Capitol Hill. Sometimes they substitute their judgment for that of military commanders and become one more layer of micromanagement, one more generator of issues, one more layer of review. Their concerns are much broader than the Pentagon's, and often as not the final number for a defense budget will come down to what they think will get through Congress or will serve the administration's economic policy.

Even the civilian leadership in the Pentagon is unable to keep its eye on the cost of Armageddon without looking at its political aspects. In the Reagan years especially, concern has rested with how a weapons program will sit with Congress, not with whether it is right technically. Putting image before substance would not be so disconcerting were it not for the lack of clearly defined objectives for U.S. military forces, which shape what weapons are bought. Compounding the problem is the fact that in growing into a supramilitary organization running the military, the Defense Department's political appointees, not to mention those down in the service tier, are often inexperienced in technical matters and industrial management.

Congress itself put the politician in the Pentagon. In the late 1970s, in its ethics in government legislation—designed to prevent Pentagon managers from going to work for companies they dealt with in contracting—Congress made it virtually impossible to attract technical talent from industry to middle- and top-level jobs in the Pentagon by foreclosing their return to a former employer or to a defense company of any stripe. Blocked from this traditional source of technologists, the Reagan administration went to Capitol Hill or nondefense businesses, and naturally what it got were not engineers and scientists but politicians. So Congress helped to create the very management mess it so vehemently denounced later on. With an equal lack of industrial and technical experience in Congress and in its staffs, the combination is hypergolic (self-igniting like some rocket fuels) for skewed decisions. Nor did the ethics in government legislation correct a related and serious problem—the legions of experienced military and civilian personnel departing the service.

The Defense Department has fattened into a ponderous bureaucracy. It has become an operating command of super-senior military decisionmakers on top of all the military operating commands, duplicating the functions of the services while ceding its more important policy functions to the National Security Council in the White House. One example is the Strategic Defense Initiative (Star Wars), which was born in the White House and handed to the Pentagon—to like or lump.

From its beginning as a small advisory group to the president, the National Security Council has become crisis manager and technical analyzer, handling the kinds of political and policy decisions that the Defense Department—and State Department—once made. The underlying significance of the Ollie North affair, mostly missed in the hearings and the media, was that presidents have lost patience with the Defense and State Department bureaucracies—even with the Central Intelligence Agency—when they want to do something difficult, politically sensitive, and risky—and do it in a hurry. When presidents want to act, they won't put up with position papers and endless reviews, and the Ollie Norths of this world fill the sometimes desperate needs of the executive for a get-it-done man who won't ask a million questions or raise a thousand objections or tell him about the corners he is cutting to do the job. North touched a responsive chord with the public as well: its frustration with bureaucratic barriers to getting something done, anything done—even something rash—with ever more legislation, regulation, and review.

At the Irangate hearings, Secretary of State George P. Shultz mused to Congress about the remoteness—in spirit, not distance—of his office in Foggy Bottom and of the office of the secretary of defense in the Pentagon from the president, while an army of White House aides in the old State Department building feeds advice to the chief executive. That old building ought to be cleaned out, he observed, and the cabinet installed there as the real presidential staff it was intended to be. Those remarks say more about what is wrong with the federal government and how it functions than a bookcase full of studies and reports.

Congress has its own bureaucracy of defense experts, too, in staffs that have been multiplying to an estimated 20,000 people. Of all the complaints in the Pentagon and in the defense industry about the impact of Congress on military decisionmaking, the most indignant have been about the role of congressional staffs.

Few of these complaints are about the intelligence, or even the motivations, of these people; they center on their zeal uncomplicated by experience, their lack of firsthand familiarity with how the military works, how wars are fought, how business is conducted in general, and how a laboratory concept is turned into an assembly-line product. Although the House and Senate Armed Services Committees that once almost solely controlled military budgets still have senior members who belie such generalizations, their numbers are gradually being thinned by retirements and outside offers. Congressional staffs are notoriously underpaid by Washington standards. Replacements tend to come with law or political science training, perhaps some seasoning in political campaigns, but little else. Not only are veteran staffers departing, but so are veteran members who understood defense—either by retirement, like Senator Barry Goldwater, or death, like the late representative Melvin Price.

The Trend toward Overmanagement

Another change that is affecting the way Congress deals with the military budget is a trend toward turf battles and factional argument over specific line items that is not in the best public interest. According to the Packard Commission:

> Today's congressional authorization and appropriation processes have become mired in jurisdictional disputes, leading to overlapping review of thousands of line items within the defense budget. A growing rivalry between the Armed Services Committees and the Defense Appropriations Subcommittees over the line-item makeup of the defense budget has played a major role in moving congressional review of the defense budget toward narrowly focused financial action on individual items and away from oversight based on operational concepts and military effectiveness. During the review of the 1985 defense budget, for example, Congress made changes to over 1,800 separate defense programs and directed the Department of Defense to conduct 458 studies ranging from the feasibility of selling lamb products in commissaries to the status of retirement benefits for Philippine scouts (page 21–22 of the final report).

The sheer magnitude of administrative chores laid on the Pentagon by Congress is awesome. The 458 studies requested by Congress in 1985 from the Pentagon was over 1,000 percent more than fifteen years earlier. According to a Center for Strategic and International Studies report, "In 1984, the Department of Defense sent 1,300 witnesses to provide 1,500 hours of testimony at 450 hearings before 29 standing committees and 55 subcommittees of Congress. This level of the Defense Department must annually respond to more than 120,000 written requests and 600,000 phone calls from Congress—all totally uncoordinated with each other" (page 20). That was 1984. No doubt the total has risen since. Why does the Pentagon need so many people, asked former secretary of the navy John Lehman, Jr., early in the Reagan administration? A lot of them, he replied, answer all those telephone calls and letters.

Congress considered at least one hundred and fifty pieces of contract legislation in 1986, and enacted many of them. Lieutenant General John M. Loh, commander of the Air Force Systems Command's Aeronautical Systems Division, recounted in a speech at an air force conference that the Defense Department had to respond to more than one thousand congressional and White House inquiries that year and was faced with more than six hundred audits from the Congressional General Accounting Office, the Defense Department inspector general, and the Defense Contract Audit Agency. Individual legislative changes in the whole process of procurement reform can be justified, he said, "but, in the aggregate, when they are all piled on top of the other, they represent collectively a severe constraint on the flexibility of both of us to do smart, and common sense, sorts of things." Moreover, they compound the risk for defense contractors. As Loh summed up the situation: "We are concerned that many . . . may consider dropping out of the defense sector because of the extended time it may take to earn a profit or obtain adequate return on very costly investments." His comments on new legislation could apply to changes made over the past twenty-five years.

The fact that Loh spoke on the record in as blunt terms as he did reflects the incipient revolt percolating in industry and the military over the way weapons acquisition has been overmanaged into a mess. Both industry and the military contributed to this mess to the extent that they did not rise up earlier, before the deterioration went as far as it did. What form the revolt may take is hard to envision, but the possibility of contractors gradually bailing out already has been noted. The United States lost about half of its defense-contractor base as a result of the funding cuts in the 1970s, and another bloodletting may be coming in the 1990s. Obviously, this is a worrisome threat for national security. On the military front, the reaction may take the form of further early retirements, resignations, and departures. Morale is down in the acquisition ranks and the exodus of experienced hands could reach flood level.

Increasing Oversight

The weapons-acquisition system has not only been hard hit by new legislation but also by the increasing oversight of congressional committees and subcommittees. As a result, over the past fifteen years, the number of changes in program authorization increased seven times and the number of changes in appropriations nearly tripled, with considerable impact on program stability. The competition between the Armed Services and Appropriations Committees was one reason for these increases, but the dabbling by various other committees in defense affairs also was felt. In one recent case, Representative John Dingell's Oversight and Investigations Subcommittee, which has no charter in national security, took the position that black programs (secret research and development efforts) get too little scrutiny by internal or external auditors. But what good might come of more public accountability for secret programs could well be offset by their exposure to intensified red tape and oversight.

Still more confusion over weapons programs exists within Congress. As the Packard Commission noted, "the Defense Department now finds itself involved in a new congressional budgeting phenomenon in which the Appropriations Committees have funded programs that the Armed Services Committees have not authorized. In fiscal year 1986, the Defense Department Appropriation Act included over 150 line items, valued at $5.7 billion, that were authorized at a lower level or were not authorized at all" (page 22 of the final report). While the committee disagreement continued, the Pentagon was left hanging—unable to commit money or complete contract negotiations. Thus while Congress fiddles, industry has employees on the payroll who have to be paid and vendors and subcontractors are left hanging by their thumbs.

Congress is, without doubt, as much a contributor to the foibles of the military-buying system as the Pentagon or the defense industry—if not more. The Packard Commission's comments summarize some of the reasons, but only scratch the surface of the multitudinous ways in which Congress is complicating the buying process, adding an enormous burden on an already encumbered system.

The Warranty Misunderstanding

For example, take the case of the crusade by Senator Mark Andrews of North Dakota to force the military to mandate warranties for its equipment. His idea was simple: If the tractor on his farm in North Dakota was covered by a warranty, if all he had to do was call the dealer and it was fixed, why couldn't the military, which was spending billions of dollars more than he was, do the same thing? Congress did mandate warranties on defense equipment, but only after more experienced hands in the legislature caught the fact that the original proposal did not exclude combat damage as a warrantable item—something patently ridiculous. By its usual grinding and digestion process, the bureaucracy was able to stall off some of the more imprudent features of this mandate. Whether, in principle, the idea of warranties for military equipment is a good one, depends on the circumstances—that is, whether the cost of the warranty is worth the expense. Some in Congress seemed to think they came for free.

The campaign for warranties did not start in Congress at all. The air force, for one, was working on a warranty system for flight instruments in the early 1960s, when the concept was revolutionary. That initial dip into the water was cautious, focusing on a single instrument—a barometric altimeter of the type that had been in aircraft since the early days of aviation. It was a simple instrument, nothing fancy that used radar or other exotic sensing technology, to determine height—in other words, a good test case. Terms and conditions were carefully spelled out, far differently from the way Congress charged into the warranty arena.

One item the legislators overlooked in trying to duplicate commercial warranties for the services was that commercial warranties require that periodic maintenance and repair be performed by factory-authorized facilities. The military performs its own maintenance, whether for conventional half-ton trucks or for very sophisticated electronic equipment, whether for a simple electronic-board change made on an aircraft or a major overhaul or modification executed in an industrial depot or navy shipyard. Manufacturers are reluctant to provide much in the way of warranty coverage on equipment out of their servicing control.

Then there is the question of cost. Manufacturers do not provide warranty coverage—commercial or otherwise—without prorating it into the selling price. Obviously, manufacturers can build enough into the contract cost to take care of warranty coverage, no matter who does the maintenance. Thus, as Pentagon acquisition experts were aware, the services might be forced to buy more warranty coverage than they could use. While the services generally were dismayed by this pressure from Congress, nothing is black or white in this business; to some extent the services welcomed the push, for it gave them a bargaining lever with industry for the warranty coverage that they did want.

The whole affair was a prime example of how good intentions in Congress and long experience in the military deal with an idea that, in the end, does some good but also raises costs and creates misunderstanding between the Pentagon and the legislature. Where the difficulty comes is in estimating whether the added costs are worth the benefit. The jury will be out for quite a while on the warranty case. In addition, consideration might be given to the fact that warranties as a single mandate are one thing; laid on the acquisition system with a batch of others, they are quite another.

The more critical policy question is who really should be managing what. Should Congress confine itself to spending levels and let the services decide how that money is apportioned? Or should Congress get into the details of military buying, on the grounds that it cannot make funding decisions if it does not understand the bits and pieces? If Congress is not convinced of the judgment and wisdom of those running the Defense Department, surely it will continue to insist on thrusting its hand into equipment buying.

Right now, Congress has come to pervade in military buying. As

Willis J. Willoughby, the navy's overseer of quality control, sees it, people in the service spend hours in secret devising clever strategy in hardware acquisition, all a delusion: "Congress has it all. Most program managers just sit and brief. They have very little control of what they've got."

The Credibility Gap

While Congress deserves the criticism it gets for micromanagement, it cannot be blamed for losing confidence in Defense Department leadership. McNamara awed Congress and the public with his command of figures and the air of the infallible technocrat in his early years. But when his promises and predictions didn't work out, when he ignored anything that couldn't be expressed in numbers, Congress became skeptical. Capitol Hill deals in people and distrusts statistics; McNamara's fixation on statistics opened a fissure.

The credibility gap was far from closed when Ronald Reagan was elected in 1980 on a platform of rebuilding U.S. defenses. Reagan's nomination of Caspar Weinberger did not seem to fit with his defense goals, for in Weinberger (known as Cap the Knife from his earlier service as budget director in the Nixon administration), Reagan had picked a tough bean counter to keep the Pentagon fiscally in line when the defense buildup got under way.

In the beginning, Weinberger and the Defense Department rode on the crest of a tenuous consensus that the United States had lagged behind the Soviet Union in modernizing its armed forces. He staunchly defended the decisions of the Defense Department, but never seemed as if he were part of them. He showed more interest in international affairs, and his attitude with Congress was didactic and inflexible. His ratings on Capitol Hill can be charted by the size of the defense budget increases he wrung from Congress—double digit percentages in the early years, zero if he was lucky toward the end. Even those legislators most expert on defense—like former senator Barry Goldwater and those congressional committee staff members with extensive experience with the military—were profoundly irritated by Weinberger's hard-line intransigence, his unresponsiveness, his lack of give-and-take that oils business on Capitol Hill. Weinberger won many admirers in the

Pentagon with his budget tactics. But in the argot of Washington, Weinberger broke his pick with Congress in the process.

To be fair to Weinberger, there was something else at work—something that gets right to the core of why Congress has been so lethal to the acquisition process. A now-retired senior officer told me that at one point Weinberger was ready to compromise with Congress on the budget. But no one in Congress could cut the deal. Even Goldwater, so the story goes, could not promise more than one vote—his own—and that left 534 others to work on. Congress is so disorganized, so bound with internecine upstaging, so leaderless that it cannot carry its own water to the conference table. Any deal on the budget that Weinberger might have made would simply have become the new level from which one committee or another, or one member or another, would subtract.

When the attack came from Congress on waste, fraud, and abuse, Weinberger's ability to cope with it was limited. Weinberger plunged into international defense politics, but, as had been customary, left the Pentagon's immense buying operation to his deputy. The first was Frank Carlucci, a fellow trouper from his budget-bureau days, a loyal and competent bureaucrat whose knowledge of acquisition details was probably no more extensive than Weinberger's. Nonetheless, Carlucci started off his term with a list of improvements to the acquisition process. Called the Carlucci initiatives, these were all welcomed by the professionals, but few had any long-term appeal to Capitol Hill and there were few that anyone in industry expected to survive. Some did—like multiyear contracting, where Congress appropriates for several years' worth of program contracting—but not most. They were a brave start on fixing what the professionals thought was wrong with the acquisition system, but they were soon overwhelmed by horror stories of waste, fraud, and abuse.

Carlucci left for private industry and Weinberger chose a successor from the standpoint of getting someone who understood the industrial process and military research and development. This was Paul Thayer, a former test pilot, who, as chairman of LTV, had confounded his company board by flying an overhauled World War II Corsair fighter for the fun of it—until its engine quit and, no ordinary chairman of the board, he got the airplane down successfully onto a farm field. But Thayer had been in office only a few months when he was accused by the Securities and Exchange Commission of leaking insider information to the considerable profit of a swinging Dallas crowd. Thayer resigned from the Defense Department and later went to jail. With his departure was lost an experienced and knowledgeable deputy secretary of defense for acquisition that the Defense Department and industry needed in winning the respect of, and dealing with, Congress. Thayer's successor, William H. Taft IV (another Weinberger protégé) was a lawyer who, again, had little acquaintance with the military-buying system.

It should be noted that when Carlucci came back to government—first as White House National Security Adviser after the Irangate debacle, and then to replace his former chief as defense secretary—his tack with Congress was conciliatory. His early testimony on Capitol Hill seemed to reflect not only a willingness to be open-minded on such things as budget cuts, but also a definite attempt to erase the image of Weinberger intransigence.

While Congress may not be expert on how the military-acquisition system works, it is acutely perceptive to what its constituents are thinking. There is no question that Congress is reflecting the distrust of the public in its flailing of the military-buying system. At the same time, the Pentagon has lost confidence in the ability of Congress to weigh and act. This mutual loss of confidence is, by far, the most insidious threat to the viability of the military-acquisition system.

Filling the Vacuum

Congress has not been hesitant to fill the vacuum left by civilian leadership in the Pentagon. Individual congressmen have worked up their own agendas. One was an attack on the adequacy of the testing of the Aegis guided missile cruiser, long under development by the navy to automate and extend the range of the fleet's air defense. Another was to use small submarines to launch ballistic missiles instead of the behemoths the navy is building for the Trident system.

A rather typical case is that of a new radar-targeting system—the Joint Surveillance Targeting Attack Radar System (Joint STARS)—under joint development by the air force and the army.

The new radar is to be flown behind the front lines on an aircraft used to detect enemy air and ground movements near a battle zone. The air force selected a reconditioned Boeing 707 to carry the radar. While more fuel-efficient aircraft have superseded the 707 in commercial airline fleets, it is a rugged airplane with a long life expectancy and a good buy for this purpose. Used airplanes bought from the airlines at far less cost than a new aircraft were to be sent to Boeing, fitted with the radar and a cabin full of control consoles, and then sent to the field for use.

But Congress had other ideas—essentially those of Anthony Battista, a veteran staff member on the House Armed Services Committee and as expert on the military and its buying as anyone on Capitol Hill. Among other things, Battista thought the big, transport-size aircraft was too easy for an enemy to detect and shoot down, destroying the whole tactical targeting system in the process. He suggested an alternative that he believed had a greater chance at survival: putting the radar on a reconnaissance aircraft—specifically a new version of the famous Lockheed U-2, which is smaller and can operate at much higher, and presumably safer, altitudes than the 707. Where to put the control consoles and communications was something of a problem, but ground basing was an option.

Survivability, in the view of the air force, was a legitimate issue, one that deserved attention. As anyone with a nodding acquaintance of air combat knows, any airplane can be shot down if the enemy tries hard enough. But there are ways to increase survivability in combat through the location of an airplane and the way it is defended.

It all boils down to this: Should Congress be substituting its own judgment for that of the services on a technical question? Or is this kind of congressional decisionmaking a way to force the services to refine their thinking, to reevaluate their own decisions, and to ensure that viable combat hardware is delivered to the troops?

The crux is where Congress's role as board of directors ends and mere meddling begins. There is evidence that Congress has crossed that line. For the past several years, bills dealing with weapons acquisition—that is, methods not policy—have proliferated in Congress to the tune of at least a hundred, perhaps as many as two hundred, per session. It is hard to imagine how that many individual bills, introduced by scores of congressmen who often have only rudimentary ideas of how the military or industry works, could possibly improve military weapons buying. What emerges instead is disorganized tinkering. While most of these bills stagnate in committee back rooms, some, like the warranty legislation, find their way into the statute books. And, for ill or good, the services carry out their provisions. But piecemeal legislation of this kind is what has heaped onto an already overburdened acquisition system an even larger mass of procedures and regulations.

Not all congressional ideas on acquisition are bad by any means. For example, Congress has encouraged the services to use commercial off-the-shelf equipment, a less expensive route in development. Use of modified commercial IBM personal computers to modernize the military's global communication network is one successful case in point.

Still the sheer bulk of legislative activity in acquisition is not only well nigh impossible to cope with but also self-defeating. If anything sums up the core of the weapons-buying problem for the nation, it is too much outside advice. More and more, the people who have to carry out the work, either in the military or industry, find themselves hamstrung. Instead of the "can do" spirit that once marked the development of new technology, the process has become a ponderous waltz of the elephants, much to the distress of a good many participants. In the zeal to fix the system, Congress has compromised its role in weapons acquisition.

Congress has to get its act together. Rival committees devoted to thumping the Pentagon may capture the headlines, but this contributes nothing to the oversight of the defense enterprise. Disorganization in Congress makes compromises on weapons and budget almost futile. Congress cannot continue to drop tons of random legislation on the acquisition apparatus without adding to what one military manager said is already an unholy mess.

Further, Congress and the executive branch cannot ride off in opposite directions, leaving the government acquisition troops and their industrial suppliers guessing at policy. Policymakers must send a clear message as to what they collectively want in weapons. In addition, Congress must demand that the executive branch define its broad strategic objectives clearly. Congress cannot reconcile dollars and strategy if policy is vaguely defined.

5

Contracts and Specifications: The Paper Mill

ONCE a requirement for military hardware is cast in concrete, once the money filters through the congressional sieve, the program will go to contract. Like everything else in the defense business, contracts are a complicated matter.

There are three tiers in supplying military hardware. At the apex are the prime contractors. Prime simply means that the contract is directly with the government. Prime contractors, in turn, buy complex and expensive subsystems from subcontractors, the second tier in the defense industry. Government, its prime contractors, and subcontractors all buy from the third tier: vendors and suppliers. These third-tier companies sell more or less standard, catalog types of equipment.

Because the government considers direct technical and financial control over vital, high-value equipment to be important, it does not always have prime contractors buy all the subsystems. Quite often it will contract directly with a manufacturer for technically advanced electronic equipment. This will then be supplied to the prime contractor as government-furnished equipment, for whose quality the government is responsible. This arrangement is a breeding ground for disputes between prime contractor and government over schedule delays in, and the reliability of, government-furnished equipment.

Further, not every major weapons system has a prime contractor. Sometimes the military buyer will divide work among a group of associate contractors, none of which has overall responsibility for design and performance. The air force used this arrangement quite successfully for the Titan 3 space-launch vehicle.

Winning a Contract

The government normally invites industry into a program following the defense secretary's authorization for the effort to proceed. The formal invitation is the request for proposals. For catalog kinds of hardware bought from vendors, the government will issue a far less complex document called a request for quotation. Despite years of attempts to reduce their size, requests for proposals for big-ticket systems are massive—hundreds or thousands of pages that spell out performance requirements, timetables for development and delivery, contractor qualifications, deadlines for submission, prospective contract-award data, and so on and on and on. The request for proposals can itself increase costs because it is expensive to reproduce in quantity and then expensive to deal with the proposals that result. For this reason, the services once tried to limit distribution of proposal requests. But with increasing emphasis on competition, the trend now is to ask in all comers, which at least pleases Congress and the Pentagon hierarchy, even if it doesn't generate a better price.

If the requests for proposals are long, the responses from contractors usually are far longer. While a diligent campaign has been waged by the services to limit proposals to about one hundred pages, contractors get around this by providing a short summary and then pound upon pound of annexes and appendixes—their thickness measured in feet, not folios. The contractor who sold the technical idea to begin with has been preparing for the advent of the request for proposals; he is not about to shortchange his preliminary research and development, let alone threaten his survival, by lack of documentation. Neither are his rivals.

Contractors will have been alerted by their new-business intelligence operatives that there is interest in some new technology, that a request for proposals is in the mill. The government itself sometimes issues advance notice that a request for proposals is in gestation, a device to encourage interest on the part of a wider circle of competitors—especially those new to defense contracting. Work on the technology will be under way, with government or private money.

Winning a contract is the final chapter in a demanding technical and business exercise, an exhilarating battle to engineering and financial teams in a high-stakes poker game that culminates in an award. These teams will spend months working (including hours of overtime) on engineering, conducting tests in the laboratory, or in the field if possible, applying sharp pencils to cost estimates. Neither price nor performance alone will carry the day, but usually a combination of both, laced with optimism and a bit of luck of the draw.

Sometimes, if a contractor has a particular lead in the technology involved, a contract can be awarded with no competition—called, in acquisition vernacular, *sole source*. If a company has invented or developed a system radically new and different, sole source is actually the fair way to proceed. Other contractors may be given research money just to provide the semblance of competition, even if the customer knows who will eventually get the contract. Congress long ago established wickets the government must pass through before going sole source instead of competitive bid. Now with the Competition in Contracting Act the pressure is to go competition. Still, the services try to avoid competition where it is downright uneconomic—that is, with small-quantity programs.

But sole source is the exception. In the typical situation, massive proposals arrive from competing contractors. Evaluating the pile of paper that results is an awesome task. Nominally, source selection is the task of the services' acquisition commands. Usually, even for relatively small programs, advisory boards or committees in acquisition commands are assigned. Obviously, the proposal submission and evaluation process further stretches out the development time of acquisitions. While some recent efforts have begun to trim the number of advisers and shorten evaluation time on less complex acquisitions, the sheer magnitude of paper on a multibillion-dollar program mitigates against speed.

If a program is large enough, a blue ribbon source-selection board may be drawn from various service commands. Pentagon political-level appointees then either accept the source-selection team's recommendation for award or not. With so much public money involved in larger weapon systems, these decisions are escalated up the line to the point where the White House or Congress will at least be advised, if not consulted, on the most expensive.

Again, for a major system, there will be a process called down selection. At least two contractors will be kept in the running to the end, so that the government can squeeze out the best possible price before it makes its final judgment. Sometimes contenders are asked for their best and final offers in the form of a signed contract; the government makes the award by executing the contract, converting the contractor's promises, however optimistic, into legally binding terms. Other times the final terms and conditions will be negotiated after the contractor is chosen. The selected contractor is not always the same as the winner of the technical evaluation. Price may override technical superiority, or politics may carry the day.

Bid-and-proposal submissions of this kind cost millions. These millions are financed in part by the government as a charge against other contracts a company may have, analogous to the way it covers independent research and development costs. In the past two or three years, the government has tried to lump the two charges into one, in effect reducing independent research and development allowances—and dismaying contractors. How much the government may allow for independent research and for bid-and-proposal costs is thus a matter of controversy—particularly in cases when a contractor suspects it is being pushed into bidding on a program where its chances are slim just to dress up the competition.

Periodically, Congress gets upset about the independent research and bid-and-proposal expense on the ground that it is a free ride or subsidy for the defense industry. Further, compounding the problem is the fact that defense contracts cover termination charges for work in progress should a program be cancelled for government convenience—charges that may be so extensive as to make termination more expensive, at least in the short term, than continuation. With cost-plus contracting—to be discussed shortly—the defense business easily may appear to be a combination subsidy and boondoggle. Sometimes programs turn out to be just that, but more often they don't.

The Nitty-Gritty

Once the award is made, contracting becomes the nitty-gritty push-and-shove of how government and private industry produce and deliver military hardware. Unlike commercial contracting, government contracting is an arcane world, peopled by cost analysts, lawyers, and multiple layers of officers, auditors, and comptrollers. In this world of weapons buying, dominated by standards and regulations, buyer and seller live by the letter of the contract. They have little choice. How well or how badly the contract is structured is a determinant of how well or how badly the program goes, how well or how badly the equipment serves the user. If the contract is murky and complex, as most tend to be in government business, if the statement of work the contractor is to accomplish is imprecise, it then becomes the source of dispute and misunderstanding.

Defense contracting has become synonymous with cost-plus contracting, but there are almost a hundred different types of contract instruments used in government business. Most are variations on a theme of three or four main contract types. Cost-plus contracting is one broad category; it has acquired the pejorative connotation of fat-cat contractors feeding at the government trough. Nonetheless, cost-plus contracts—or, more broadly, cost-type contracts—continue to survive, because they provide an incentive to producers in what would otherwise be too risky a situation—the quest for advanced-technology equipment that has never been built before in this particular form for a narrow market (perhaps a single customer) that can, and does, change its mind. Thus cost-plus contracts allow for the financing of programs that a private contractor would not otherwise take on.

The differences between government and commercial development may be illustrated as follows. Say the Ford Motor Company decides to introduce an automobile with increased aerodynamic sleekness that will reduce air resistance on the road and improve fuel consumption. The project will require costly research in aircraft wind tunnels, and a high degree of manufacturing finish and fit to eliminate gaps, bulges, and rough edges. Ford knows from past experience how much money it will take to pay for new car development, although, given the unknowns of this particular project, costs probably will come out higher or lower than predicted—probably higher. Within reason, these differences are not disastrous, because Ford can spread development costs over a commercial market of millions of vehicles, getting its investment back tidbits at a time. The product may turn out to be a successful Taurus—or an Edsel—but Ford has millions of potential customers and a reasonable bet that enough of them will see the product its way to warrant the investment.

Then imagine that Boeing decides to build a new generation of commercial transport airplanes, like its 757 or 767. It knows from past experience how much the research and development of a new commercial aircraft costs, but there still will be glitches and mistakes and the unexpected. Just as was the case with Ford, Boeing's estimate of the costs of engineering, wind tunnel work, materials testing, and government certification will no doubt come out higher or lower than projected—probably higher. Boeing, too, can spread its development costs over a commercial market, but unlike Ford's millions of automobiles, Boeing will produce only hundreds of—or, if it is lucky, a thousand or so—airplanes for the airlines. Because a much smaller number of vehicles will be sold, the penalty for overestimating the potential market is far more severe, and the risk involved is sportier. Still the risk is spread over a market of hundreds of airlines.

Now take the case of defense contractors who agree to design and develop a new airplane or missile for the government. They can estimate from past experience how much it will cost to get the project to the assembly-line stage. Again, there will be surprises, mistakes, and, more pronounced in the defense business, changes mandated by the customer. If the project involves new technology, there will be a lot of surprises, unknowns, and recalcitrant problems. The government may or may not know how many it will buy, and it may or may not tell the contractor. Even if the contractor is given a precise market size for the product, budgets may be cut or redirected by Congress, and the government may cancel the contract at any time. Although the product may be bought by other military services or overseas customers, the defense contractor still faces uncertainty over what kind of a production run he will have—that is, how many units he will sell against which he can levy an incremental charge to recover his research and development. His risk, then, is prohibitive—unless the government agrees to underwrite the bulk of the costs.

Northrop's Tigershark

What happened to the Northrop Corporation in the 1980s is illustrative of what defense contractors who invest in their own programs are in for. Some years ago, Northrop built a high-speed, light trainer aircraft, called the T-38, for the U.S. Air Force. Because of its maneuverability, supersonic speed, and simplicity, the T-38 became a nucleus around which Northrop invested its own money to develop a single-seat strike-fighter version, designated the F-5. Only a handful of F-5s found their way into the U.S. military—used as proxies for Soviet MiG-21 fighters in simulated combat training. But air forces around the world found the F-5 to be just what they wanted: a relatively inexpensive airplane, maintainable by native forces with limited skills, agile, and fun to fly. From the time of initial delivery in 1964, Northrop built more than 2,600 for 31 countries; in the 1980s alone, Northrop delivered almost 300. The F-5 was, in the company's words, a very successful program. A thousand or two is a big production run for aircraft, while commercial companies think in millions of units.

Encouraged by this success, and beguiled by President Carter's policy of protecting small nations from themselves by limiting U.S. fighter exports to something less than first-line air force F-16s or navy F-18s, Northrop invested its money in an advanced version, called the Tigershark. Again, it was a highly maneuverable, joy-to-fly airplane, but times had changed. Overseas customers balked at buying an airplane that was not in U.S. military service, because that meant they could not tap the resources and organization of the global American supply-and-support network. Further, friendly nations resented being told they could not have F-16s, that they should buy something less sophisticated that their own troops—by implication, less intelligent—could manage.

The airplane did not sell overseas—even with its later-acquired designation of F-20 to give it clothing as American military hardware in fighting its image battle. While some countries, like Saudi Arabia or Korea, liked the Tigershark, they did not want to assume the burden of being the first customer—that is, the expense of introducing a new airplane into service and setting up a supply apparatus. Even if they had, Northrop could not open a production line for a single, relatively small overseas order.

Northrop tried and failed to sell the aircraft to the U.S. Air Force as a close-support fighter and later an air-defense fighter, either of which would have been a large enough buy to support the costs of tooling up for assembly. But the air force already had paid for development of aircraft like the F-16 and did not, like the countries overseas, want to pay the costs of introducing a new aircraft into the supply system. By the time it lost the air force competition, Northrop had invested a billion dollars of its money in the Tigershark. As soon as the air force decision came down, Northrop terminated the F-20 program. It will not recover any of its investment outside of tax credits for its losses.

A Look Back

In the days before World War II, when aircraft companies were small and the costs of building a prototype airplane amounted to a few thousand dollars, investors could take the development gamble on the chance that the military would like the result and buy a few. When the war broke out, the magnitude of defense orders and the acceleration of development and production timetables made it impossible for this practice to continue. And aircraft, expensive as they might be, are a drop in the bucket compared to other military equipment. Thus the cost-plus contract was born. Government agreed to pay the contractor's audited costs, plus a negotiated fixed fee to serve as his profit. Further, the government made payments as work progressed, to cover the costs of materials bought by the contractor and the costs of labor on work in progress at the plant. In those days, defense companies were so ephemeral that they had trouble qualifying for loans from banks, and, besides, the government did not want to reimburse contractors for interest charges, so it found it cheaper to go the progress-payments route. This basic system continues today.

Defense contractors behaved like construction contractors into the 1950s. They hired production workers and engineers for specific programs and laid them off when the job was over. They could not—or would not—sell bonds for buildings and tools for defense work, so the government bought both and assigned or leased them for specific programs. Outside of a core of technical and administrative people, defense contractors often had little by way of permanent employee rosters or fixed assets.

As the cold war became a fixture, as the defense business evolved from boom or bust, from feast or famine, to a steady diet, contractors began to change. Their engineering staffs ballooned and acquired a permanence. Government contract-award criteria rated big engineering rosters as good, so defense contractors became big engineering employers. The government got tired of buying plant and tooling for what had grown into large enterprises with good credit ratings. It began to sell off what it had to contractors or made them buy their own factories. Bankers and institutional investors began to see defense as an established business and were willing to advance long-term money for fixed assets. Defense costs and a defense industry were becoming embedded in the national economy.

Where the most fundamental change came, though, was in the government's attitude toward cost-plus contracts. Useful as these had been during the wartime emergency, they had drawbacks. For one thing, cost-plus fixed-fee contracts based profit on a percentage of cost—explicitly or implicitly. Thus contractors had little financial incentive to minimize costs—or worse, they had an incentive to maximize costs, because as costs rose, so did their profits. In addition, government buyers found themselves in the position of signing a blank check. If a producer stumbled delivering equipment that had become a national priority, it was faster and cheaper to help, or force, the original contractor to deliver rather than to try to bring on another one.

Nonetheless, there was no easy way to change the system. Any contractor in his right mind was reluctant to take on a project on anything other than a cost-plus basis when he had no way to estimate either his costs or the size of his market accurately—or even to know that there would be a market.

In the 1960s, Robert S. McNamara and his whiz kids set out to break the cost-plus habit. One remedy was simply to use more fixed-price contracts. Another was the introduction of the incentive-type contract. Incentive-type contracts usually are a variation of cost-plus, but they can be fixed-price as well. Instead of a fixed percentage, they tie profit to meeting a project's goals—such as performance, delivery schedule, or cost. A common form of incentive-type contract ties profit to a target price or price band. If the contractor delivers the hardware at less than target price, he takes part of the saving as profit. If he slips over the target price, he shares in the cost; this is calculated on a sliding scale that, above an upper limit, makes the contractor pay 100 percent of the overrun. The dividing line is called the share line.

On the positive side, incentives introduce a sort of artificial but useful commercial discipline in military work, since they extract the kind of penalty the market does for misjudgments. They also work to motivate profit-minded companies, which can improve their profit margins by exceeding targets. But there is a negative side, too, if the focus is on what turns out later to be the wrong incentive—for example, a focus on quick delivery when better performance would have resulted from extra effort. Nonetheless, incentive contracts have become fairly standard for development work, particularly when technology is reasonably familiar.

Fixed-price contracts are hardly novel, in or out of the defense business. Traditionally, in the defense business, they have been used when the surprises presumably are over, when research and development is complete and the assembly line is up and running. In other words, when the project has reached a stage where cost estimates can be realistic and the contractor is willing, or at least should be willing, to share some of the risks the government had borne by itself in earlier stages of development.

Generally, fixed-price contracts work out well for both government and contractor. Sometimes the contractor makes a nice profit and sometimes his learning-curve estimates go awry and he loses a bundle. At least, within the framework of the fixed-price contract, the contractor is master of his own destiny. Over the long term, for a competent contractor with a diversified bag of programs, it all balances out. As one veteran battler with contractors observed: "Finance is like a bowl of jelly no matter what you do. If you push it in on one side, it pushes out on another." That is, if a contractor loses his shirt on one government program, he will find a way to afford a new one on the next program. He has to, or he won't be in business long, hence some of the mischarging scandals.

Jousting over Prices

In the mid-1980s, the Defense Department, prodded directly or indirectly by Congress, began to jiggle and fiddle with this uneasy balance. The navy suggested that contractors ought to buy their own tooling for research and development or, better, do research and development on fixed-price terms. Contractors were aghast at the idea of making that kind of investment in programs incorporating new, complex, and untested technology. To the contractors, accustomed to contractor-government cost sharing on research and development, it looked as though government was shifting over to them the signing of blank checks—like an invitation to go broke since their pockets were not nearly as deep.

Another technique that stemmed from congressional heartburn over defense buying is defective pricing. Spawned of indignation over cost overruns, defective pricing seemed the ideal way for the government to fight back. What it does, in essence, is give the government the authority to demand some of its money back—even with a fixed-price contract—if it can show that the contractor quoted erroneous or false cost figures or if he knew of impending changes that would affect his costs. Truth in negotiations, mandated by Congress back in 1962, became the cornerstone to defective pricing. Contractors must certify, under penalty of law, that the cost data furnished in contract negotiations is accurate. If it turns out later that the cost data was lacking in precision, the government can demand refunds.

To the government, defective pricing was viewed as a preventive against gouging. To the contractor, it looked like a no-win situation, in which the government stuck to a fixed price if it came out ahead, but cried foul and readjusted the price if the contractor, by luck, came out ahead. In effect, the provision allows no differences of interpretation over estimated costs. It reduces contract negotiations to haggling over what the contractor's profit percentage will be, and those percentages are limited by the government.

Defense Department guidelines for contractors' profits specify a range of 2 percent or 3 percent to as much as 6 percent on sales—generally lower profit margins on sales than business as a whole. In the past, contractors' profit margins on equity were larger than average because of their low net worth and because they used government-furnished tools and facilities. But that is changing as government demands more contractor investment. Profit margins on equity have declined and profit margins on sales have drifted upward for those who have boosted capital spending. Recent studies by the navy and by the General Accounting Office contend that profits on sales have drifted up too far. To the contractor, truth in negotiations, defective pricing, and profit guidelines have a sniff of heads-I-win, tails-you-lose. If the government holds down costs and profit margins, it is happy; if the contractor does better than expected, the government wants a refund.

Regardless of all this jousting over fixed prices, defective prices, should-cost estimates, and pricing policy in general, profits are still tied to costs and costs are still reviewed and audited by the government. Not only does pegging profits to costs leave intact the incentive to goldplate hardware (to make it more technologically sophisticated than necessary), but also it means that the fundamental idea of fixed-price contracting is subverted. Fixed-price contracting is supposed to emulate commercial practices, where the company agrees to supply an article and then lives with the accuracy of its cost and market-size estimates. But if the government wants to use commercial-buying methods, then it cannot turn around and insist that all the specifications and standards in its voluminous regulations are adhered to and that it can have access to a contractor's internal records to check on prices. Commercial-product development practices and hordes of government auditors checking a contractor's every step are mutually exclusive. The government can have it one way or the other, but not both ways at once.

There is yet another problem. Pentagon auditors and congressional staffers talk about profit levels as if they are immutable, as if they are grants of a beneficent government. What they are actually talking about are negotiated profit margins included in a contract, or going-in profits. Coming-out profits, when actual costs are in and hardware is delivered, are different—usually lower. So when the General Accounting Office talks, as it has done recently, about the need to reduce contractor profits by more than 1 percent to bring them in line with those of durable-goods manufacturers in general, defense companies are confident the end reduction will be more like 2 percent or 3 percent, or perhaps more.

There are many other ways to analyze profitability besides margins on sales volume. In its latest profit study, the Defense Department uses profit margins as a percentage return on assets, which can be defined differently than the return on equity normally used in financial analysis. Since return on assets attempts to reflect and credit contractor investment in facilities, its goal is to reduce emphasis on costs as a profit driver.

Generally, the public perceives defense contracts as lucrative. While this is true in terms of revenues, it is not necessarily so in terms of profits. When contract profits are good, they are very good; but when they are bad, they are horrid. They can swing from comfortable, with cost-plus guarantees, to losses that can bankrupt a manufacturer whose fixed-price contracts were bid too low. The subdued behavior of defense-company stocks in the bull market of the 1980s is a measure of what the investor thinks of their profits.

The way of doing business in the defense arena is changing. As Brigadier General Charles R. Henry, the army's competition expert, observed, the government used to decide what it wanted. Then it hired a contractor with the talent to do the job, and set him up in business under a cost-plus, sole-source contract, perhaps even built a plant and bought tools for him to do the work. Now, spurred by the Competition in Contracting Act enacted in 1984, the government is literally beating the bushes to scare up competitors—conducting market studies to locate suppliers who don't volunteer, and encouraging suppliers to come forward with offers. Plus, the probability is that the work will be put out to competition a year or two later.

Thus an elementary tenet of defense contracting seldom understood by outsiders is that "lucrative" defense contracts are liabilities. They do not become assets until the last nut is tightened, the last widgets delivered, and the producer has recovered all his costs—if he ever does.

Defense contracts have another barbed hook when prices come unhinged as they did in the inflation of the 1970s. Contractors with cost-type arrangements managed to stay afloat, but those on fixed-price with modest escalation clauses were in trouble. They simply did not have the adjustments available to commercial business—hiking up prices, reducing the size of the candy bar, or substituting cheaper materials and processes. Because contractors were legally tied, by contract, to performance and material specifications, to government specifications and standards, they did not have the flexibility to absorb inflation. Contractors who tried substitutions or smaller sizes soon found auditors and prosecutors on the doorstep.

The Regulatory Tangle

Aside from government specifications, contractors also must adhere to government contracting regulations. Contracting regulations are a mare's nest, stemming, again, from well-intentioned congressional action taken a decade ago. At that time, the Pentagon had a set of directives, called the Armed Services Procurement Regulations. Each individual service also had its own supplementary regulations in accordance with the main body of rules. The civilian agencies had their own rules, but because they bought less, they were usually not as refined. Congress thought the hodgepodge of individual regulations was a bad idea. So it mandated a common set, which came into being as Federal Acquisition Regulations that covered everybody. Since the Pentagon had more complex buying to contend with, it developed its own supplement, called Defense Federal Acquisition Regulations. But in creating a total government system, Congress also created a coordination monster—a bigger hodgepodge.

Back in the days of the relatively simple Armed Services Procurement Regulations—what the Pentagon regulatory troops tend to call the good old days—regulatory changes were made within the Pentagon itself. Now, changes must be cleared through an interagency board, augmenting the possibility of disagreement and delay. Further, public comment is now required; this means publication, in the *Federal Register*, of modifications or new regulations and waiting for comments from those affected. While public comment has been beneficial to the regulation-drafting process, it also carries drawbacks. It takes months to make a necessary fix. Thus, ironically, as burgeoning regulations become entangled in their own stretched-out timetable, they contribute to the length and cost of the weapons-buying cycle. Still, contradictions and ambiguity in the statutory changes, which handicap government and contractor alike, must be ironed out. Pentagon regulators make no bones about the fact that rushing from legislation into regulation has brought mistakes and confusion.

These regulations are only part of the picture. Not only do the individual services still have their own guidelines that, in the final analysis, guide their operations, but also they must follow the broad policy directives issued by the Office of the Secretary of Defense. In the case of acquisition, this means the 5000 series of directives, reissued to take the recommendations of the Packard Commission into account. As one Pentagon veteran observed, however, these policy directives are academic until—and unless—the provisions are incorporated in the individual service regulations that program officers abide by. If the bureaucracy so chooses, frustrating good intentions is easy.

Pentagon regulations specify, often in exquisite detail, exactly what charges against contracts are acceptable—that is, allowability. Costs of labor are an obvious allowable cost, but overhead—which includes general and administrative costs such as heating and lighting the factory, the travel and entertainment expenses of the marketing troops, and the salaries of the clerks who prepare the bills—is another matter. Overhead is part of the cost of doing business, but it easily can get out of hand and penalize efficiency, or worse, court fraud.

There are other kinds of overhead that infuriate Congress. One of the most recent statutory enactments was an outright prohibition against charging the cost of alcoholic beverages against defense contracts. This meddling into petty detail by Congress made for a simple regulatory change; it also started a disproportionate round of contractor management-policy meetings to decide how to deal with the regulation. All of this will end up costing more than the forbidden drinks. Again, it is chasing nickels and dimes while the billions march out the door.

There are larger implications to regulating in such picayune detail. If it is this complicated to deal with a contractor's drink with dinner or his hotel bill, how many times more confounding is it to deal with big-dollar questions? Again, it is a matter of policy run amok. Statutes governing contracting are beginning to look amazingly like regulations. Policy, abetted by Congress, has delved down into a level of detail where it has brought complexity and confusion instead of order. Instead of relying, or, more accurately, insisting on good judgment on the part of the program manager, the government has resorted to procedure and regulation to do what it cannot do: mandate wisdom.

Byzantine military specifications and standards also set the boundaries of contracting. Two distinct categories of specifications exist. The standard military specification sets forth technical yardsticks that products must meet—such as minimum or maximum temperature limits for lubricants, or size, weight, and durability requirements. It is incorporated into contracts as boilerplate. The other is a specification tailored for the particular job at hand and concerns the scope of work. Military standards are complementary to specifications. If specifications are considered the "what," standards are the "how." Specifications tell the contractor what kind of wire to use in an electrical circuit. Standards tell him how the wire should be fastened to a terminal or how its solder joint should look. Endless specifications are not just a military foible. The General Services Administration, for example, the centralized agency for federal commodity purchases, has issued a fair-sized volume on the specifications for just one of several kinds of hammers the government buys.

Specifications and standards shape weapons acquisition as fundamentally as requirements. Specifications and standards, as part of contracts, also have the force of law, but apply to technology rather than finance or management. Much as specifications and standards complicate contracting, durability, commonality, and standardization are vital to the troops in the field. Where specifications and standards begin to cause trouble is when they go into too much detail, when their application is irrelevant, and, most important, when they become obsolete.

In the mid-1980s, in recognition of these problems, efforts got under way in the Pentagon to streamline and cut through unnecessary specifications and standards. Naturally, progress was slow, for there was resistance. The navy's outspoken chief of reliability and quality control, Will Willoughby, took on a personal crusade to get rid of just one standard—MIL-Q-9858A—which sets requirements for quality-assurance programs in contractor plants and how the military services should administer them. Quality assurance refers to eliminating such problems as car windows that sink into recesses in doors, never to be seen again; seals that fall off refrigerator doors; compressors that burn out in air conditioning systems; pumps that fail; missiles that won't fire; or electronic chips that short out. Inspection and quality control are supposed to prevent this kind of stuff from getting out of the plant, but they don't always.

According to Willoughby, nothing was wrong with MIL-Q-9858A when it rolled out of the Pentagon in 1963, and the defense industry was young. But twenty-five years later, industry has matured and should be responsible enough to discharge that obligation. Within the Pentagon, some argued that doing away with MIL-Q-9858A might be throwing out the baby with the bath water. Willoughby believes that "it is time a twenty-five-year-old baby got up and walked." Too much of the burden for quality, Willoughby argues, is placed on the government by this standard, and that burden, he contends, should be placed on the contractor.

Willoughby's navy-launched battle over MIL-Q-9858A never got very far. His motives may have been mixed anyway, since this standard has its partisans in the air force. As an industry quality-control expert said, "It looked as if Willoughby was trying to break somebody else's rice bowl." Whatever the politics in this case, those inside the Pentagon who joust with the bureaucracy know why it resists streamlining: Less regulation means less work; jobs will be lost, turf will vanish; somebody's rice bowl will be empty.

Specifications and standards are two of the legs in a weapons acquisition tripod. Oversight—how they are administered—is the third. The services send representatives to prime contractors' plants to ensure compliance with each dotted *i* and crossed *t* of each specification and standard included in contracts. Subcontractors, who supply the primes, usually fall under the jurisdiction of the Defense Contract Administration Service, which is part of the Defense Department's Defense Logistics Agency. A once relatively simple plant-representative system has evolved over the years into multiple oversight by other service or defense auditing agencies, so that now a contractor may find himself dealing with monthly review visits by teams from one or another of them or with various agencies in the nearest regional office. What has come to pass is a contest between auditors and oversight teams of the services and the defense agencies to see who can be the toughest, who can emerge as dominant, and who can survive if Congress chooses to create a separate acquisition agency.

The tale is told of a subcontractor specializing in environmental control systems who presented a piece of hardware to a government inspector from the Defense Logistics Agency for delivery acceptance. The inspector, noting that the words "serial number" were to be spelled out on the identification plate, but that the actual name plate had just the initials "S/N" before the numbers, rejected the hardware. This hair-splitting quality-control rejection, added to the subcontractor's internal shortcomings in meeting its schedule, put it behind on deliveries. In the commercial business, retribution is swift and certain for such failings, though less devastating in the long run than failures in government contracting. As ludicrous as this story sounds, it left the company—and similar situations are leaving other smaller companies—wondering if it can afford to stay in the business of supplying the government.

Another problem is that sometimes, even when specifications are met, the system simply doesn't hold together. Industry and government are painfully aware of cases where, for instance in electronics, the individual chips meet specifications but when plugged into a circuit board together the system doesn't work. It could be that the soldering machine just missed a connection, or it could be that the specification asked for the wrong things.

Willoughby was instrumental in shutting down a production line in Tucson, Arizona, where Hughes Aircraft was building the navy's Phoenix missile that arms the Grumman F-14 fighter. "When Phoenix was stopped," Willoughby explained at an American Defense Preparedness Association meeting in the Boston area in 1986, "we were told the missile has met all milspecs, but it was totally deficient. Why? All the paper was right, but it bore no relation to the hardware. The system is now so full of paper that the hardware is never seen. We have got to keep an eye on the hardware, where the problem is, and not concentrate on whether the paper is filled out right."

Willoughby showed me some of the photographs of the electronic insides of Phoenix missiles that had precipitated the shutdown. There were wires terminating in the air instead of on connections, and bits of solder and insulation were lying around loose on circuit boards. Lest this sound like Hughes was grossly slipshod, it should be said that this kind of situation besets every industrial electronics operation. Loose bits of solder may be a failure waiting to happen in service, or they may be inconsequential.

Hughes is still in shock over the Phoenix compliance consequences. It shut down the production line and delivered nothing for a year, bearing the expense of operating the plant with no revenue. It spent its own money, besides, in developing manuals in exquisite detail for workers to follow, step-by-step, to ensure every minute detail in specifications was carried out. While it was able to convince the air force to modify specifications for easier compliance, the navy would not go along.

Though Hughes is backing away from confrontation with the customer, privately it is bitter over the way Willoughby and the navy handled the Phoenix affair. Compliance with multitudinous specifications and standards was the crux, in its view—not quality, not performance in the field. This is a very contentious issue with industry and government. So many specifications and standards bristle in contracts and so many government inspection and review teams are checking them that dissenters in industry and government argue the original idea—to get reasonably reliable stuff into the hands of the fighting forces—is being obscured. Where the balance lies is in how serious a divergence from specification or standard is taken. Government, driven by a congressional lash, considers any departure as prima facie evidence of failure; industry's attitude is that specifications or standards are a sometime thing.

To take an extreme case, the army and the Federal Bureau of Investigation conducted a criminal investigation into whether a Texas contractor, E-Systems Inc., falsified test results on radios it built to get them past government inspection. E-Systems contended that it had to make changes in the radios, that if it had built the radios to conform with specifications they would not have worked.

Inspection has quirks of its own. Following the Phoenix shutdown, a raft of plant inspections by the services took place all over the country. In one case involving an electronics supplier, microscopic-inspection standards were raised by government plant representatives so that they could not be accused of laxness by a visiting audit team. (If inspectors had been using 2X magnification for checking circuit boards, 20X had to be better.) Predictably, inspections at higher magnifications found junk, scattered around. But no one knew for sure whether the debris really meant anything—especially when the boards were passing turn-on acceptance tests and the equipment they became part of also worked.

Curing the Ills

Government contractors are not immune to the ills of the rest of the U.S. industrial establishment. The long list includes a lack of dedication in the work force, inability to control quality, obsolescence of facilities, a next-quarter outlook on earnings, and the ascendancy of the clever but technically inept master of business administration over the engineer. Nor have government contractors escaped the general malaise of U.S. industry with obsolescent manufacturing facilities, high pay scales, and technically complex equipment that fails early in its life cycle and can be tough and costly to fix in the field. At the root of U.S. product-quality troubles, some authorities believe, is the subordination of manufacturing to, or its divorce from, design engineering. Defense companies and their obsession with high technology are prone to this approach—something that quality-conscious Japanese industry avoids.

Low production volumes and all the sorry, hard-to-explain productivity statistics that result are complicating the defense contractor's lot. Military customers have taken differing approaches to the problem of fostering productivity among contractors. The air force has encouraged investment in new equipment by letting the manufacturer keep some of the savings that result from the lower costs made possible by more efficient, new machinery, and it has helped to fund automation. The navy, on the other hand, is cool to funding manufacturing technology and has turned to competition to force contractors to invest to survive. Both techniques can play a useful role.

There is a Pentagon-wide program to cut down on the number of standards and specifications included in defense contracts. For example, in the air force C-17 cargo-transport program now under way, the list of specifications was cut from over a thousand to about four hundred. Still, it is faster and easier, sometimes unavoidable in a high-priority program, to pick up the boilerplate from the last contract rather than to work slowly through the long list to see which specifications and standards actually are useful and necessary. But simplification, while difficult, can be done. The problem is that, in a waste, fraud, and abuse regime, heroes are made not by reducing specifications and standards but by multiplying them.

Besides, good reason exists for the government to use care in tinkering with specifications. For example, the government must guard against unsafe substitutions of material—for example, alloys that have not been properly heat-treated so that they do not meet strength requirements. All kinds of contractors inhabit the defense world, mammoth ones with armies of engineers to watch quality, small ones who may just be squeaking by; those with long traditions of integrity, and those without. Material substitution can be a breakthrough, or it may be a case of a contractor trying to slip by a cheap substitute for a fast buck.

Still, the government will have to do something about the burden of paper. Intrinsic in reams of regulations, specifications, standards, and contracting documents is that the acquisition system is buried in processed pulp. A decade ago, an aircraft company president marveled sadly at the fact that 27 percent of the flyaway cost of an airplane was for documentation, specification, forms; that is, for preparation of all kinds of paper.

Clearly, regulations and specifications are necessary in big organizations. But it must be remembered that they are a means to an end that is only as good as the people who administer and execute them. Multitudinous military specifications, which may not even be focused on the right question, have not prevented quality problems. Further, contracting terms and procedures have become too complex, and their ambiguousness contributes to misunderstanding, cases of defense fraud, and the intensifying and counterproductive paper blizzard. Any political administration that wants to deal with military-buying efficiency must attack the paper monster and its long-term impact on the acquisition system.

6

Provisioning: A Fount of Horror Stories

WHEN an aircraft, missile, or tank reaches the stage of detailed engineering design, and the first tenuous steps are under way in cutting metal and assembling circuit boards to get things going in the factory, the more prosaic nuts-and-bolts process of provisioning is also getting started. This is the routine clerk work that deals with how many and what kind of spare parts the vehicle will need, how it will be maintained and overhauled, and what sort of auxiliary equipment will be required for testing, access, and repair.

Boring stuff for anyone outside the program, provisioning rocked along in obscurity until the mid-1980s, when headlines hit about $600 ashtrays and $5,000 coffeepots. With a few exceptions, the Defense Department hierarchy did not understand this part of the acquisition system well enough to explain it quickly to the critics. Neither did the White House for that matter, and the administration's immediate mea culpa before ferreting out the facts only started Congress salivating. Within two years of the initial stories, public confidence in the defense industry, measured by a Packard Commission survey, was disappearing. Some in the Pentagon blame the uproar for the loss of billions of dollars in defense appropriations in the fiscal years following the revelations—1986 and 1987.

Early leaks to the Washington press corps came from an organization called the Project for Military Procurement, headed by a woman named Dina Rasor. Washington is crawling with lobbying organizations of every political stripe, half a dozen of which deal full or part-time with national security. Some, like the Heritage

Foundation, support a defense buildup, and some, like the Project for Military Procurement, are opponents. It is hard to establish where the more propaganda-oriented groups get their financial support, but there are those in the Pentagon who believe the Project for Military Procurement is financed by Stewart Mott, the leftist, anti-defense General Motors heir.

The campaign was the most successful anti-military propaganda effort since the merchants-of-death days of the 1920s and 1930s. Rather than take on the U.S. military buildup head on—a dubious political prospect given Ronald Reagan's election on a strong defense plank—the opposition circled around behind, attacking the Pentagon on waste and mismanagement. Secretary of Defense Caspar Weinberger, the service secretaries, and the administration all fell into the trap one way or another.

At first, Weinberger treated the situation as the usual flap in Congress that would blow over after he made polite apologies and promised stern action to fix the problems. But Congress took his reaction as an admission of guilt and turned up more horror stories. While Congress may not understand all the complexities of military technology and how it is developed, it is acutely aware of what the folks back home are thinking and what generates a headline. Flogging the Pentagon took care of both, and political Armageddon was at hand for military buyers and defense contractors. The very drabness of the subject helped the critics. Neither Weinberger, who wanted to deal in big international security issues, nor the public wanted to hear the tedious, convoluted explanations that sounded screwy half the time anyway.

One of the exposés concerned a report of the Pentagon inspector general on drastic price increases imposed by Pratt & Whitney for jet engines parts for air force fighters like the F-15 and F-16. It had not been officially disclosed by Joseph Sherick, who was then consolidating the inspector general's office after a reorganization; it was leaked to the press by the Project for Military Procurement. At the time, I spoke to an air force civilian in the drab innards of the Pentagon who had been in the military-buying business for twenty years. His reaction confirmed what I suspected. The inspector general's report was a mess that suggested inexperience or organizational confusion: Columns of figures had been reversed, so that price declines were turned into increases; dates were wrong, so that price changes that took place over decades looked as though they occurred over a couple of years. Documents like this usually are sent around the Pentagon for staffing—that is, for checking by, and comment from, various specialists. But the report had been leaked before it had gone through the staffing process. Sherick later had to get up before the Pentagon press contingent and admit there had been errors. But his recantation never caught up with the story; Congress was not about to let go of a burning issue.

The inspector general's office also figured in subsequent disclosures. Around the halls of the Pentagon, the gossip was that the military had outstrategized itself. By hiring a crusading staffer on Capitol Hill—Derek J. VanderSchaaf—for a top job in the inspector general's office, it had sought to neutralize him. Now, the crusader had an inside mine of information and was giving the Pentagon more heartburn than he had in the halls of Congress. All kinds of astronomical prices graced the news columns and the television screens.

To understand what they mean, however, it is necessary to go deeper into how provisioning works. There are two distinct activities at issue—replacement parts and support equipment—and buying practices and pricing are different for each. Replacement parts, called consumables or rotables by the airlines, are those pieces needed to take the place of components that have worn out. For example, they replace the turbine blades of a jet engine that, after rotating at high speeds in temperatures over 1,000 degrees, erode or even disintegrate. Support equipment is what is required to operate high-tech ships or aircraft. The days are long gone when a barnstormer could fly his 90-mile-an-hour Jenny into a farm pasture and then ask a bystander to restart the engine by swinging the propeller. Before an aircraft takes off today, its electronics systems must be tested by multimillion-dollar pieces of equipment; pilots require special ladders to climb into the cockpit and both special tools for repair in the field and common hand tools, like pliers or hammers, for routine maintenance.

Sticking with the example of an aircraft, since most of the horror stories centered there: When an aircraft is designed and developed, teams of engineers at the contractor's plant and teams of technical and logistics experts for the customer begin to lay out how the vehicle will be maintained and what will be required by way of replacement parts and support equipment. This is a complicated operation, involving estimates on how much maintenance will be required, what tools will be needed where, and how fast parts will wear out. Underestimates of spares consumption mean that the aircraft will be grounded, not ready for combat; overestimates mean the waste of funds and storage space. In an effort to beat the system, contractors are given maintenance targets in terms of minimum failure-rates for equipment and maximum man-hours for maintenance.

Buying Spares

Initial spare parts provisioning takes place during development; critical subsystems or parts are ordered as part of early production options. For example, aircraft engines are bought from the beginning in batches—both for the first production block of aircraft and as extras to serve as spares. New engine orders may be placed on the basis of one spare engine for every two engines that go into actual production. As engine-reliability experience accumulates, the spares ratio might drop to 20 percent or 25 percent, and decline further over time as bugs are worked out. Commercial airlines follow similar practices for initial spares provisioning.

In the case of the U.S. Air Force, its Systems Command, which manages development, also buys the first round of spares. Once development is complete and the equipment is in service in the field, Systems Command turns over spares buying to the Air Force Logistics Command, which runs a half-dozen supply-and-maintenance depots around the country. Other services have analogous operations. The navy, for example, has what it calls rework facilities, where it does aircraft overhaul, and it also has its navy yards for refurbishment of its ships.

The Logistics Command—and comparable organizations in other services—buys spare parts differently from the way they are bought in initial provisioning. Systems Command routinely buys spare parts from the prime contractors as add-ons to production—an economical way to make purchases, taking advantage of the larger volumes of functioning production lines. The Logistics Command, on the other hand, is more likely to go out for competitive bids—especially for equipment that falls into the category of commodity items, like tires and wheels. An enormous amount of controversy has arisen over these spare parts buying practices, and it is a source of considerable bitterness on the part of both government buyer and contractor.

One argument stems from the fact that the prime contractor, which handles the ordering of all the bits and pieces from subcontractors or vendors, tacks onto the price from the supplier, which includes the supplier's profit, charges for handling, packaging, and, last of all, a percentage for the prime contractor's own profit. Congress has bridled for years over what it considered pyramiding of profits in this game. Fueling its opposition was suspicion that contractors were bidding low—perhaps at a loss on development—buying the business, and then charging stiff prices for spare parts to "get well." When the spare parts "scandals" erupted in Congress, the Pentagon reacted by demanding breakout—that is, that prime contractors get out of the middleman's role. The government wanted to deal directly with component suppliers.

Intimately related to breakout came the war over data rights. Data rights refer, in essence, to who owns what in defense contracting. Even though development contractors are funded by the government, they consider the product, which results from their engineering, technical, and innovative skills, to be their property. Manufacturing drawings would carry legends to the effect that they were the property of the contractor and could not be passed along outside the company. As long as weapons development remained a sole-source proposition, data rights were not a big issue. But with the rise of competitive buying, which happened in defense contracting long before the Reagan administration turned it into a buzzword, skirmishing over data rights began.

To solicit competing bids for hardware—whether a missile to arm a fighter or a tiny hydraulic valve—the government had to have detailed data and drawings from the original supplier to give to prospective suppliers. If there were restrictive legends on drawings, a legal question arose over ownership and rights for distribution to others—one akin to copyright of a book or painting.

Without the rights to the drawings, there could be no competition for follow-on production. In cases of wholly government-funded development contracts, the government could claim rights to all resulting data. Alternately, if the contractor had a strong claim to ownership, if the product was developed with its own money, the government could buy the data from the contractor, the way one company buys technology from another.

Because in breakout the government wanted to deal directly with the vendors of the thousands of components in weapons systems, and because it wanted to open more production to competitive bidding, it had to have the drawings and the data. It began insisting that prime contractors, in their development of hardware, challenge the restrictive legends on the drawings of their suppliers. Cries of outrage came from the scores of small companies that developed bits and pieces with a mix of their own money and government contract funds. These companies, often too small to maintain the extensive historical records to establish patent protection or exactly whose money did what, formed an association to fight their cause, and, surprisingly, managed to make a dent in Congress and the Pentagon where there was little knowledge of what went on down in the bottom tiers of defense contracting.

Meanwhile, the prime contractor's role in buying spares came under fire. Congress complained mightily about prime contractors tacking their markups on vendor equipment. But contractors are in business to make money and they won't employ their assets—equipment or people—for nothing. Suppose, for example, that a prime contractor, acting on a government order, buys a temperature sensor costing $10. The overhead associated with processing that order in a giant organization would bring the cost up to about $60. The sensor probably would have to be packaged for long-term storage, which requires special containers, preservative coatings, and the like. Suppose this packaging cost another $20. Then the prime contractor tacks on his profit—10 percent or 15 percent before taxes—and by that time the $10 sensor bill has risen to $100. Yet nobody has cheated anybody. Further, the prime contractor is performing a service—particularly in handling quality control and inspection of thousands of small items for the customer. Substandard or bogus parts are a real danger in the field.

Buying Support Equipment

Before breakout, support equipment had been bought in analogous fashion to spare parts—through the prime contractor or original supplier. While in theory the services could determine what kind of test equipment an aircraft, missile, tank, or ship will need, what kind of maintenance tooling it ought to have in the field, and then ask for bids, in practice it didn't work out this way. In the military budget squeeze after the Vietnam War—caused by either outright reductions or failure to keep pace with inflation—the military lost scores of procurement people through attrition. The prime contractor, on the other hand, had an organization in place that could deal with a cross section of vendors—from the *Fortune* 500 conglomerates to mom-and-pop job shops. It seemed more practical for the services to contract with prime contractors who could manage the gaggle of bits and pieces that comprise the low-end part of support equipment: buying it; keeping after the suppliers to deliver; doing the billing, packaging, shipping, and all the rest so that troops in the field would have what they needed. Reluctantly, often enough, the primes did so. But they charged for the service, including for the time of the well-paid engineers who did the analysis and specification. The services then concentrated their manpower and attention on the high-value, expensive equipment. Breakout, of course, is sure to change this.

The final chapter in the breakout and data-rights story is yet to unfold. Contractors and some government buyers have misgivings about direct buying from the supplier on the ground that, without the prime contractor's supervision of parts quality and conformance to specifications, without his ability to deal with the vendors' varying degrees of schedule and production competence, substandard parts or substitution of specified material will follow. The army's General Henry, on the other hand, pooh-poohs the dangers of dealing directly with small companies; cutting out the middleman, reluctant or otherwise, will mean big cost savings, he believes.

Whatever the merits of these arguments, both spares and support equipment created the grist for the waste, fraud, and abuse campaign-mill that hit both government and contractor so severely. They have one overarching theme: they are relative nickel-and-dime situations. Some examples follow.

The $5,000 Coffeepot

True enough, the air force did pay that much, or at least was quoted a price that high, but for a more elaborate coffee maker (more like restaurant equipment or a small galley aboard a transport airplane) than what Congress took to be a $10 or $20 percolator or a Mr. Coffee kind of unit. It also was for the first version of the C-5 transport, built back in the 1970s. When the air force reopened the C-5 production line in April 1984, it went to a commercial airline coffee maker. At the time the $5,000 price was disclosed, the air force actually was paying about $3,000—slightly less than these units cost the airlines. Using commercial rather than military-specification equipment to get this price was no minor achievement, for logisticians have reservations about nonstandard hardware in the rigors of military operations.

The reason why the airlines as well as the air force were paying $3,000 for a coffee maker that even for industrial uses might cost a hundred dollars or so is that equipment bought by airlines—and this includes coffee makers as well as engines—has to be certified for safety by the Federal Aviation Administration. In the case of the coffee maker, it had to be designed so that it would not spill in rough air and burn passengers, it had to be strong enough not to explode if the cabin depressurized at high altitudes, and it had to withstand impact forces in the unfortunate event of a crash so that it would not break loose and become a lethal missile. Aircraft quality hardware is, in general, expensive stuff.

Although granting these reasons for the high price of the coffeepot, General Robert Russ, then air force deputy chief of staff for research, development, and acquisition and later commander of the Tactical Air Command, was indignant about the specification to begin with. Why, he asked, was it necessary to design a coffee maker to withstand crash impact forces fatal to humans? That goes to the question of requirements and to the way goldplating creeps in, so that equipment is designed to be the ultimate in technology rather than good enough to do the job. Requirements, Russ observed at the time, were the source of a lot of grief for the services in the waste, fraud, and abuse cases. "Sure, we can explain why the coffee maker cost what it did," Russ agreed. "But we would look like fools no matter how much and how well we explained." As in many of these cases, the military just chose to keep quiet and take the lumps.

The $2,000 Pliers

The case of the $2,000 pliers gets to the heart of a central issue in defense buying: commercial pricing versus contract pricing. In commercial pricing, full costs, including overhead, are recovered on the company's long-run production. When a commercial company prices a product, it looks at start-up costs, recurring costs, overhead, and the like. It fixes a price that accepts a loss on early production but anticipates that once past a break-even point, profits will begin to accelerate. Big profits on hot items subsidize losses on flops.

Military contract pricing is another kind of cat. For big-ticket hardware, the contractor has to recover all his costs on that job. They cannot, as in the commercial world, be spread over thousands or millions of units in a production run. Costs must be recovered on the number of units in the contract at hand, not those that might be built under another subsequent contract.

Another vital difference is that military contract pricing is covered by the Pentagon's Cost Accounting Standards. Contractors are told how to allocate their overhead to different items—right down to nuts and bolts. More than anything else, it is these accounting standards that confused the spares issue. It even confused military buyers down in the ranks, who were the source of many complaints about astronomical prices for spare parts.

In military contract pricing, it was the little stuff like the hammers and the pliers that left the admirals and the generals standing outside in their drawers before a hostile public. Buying hammers and pliers from a multibillion-dollar prime contractor is a little like using an elephant to pick up a flea. Just for openers, it costs a big company $50 or more to shuffle the paperwork on a military order. Still, it may be the best way to buy support equipment. Contractors have engineering staffs in place to do the specifications, and they know the vendors and what they can do. Small job shops go in and out of business, and keeping track of orders and finding alternates if a bankruptcy intervenes can be handled more flexibly by a contractor than through cumbersome government-procurement procedures. Further, a contractor can lay off people if work disappears; civil servants are hired for life.

The pliers in question were support equipment, part of a maintenance kit for a new engine—the CFM56 built in a joint venture between General Electric and a French company—for the KC-135 tanker operated for aeons by the air force. Since Boeing was serving as prime contractor for the modification work, it also wound up doing the engineering for the support equipment. It put a team to work analyzing requirements and developed a long list that included routine, hardware-store items—including two pairs of duckbill pliers. In fact, the pliers were bought by Boeing from Channellock, Inc., of Meadville, Pennsylvania, a commercial hardware supplier.

But one of the tasks to be performed by the pliers was to fish a precision wire from a supercold cryogenic container. In order for the pliers to do this, a groove had to be cut in the head to hold the wire, and a coating applied to prevent corrosion in the cryogenic bath. Buying pliers off a production line at commercial pricing is one thing. Taking the same $10 or $20 pliers, having a groove custom cut in it, and having a coating custom applied is another. Since only two pliers were involved, there were no economies of scale. The specially modified pliers had to carry full labor cost and overhead for customizing as well as the pyramiding profit markup. At this point, the cost of buying and modifying the pliers had risen to something like $80 or $90. Precise costs for the pliers never were very clear through the whole imbroglio, because of a succession of asking-and-getting negotiations.

More was yet to come—specifically, the matter of how to allocate the engineering costs, the direct expenses for analyzing maintenance requirements and specifying special tools. Spreading the engineering costs over each of the bits and pieces brought the price of a pair of pliers to $80, $160, $180, $748, or $2,548, depending on which newspaper account or which allocation of costs.

Since there was plenty of potential for a new military waste/horror story, the air force and the contractor decided not to spread these engineering costs as part of the price of the hardware but to negotiate it as a separate block item. So the air force managed to negotiate these charges for management support from the $398,000 that the contractor wanted to $143,000. By not spreading the costs, though, more confusion resulted. An air force general sat down with two *Washington Post* reporters to try to explain the cost allocation for the pliers. The story that appeared made it sound not only as if the contractor had dropped in a phoney $143,000 charge for overhead, which it had not, but also that the contractor and air force had arbitrarily cut the price of the pliers when Congress got a sniff of the costs and then tried to slip $143,000 under the rug. By that time, the air force and the contractor were so shell-shocked that they refused to discuss the pliers any further.

The $1,000 Allen Wrench

An Allen wrench is an L-shaped piece of hexagonal rod that fits into matching hexagonal recesses in special nuts. They are popular for use in confined spaces because the small wrench fits into, instead of over, the nut, making it easier to slip into tight spaces. A kit of various-sized Allen wrenches can be bought in a hardware store for relative pennies. When it looked like the Pentagon paid over $1,000 for one, eyebrows lifted.

Major Thomas W. Mahler, Jr., who had done a briefing paper on the controversy for the Pentagon hierarchy, had a breakdown done on the man-hour cost allocations for the Allen wrench and two other support items (see table 6–1).

Even a cursory reading shows that the man-hours for each item were exactly the same. Obviously, this is an arbitrary allocation of man-hours to each piece of hardware, irrespective of how many were actually devoted to one or the other. Equal spreading of these costs is required by the Pentagon's Cost Accounting Standards, and it is a relatively easy way to handle a passel of nickel-and-dime charges. Nobody will argue with the fact that it looks dumb. After

Table 6–1
SUPPORT ENGINEERING DIRECT MAN–HOURS

	Antenna Pulley Puller	*Allen Wrench*	*Alignment Pin*
Special engineering staff	1	1	1
System safety	5	5	5
Parts engineering	7	7	7
Support systems staff	2	2	2
Electrical sustaining engineering	42	42	42
Sustaining engineering program staff	3	3	3
Computer aided design	1	1	1
Ancillary design support	1	1	1
Total man-hours	62	62	62

the volcano erupted, the air force stopped equal cost allocations and went to value-basing, so that inconsequential items would. in fact, have more reasonable prices. The bill for sixty-two manhours was $1,034.64. That amounts to $16.68 per hour, or an average annual salary of $34,710—not an exceptional salary for an experienced graduate engineer. Added to the commercial price of an Allen wrench, it looked like no bargain.

Further, there is more to the cost of the Allen wrench: the overhead and the miscellaneous charges (see table 6–2). Again, these figures all smell of arbitrary allocation, not the specific cost of one twenty-five-cent item or another. Depending on how these costs are prorated, as much as $3,000 could be added to the price of this indefensible little Allen wrench. Its only crime was a slight cant to its slimmer-than-usual head—modifications that did take it out of the $2-a-copy category but not to the price point it ultimately reached. Small wonder that Congress and the public have apoplexy when confronted with $2,000 wrenches or $400 hammers.

Table 6–2
SUPPORT ENGINEERING ALLOCATED COSTS

Support engineering	$1,034.16
Engineering overhead	503.64
Fringe benefits	507.52
Travel and per diem	73.78
Graphics services	31.00
Logistics support	10.80
Configuration status accounting	160.00
Computer aided design	20.00
Program office	6.20
Miscellaneous	15.84
General and Administrative	149.14
Profit	388.79
Capital cost of facilities	12.98
Total	$2,913.85

The Coat Hanger Wire-Alignment Tool and the Milk Carton Shim

Representative John Dingell used his subcommittee's tenuous oversight of the Securities and Exchange Commission as an excuse to put himself smack into the middle of the Pentagon's buying habits and defense policymaking. Ostensibly, his investigation was on the grounds that contractors like General Dynamics, accused of shenanigans in submarine construction for the navy, may have misled the investing public. Dingell's hearings were an out-and-out rump court.

What made hot copy for the papers was a deposition from a technician at an air force depot where F-16 fighters are overhauled. He allegedly did not need or use the expensive cylindrical tool Westinghouse had supplied for alignment of the F-16's radar; instead, he used a coat hanger—or so the subcommittee investigators reported. The technician himself was called before the subcommittee, and testified that he had not used a coat hanger wire at all, but a piece he had cut from bar stock. The attitude of the front office was reflected in the retort of Major General George L. Monahan, Jr., then the program manager for the F-16, who explained that the air force was building a tool kit for major overhaul of the multibillion dollar F-16 fighter force with a multimillion dollar radar. "We don't use wooden pins," he said. "We don't use coat hangers. We don't use milk cartons as tools."

But no doubt about it, mechanics on the shop floor cook up their own tools—either by preference or because the factory-designed equipment is not handy. There are tales, for example, of mechanics using cardboard scraps from milk containers for spacers instead of the factory-designed shims for equipment-installation adjustments. Managements and military officers worry about expensive equipment that might be damaged that way. In the commercial world, experienced mechanics may take short cuts with tools and methods. But with its constantly changing roster, the air force wanted a factory-designed tool kit for the F-16, to enable mechanics new to the task to draw a special tool to do the work right and not break a broken piece of equipment a second and worse way.

Special tools are nothing new; they are common in automotive-dealer garages. Harry Smith, who was running the Westinghouse operation that built the F-16 radar and its special tools at the time of the Dingell hearing, looked up the dealer's catalog of special tools for his Buick. General Motors had done the same kind of support engineering Westinghouse had in laying out what it thought was required for the maintenance of his car. Whether General Motors did so at less cost than a defense contractor is hard to tell, but the pertinent difference is that General Motors had thousands of cars on which to tack a smidgen of the price of its special tool and support-equipment bill.

The $600 Ashtray

Nor was the air force the only service with spares and support-equipment problems. Each of the services, sooner or later, one way or another, shared in the opprobrium. The navy, for example, had the $600 ashtray and the toilet seat in the same price league; strictly speaking, though, the latter was a larger structure, a shroud made of expensive composite material to save weight.

In the case of the ashtray, a navy supply facility in California ordered a couple of replacements for the cockpits of a Grumman E2C Hawkeye. This is a twin-engine, propeller-driven airplane with an enormous saucer-shaped radar antenna mounted on struts on its fuselage—one of the largest airplanes to operate off an aircraft carrier. It flies long patrols searching for hostile aircraft with its search radar, and the requirements makers and designers thoughtfully included ashtrays so the flight crews could relieve the dreary hours with a smoke.

Grumman, which was not set up to build a couple of ashtrays easily or cheaply, did not want to take the order, but agreed to do so to please the customer. It took something like eleven man-hours of labor, with handling and overhead on top, to build each ashtray and the $600 was just about what the hardware cost to custom produce. When the navy checked with one of its own facilities for an estimate on the same job, it came in at over $1,000 per ashtray. When Defense Secretary Weinberger first heard the news at a morning staff meeting, he became so apoplectic that he demanded that then secretary of the navy John Lehman do something drastic. In response, Lehman relieved both the admiral responsible for ordering the ashtrays and the supply officer involved—although he had no intention in the world of doing so when he walked into the meeting.

George Skurla, president of Grumman, told me about it over a brandy at the bar in Grumman's hospitality chalet at the Paris Air Show. (In passing, entertainment at the Paris Air Show is another red flag for Congress. Although legislators placed a statutory ban on the allowability of air-show expenses, they then obfuscated the issue by stating nothing they did was meant to stand in the way of export selling of American aircraft—one of this country's few positive balance-of-trade products.) "Lehman called me," Skurla said, "and told me he was going to take strong action against the admiral. He told me I should do the same to clean up my own house." Incredulous that he should make a goat of one of his people, Skurla answered: "Well, John, maybe you better start with me."

In the end, Lehman had to backtrack on the admiral, who was cleared by a navy investigating commission. At the peak of his irritation, Skurla looked up the cost of an automobile ashtray. For a Cadillac, the price of an ashtray and its comparable housing—presumably made in larger quantities than the navy airplane unit—was on the order of $75 to $100.

Eventually the furor died down, but the ashtray fiasco underscores one constraint of military spares: buying in ones or twos. Often enough it cannot be helped, as in cases when one or another of some ancient piece of equipment still in service malfunctions. Only one part is needed, but it is no longer in production. So it has to be built to order. Otherwise the equipment sits. By the time the factory goes through the setup to build one part, it could build a hundred for not much more money. If the military buyer does order in quantity and the lot sits in a warehouse, then an auditor or inspector raises cain. Obviously there are cases when the services could survive without a replacement part like an ashtray, but more likely it is a damned-if-you-do, damned-if-you-don't affair.

Some Trivial Reforms

The ashtray case, the Pratt & Whitney spare-parts case, and some others have a common thread. They are cases where the contractor agreed to custom build a less-than-critical part. In cases like Grumman's ashtray, companies would rather just give the part to the customer for nothing, but that is illegal or against regulations and might even be construed as an attempt at subversion or bribery.

Defense regulations do not permit a contractor to buy lunch for a military customer, or even to invite him to sit at tables the company has taken at the banquets that are a staple of the Washington, D.C., social scene. Instead, the sponsoring organization invites government guests suggested by the companies, and they are parceled out at random. By late 1986, regulations had grown so tight that government visitors at company plants were not even offered coffee and cookies as refreshments. One General Electric host described an all-afternoon affair at the plant with a foundation committee that happened to have government employees as members. "I just told them at the end of a long day," he said, "that under the new regulations we could only offer them one thing: ice water."

After the ashtray scandal, Grumman took itself out of the special-built small-parts business. Formal company policy in response to requests for such equipment was to list other manufacturers who might be willing to do the job. Such lists are hard to compile. Few companies, be they large corporations or job shops, are interested in small-volume, built-to-order business. Pratt & Whitney also took itself out of the small-parts business. It purged its catalog of about 50,000 parts and, as Grumman did, told the government who its suppliers were so that the customer could buy direct. Whether such action will serve the national interest is still an open question.

Many of these cases have still another common thread. Does support-tooling or spare parts need the intensive (and thus expensive) engineering that runs up the cost? The air force general who tried to straighten out the Boeing pliers situation for the newspaper reports himself called it dumb to buy this kind of hardware through a prime contractor. Doing so adds inexorable handling, overhead, profit, and ad infinitum charges, swamping the original cost of the item. It just doesn't seem to make sense to buy a couple of pieces of twenty-five-cent hardware from a billion-dollar company. Alternatives have their own problems, though.

About the time of the pliers case, the air force changed the way it bought support equipment, ordering its own buying organization to do the job. The order was greeted with some dismay in the ranks. In an office at Wright Field, the center where the air force manages its aircraft acquisition apparatus, I talked with a young colonel who faced the inevitable with resignation. His program office, which managed the F-15 fighter, had not done this kind of buying—the support-equipment chore. It was short of people to handle the voluminous detail entailed, and those who were available did not know the vendors the way the prime contractors did. He fully expected that essential support equipment would be lacking when squadrons took on new airplanes. The problem is that the policymakers who ordered the changes are a long way from the users in the field who wind up without the bits and pieces they need to keep operating.

There is no doubt that the services and their contractors came out looking foolish and wasteful in the uproar over spare parts and support equipment. Worst of all is that these horror stories diverted the attention of Congress and the public while the real strains of the acquisition system grew worse in reaction to them.

The Pentagon felt betrayed by its biggest contractors, the ones to which it had entrusted billions in public money. Contractors felt that the top level at the Pentagon had dumped the blame on them for the workings of the department's own regulations and its people. But while Congress and the public fumed over nickels and dimes, the billions kept marching out the door. Before the eruption subsided—it has not yet ended—the Pentagon was demanding blood oaths from contractors that there were no more foolish-looking prices on their books. Contractor lobbyists around Washington had a haunted look, for anywhere in their catalog mazes could lie another unsuspected pricing time-bomb—and acute embarrassment. Grumman, for one, had just assured the navy it had no skeletons on the eve of the ashtray disclosure.

Spares and support-equipment horror stories were misconstrued as fraud and bumbling. In fact, they were worrisome symptoms of the deeper ills of the acquisition system. Unfortunately, reform and regulation have tended to concentrate on the symptoms, not the root causes. Both government and public need to understand their real message if the military buying process is to be put back on track.

7

Making the Pentagon More Businesslike

BILLIONS do walk out the door in military acquisition, all too often as the result of attempts to improve the buying system. Two ideas, in particular, that have been favorites of reformers, led to trouble. One is the introduction of commercial practices—the checks and balances of the marketplace—into Pentagon buying. The other is greater commonality in weapons—that is, giving all the services one kind of radio, radar, or airplane.

The Packard Commission recommended commercial-management techniques as a model that should be emulated in defense-program management. Competition is now the commercial-practice buzzword in the Pentagon. It is not really a new idea to the military, and in the past has been a dandy when shrewdly used in big enough programs. But in the military, orders from the top often are executed with excess zeal at the bottom, as in the instance when $100,000 was spent to bring about competition for a $40,000 order.

Pentagon managers have been trying to cut down sole-source awards since the 1960s. But sole-source contracting is faster and easier for the working troops in acquisition; contractors with a handle on esoteric technologies are scarce and competition is potentially expensive. While the government finances competitions for big-ticket weapons through bid-and-proposal charges against existing contracts, all this means front-end investment, which can amount to millions taken from someone's budget. So it takes cajolery, edicts, and competition advocates to change the Pentagon's ways of doing business.

Still, impressive figures are quoted for competitive savings, perhaps overly impressive. Take the case of the army's Chaparral missile fire unit, the rail on which the missile is launched. The first fifty were bought at $919,491 each in 1986. When the army Missile Command ran a competition later the same year for fifty-two more for delivery in fiscal 1987, the same contractor, Ford Aerospace, bid in the job for a unit price of $532,937 each. Not all that reduction was directly the result of competition; learning-curve experience had dropped the price toward the $600,000 level. So the direct savings through competition were closer to $100,000 than $400,000 each. Still, $5 million in price reduction for the total order because of competition is nothing to quibble about.

All the services now have competition advocates—both in the Pentagon and in field commands where contracts are negotiated—to spread the gospel. Although they are salesmen of the idea, most of these competitive-buying advocates make clear that the goal is competition where it makes sense, not across the board. This does not, however, prevent them from making a hard pitch, as the army's competition advocate, Brigadier General Charles R. Henry, has in trying to get the Bradley Fighting Vehicle program number projections revised upward to justify bringing a second contractor on line.

And these advocates have been successful. General Henry says that army field commands have become sensitive to competition as a way to conserve budget funds and look smart. Competition became such a salute-the-flag item in the navy after former secretary John Lehman, Jr., seized on it as an antidote for waste, fraud, and abuse that it turned into an end in itself rather than a means. The navy's Advanced Tactical Aircraft program at one point had the look of competition for the sake of competition, rather than the aircraft.

Another technique urged by the Packard Commission, and supported in Congress, is off-the-shelf, commercial catalog buying. This countervails the military practice of buying expensive, custom-tailored equipment when workable stuff—especially things like electronic chips or personal computers—is available on the market at lower prices.

Logisticians are wary of both competition and off-the-shelf procurement. Competition can introduce nonstandard or substandard hardware into the supply pipeline that won't fit or might fail at a critical point in service. Catalog equipment may not be rugged enough for military handling and the rigors of the field or may be difficult to support. Besides, private business can change catalog equipment specifications any time it feels like it, something that disconcerts the military.

Users also tend to skepticism, summed up by an astronaut's reply to how he felt waiting for the rocket motor to ignite and launch his body into space. Just like anyone would feel, came the answer, anyone who is sitting on top of a thin-wall metal cylinder filled with tons of volatile liquefied gases and fuels, with thousands of complex electronic parts and mechanical systems all of which have to function to prevent disaster—and all bought from the lowest bidder.

Where competition can come unglued in sophisticated military weapons is in the very fact of low bids. Military buyers used to place great stress on soliciting bids only from lists of qualified suppliers. Now, with the government beating the bushes to scare up more competition, military buyers are faced with the increasing challenge of determining whether a low bid is a bargain or a delusion. Government must be cautious of arbitrary application of this commercial practice, of misapplication in a system that runs by the book and layers of oversight, not personal judgment.

The C-5A and Total-Package Procurement

Perhaps the best example of how things can go wrong with the finest of ideas is the infamous total-package procurement concept used to develop the Lockheed C-5A giant cargo jet.

Because of the uproar in the press and Congress over the C-5A's money troubles, overrun—which started life as obscure Pentagon jargon meaning that actual cost of a program exceeded estimated cost—became part of everyday lexicon. Although an overrun may result from off-target estimation of costs, not loss of control over them, it became a synonym for waste. As for the C-5A, it was a watershed. Its cost overrun crossed the billion-dollar line, thus engineering the transition of public perception of the military-buying system and the defense industry from a team that could invent anything, that could turn technology into first-rate hardware unequaled anywhere, to an apparatus that was wasteful, dishonest, and incapable of producing anything that worked or stayed within cost targets.

The C-5A was in the vanguard of wide-body transport development. Wide-body airplanes are used almost exclusively by international airlines today. Like many programs, its technical challenge was underestimated. While this also was the case with its commercial counterpart, the Boeing 747, Boeing and its suppliers swallowed the added costs of the technical unknowns in relative quiet; the government and Lockheed ran into a noisy exchange over who would pay the unexpected overage.

Total-package procurement was something of a culmination of Secretary of Defense McNamara's espousal of the commercial practices theory in the 1960s, although the idea itself came out of the office of the secretary of the air force. Specifically, total-package procurement was aimed at solving a problem government buyers faced in awarding large programs. Generally, buying was done piecemeal, in successive phases. Hungry or wily contractors found early on that they could win initial development contracts by putting in a marginally low bid; then, once they licked the technical problems, they could jack up prices because no one else was equipped to do the job. They were then the sole source for the hardware. There was a name for this practice: buying the business. It was well worth the risk to the company if the hardware was something the government was going to have to buy, something that was a priority service requirement and one clearly embedded in the budget. Once millions of dollars were committed, once the contractor had hired thousands, tooled up, and bought material, the government had little realistic option to go elsewhere.

Total-package procurement was designed to defeat the buy-into-the-business strategy that was becoming all too common to suit the government. The concept was simply to put the whole program out for bid at once: development and at least substantial blocks of subsequent production. It was meant to be a truth-in-bidding technique. There would be less opportunity for a buy-in contractor to "get well" as the sole source for later production if he had already committed himself to a long-term development-and-production price.

But in shifting the balance of risk, the government did too good a job. From the point where the government absorbed all the risk, it shifted to a position where the contractor seemed to be taking all the risk. No contractor was going to accept that on wild-blue-yonder kinds of development where there was vast uncertainty over whether technical challenges could, in fact, be overcome. The government did not really expect that from contractors either. But total-package procurement looked quite feasible for a program like the C-5A cargo jet where the technology was considered—incorrectly—as well in hand as it ever is in a development effort. And total-package procurement was introduced before the Vietnam War ignited a firestorm of inflation far beyond what government and industry were prepared for.

Within a couple of years after Lockheed won the C-5A total-package contract, the bad news began to emerge: Building a big transport airplane was not just a simple matter of replicating a smaller one in a jumbo size. Besides, the C-5 was to have an unusual drive-through main cabin, with vast cargo doors at both front and rear. In fact, the whole nose section of the airplane swung up and over the cockpit. And the landing gear could kneel, adjusting on the ground for differing loading-ramp heights. On top of that complexity, the C-5A looked like a winged centipede on the ground because of short but heavy struts supporting a couple of dozen balloon tires to allow it to land on grass fields.

These technical details figured in the subsequent disaster—a disaster, at least, in terms of lost public respect for the Pentagon and the contractor. Though it was recognized that it would cost more to design and build into the C-5A the ability to land on grass fields, the idea fit nicely with the McNamara-era philosophy of an all-purpose, common-use airplane. But once the C-5A entered service with the Military Airlift Command, it became clear that there was not much call to put three hundred tons of C-5A into the cow pastures near the front lines. In later years, the whiz kid systems analysts got blamed for the added cost and complexity of making it possible to do what turned out to be an unnecessary job.

Whether total-package procurement demanded that the air force stick rigidly to such C-5A requirements as the grass-field landing gear, to every period and comma in the contract, was debated. The total-package procurement premise is that the service will lay out an explicit set of requirements at the outset of development and then let the contractor figure out how to make good on it. To the extent that it took the government out of the business of looking over the contractor's shoulder every minute, it was a marvelous idea. Where it began to unravel was in the government's insistence on absolute, undeviating adherence to contractual periods and commas as embodied in the first C-5A delivered for service testing at Edwards Air Force Base in the California desert.

Lockheed had built plenty of cargo airplanes. Its C-130 propeller-driven transport that dates from the 1950s still is a basic U.S. military front-line supplier. It supported army and marine troops under fire in Vietnam and it is flying today as part of U.S. support to governments or rebels in the rain forests of Central America. Lockheed also built a successor to the C-130—the C-141 medium-sized cargo jet. But building a big airplane like the C-5A was not just a matter of scaling up the smaller C-141. When the increase in size passed a certain point, technical challenges and changes cropped up.

Because of the heavy structural pieces required, Lockheed ran over the weight specification for the C-5A. In times past—too often in times past—contractors missed specification targets, leaving the services with the option to take it or leave it. Sometimes, when it was evident that targets were unattainable, specifications were relaxed. Sometimes this made for scandal; other times the exact specification was not all that important. But with total-package procurement for the C-5A, the air force said, in effect, no more specification games. "Here is the weight specification you, Lockheed, contracted to meet. Use your ingenuity to meet it." As a former program manager for the C-5A told one of my colleagues at the time: "Total package procurement means we sign a contract for this airplane with hard performance specifications. Then we don't talk to the contractor again until we meet at Edwards Air Force Base for service testing of the first airplane—with our lawyers."

Lockheed complained that the weight overage—something on the order of 3,000 pounds in an airplane whose structural weight alone was over 300,000 pounds—was not all that significant, that the cost to meet the specification was not worth it. If the government had been more flexible on the weight specification, Lockheed claims, vast sums of money could have been saved. In the event, the government stuck to its requirement and the contractor used its ingenuity to meet the specification—at a price. Not only did the weight shaving contribute to the multibillion-dollar cost overrun—that is, actual cost compared with target cost—but also it came in a critical area: in the structure of the wing.

Once the air force started to fly the airplane regularly, cracks began showing up. Cracks anywhere are an ominous sign in an airplane, but this is especially so in the case of the wing. The C-5A flies at high altitudes, and the wings, which are subject to metal-fatigue stresses over time, are designed to flex. Cracks can extend to the point where the structure will fail and the aircraft will disintegrate in flight. With the C-5A, the air force had little choice but to bring the airplanes back to the factory and install a strengthened wing—at a multibillion-dollar price above and beyond the original program cost.

Nonetheless, flushed with enthusiasm about the future of big-transport airplanes, and betting on the technical know-how it gained in the C-5A program, Lockheed went on to develop the commercial L-1011 trijet at its own expense to compete with Boeing's 747 and McDonnell Douglas's DC-10. But the market for big airplanes did not grow as large or as fast in the 1970s as forecasts predicted because airline-passenger traffic did not grow as fast as projected. Rolls-Royce, the British engine supplier for the L-1011, collapsed abruptly into bankruptcy and left Lockheed at the end of a long limb. Then came the C-5A overrun, and Lockheed, faced with swallowing those costs itself, almost went into bankruptcy, too—saved only by a then-unprecedented government guarantee of a bank-loan bailout (the kind that later saved Chrysler).

Total-package procurement was blamed, in part, for this fiasco by some in both government and industry. Others disagreed. One Pentagon civilian who is intimately familiar with the C-5A program contends that the C-5A imbroglio was a combination of a lack of integrity on Lockheed's part and of personal ambition within the air force. In his view, Lockheed was attempting to play catch-up with Boeing and McDonnell Douglas. Both had been researching big-transport airplane technology on their own and through military-study contracts. Both were designing and producing commercial jet-transport airplanes, a field Lockheed had decided not to enter in the 1950s when it committed to build the turboprop Electra for airline customers. But propellers became anathema to the airlines once the more reliable, more maintenance-free pure-jet engine demonstrated what it could do in service. Lockheed, which, with its triple-tail Constellation had been a prime manufacturer for the airlines, was left out. It wanted a military-aircraft-development contract to come back, and it bid low on the C-5A total package, doing the very thing total-package procurement was designed to penalize: buying the business. To that extent, total package worked. Lockheed was indeed penalized.

In this official's view, Lockheed's technical proposal ranked third in a field of three. He contends that Lockheed's motivation and buy-the-business approach were clear to the government at the time, but that Lockheed was handed the contract anyway to win points with the late senator Richard Russell of Georgia, where the Lockheed plant was located. Russell was the powerful chairman of the Senate Armed Services Committee then, and there were many reasons—including personal ambition and future program support—for putting dollars and jobs in his home state. The string of government installations across the sunbelt, NASA as well as military, is a physical legacy of southern seniority on congressional committees and military and civilian agency politicking.

Technical troubles are the norm, not the exception, in development programs. In Lockheed's defense, it should be noted that the 747 that Boeing was developing commercially while Lockheed was building the military C-5A also ran into weight problems. When Boeing became aware of the problem, it did what most airframe builders do in such situations. It went to the engine manufacturer, Pratt & Whitney in this case, and demanded more power from the engine sooner than it would normally come along. It seemed like a quicker and cheaper course than redesigning the entire airplane to ensure that the 747 would meet its range and payload performance guarantees to airlines. Pratt & Whitney met the power demand, but without the time it wanted to prove out the changes. As a result, the 747 had a chorus of engine maintenance woes in its early years of service, and Pratt & Whitney paid out millions in warranty claims.

Lockheed could have done the same thing to solve the C-5A weight problem. An approach was made to General Electric to increase the thrust of the engine. Gerhard Neumann, who headed General Electric's engine operations at the time, told Lockheed he could get more engine thrust—with more development money.

Lockheed did not pursue it. Some say that the government—reportedly Defense Secretary McNamara himself—tired of contractors falling flat on their promises, rejected changing the engine specifications, thus holding Lockheed's feet to the fire.

Neumann had a lot to do with conceiving the big, high-bypass-ratio turbofan engine that made jumbo jets like the C-5 and the 747 possible. His account of how the idea was broached to the air force reveals a lot about how military buying once worked and how the system is now congealing into bureaucratic gel. After Neumann was certain that the high-bypass engine could double the power of then first-line jet powerplants, he requested a private meeting with now-retired air force general Marvin Demler at Systems Command, to disclose the concept in highly secret surroundings. Except for one witness, a colonel from his staff, Demler agreed. They met the next day, at which time Neumann asked Demler if the air force would be interested in doubling engine power—getting down on the floor to reel out a scroll so long it could not fit on a desk top. Such a burst of growth in power could not fail to interest the military. And the air force worked fast in those days. It put out a contract to start work on the idea, limiting response time for competitors to thirty days to give Neumann and his group some protection for whatever lead they had. There had to be a competition, though, and the air force had to fund other companies to work on the high-bypass concept. This kind of flexibility, speed, and decisiveness is doubtful in today's far more regulated, competition-above-all acquisition climate.

Wreathed in controversy as the C-5A was, the air force terminated the program in the early 1970s at the original eighty airplanes specified in the total-package contract—minus one lost at the plant in an accidental fire. In retrospect, the conclusion is inescapable that the government could have eased some of the pain of the C-5A program by giving ground on the weight specification. Whether one of the other contractors competing for the program might have done better is hypothetical and irrelevant at this stage. The fact is that all were experienced in building transport airplanes and there is no reason that any one of them should not have been able to deliver a good airplane, allowing for some cost problems resulting from technical surprises. Total-package procurement, the government, and the contractor each played a role in its demise.

Then, a decade later, the predictable happened. The Pentagon was short of airlift. The services wanted to push ahead with a new airplane—what became the C-17, a smaller, C-130 kind of replacement, in a program that went to McDonnell Douglas. Congress had resisted for several budget cycles, on the grounds that the C-17 concept was ill-defined by the Pentagon. Then the airlift shortfall became a higher priority, and the Defense Department decided it couldn't wait for the new airplane. After a battle with Boeing over the idea of buying new or refurbished 747s for a quick fix, and with the services over the C-17, the secretary of defense—not the air force—chose to put the C-5A back into production.

It was to be a modified version of the C-5A, called the C-5B, with the new, beefier wing and other changes. A contract was negotiated with Lockheed-Georgia late in 1982 for options for as many as fifty aircraft valued at $7.8 billion. More controversy ensued. Flogged by the Dingell subcommittee once again, the air force and the Defense Contract Audit Agency—one of the many audit arms for the Pentagon—decided to invoke defective pricing. As described earlier, under recent congressional truth-in-negotiations legislation, companies are required, in effect, to lay all their negotiating cards on the table. They must provide full details on all their costs and a corporate officer must certify to their authenticity and completeness—at distinct legal risk to himself. If something comes along to cast doubt on the original figures, the government can demand its money back and the corporate officer may face a grand jury. Many corporate officers have balked, on the grounds that no one manager can personally be aware of the accuracy of every detail of a contract proposal.

Government auditors from the Defense Contract Audit Agency found out that Lockheed had a labor-negotiation strategy, set for a year after the C-5B contract was signed, that would make for less inflation in C-5B building costs. Inflation is of vast consequence in military contracting, which involves large sums spent over years or decades. Back in the 1960s, the original C-5A contract had attempted to protect against inflation by a complicated formula tied to government price indexes, but both Lockheed and the government had been badly singed anyway. As of the early 1980s, they were both still wary. Questions also arose over mischarging on the costs of labor and materials.

Lockheed's response to the defective-pricing charge was that its success in the labor negotiations was problematical and that an economic-adjustment clause in the 1982 contract would reduce the contract price if its costs did come down. As of this writing, the air force is talking about $281 million or even as little as $175 million in defective pricing recovery.

If the government had stuck with the original C-5A contract and bought all the airplanes planned at inception, it probably would have saved money in the long run. Originally, the program was priced at what the dollar was worth in the late 1960s and early 1970s; now the C-5B is being paid for with inflated mid-1980s dollars at prices that have run up twice what they were in the first contract. Further, the original airplane came for a lower price, the substantial costs of restarting the shutdown assembly line would have been avoided, and the military would have had extra years of use of the full fleet—all if the initial program had been maintained.

One of Lockheed's Washington operatives summed up the years of controversy—the battles with Pentagon whistle-blower Ernest Fitzgerald, who first revealed the existence of the overrun, and the hearings before Dingell's subcommittee—by saying that the populace had probably grown sick of the whole business. "I hope," he said then, "we get those last twenty airplanes out of the barn in a couple of years, that the airplane performs beautifully for fifty years, and that I never hear of the C-5 again."

There is a footnote to the whole affair. Eventually the Pentagon went ahead with the McDonnell Douglas C-17, in addition to the revived C-5 production. Progress on the C-17, though, was halting. In 1985, Senator Sam Nunn of Georgia—where Lockheed's C-5 building plant is located—sponsored a move to kill the C-17, and almost succeeded. In 1987, Representative Wayne Owens introduced a similar amendment, but without any luck either. In a *Wall Street Journal* interview, Owens bemoaned the fact that due to lobbying on behalf of the plants that make pieces and parts for the C-17 in one hundred congressional districts in twenty-seven states, his legislation was stifled before it could even be debated. Congress has not changed much since the military courted Senator Russell over the C-5A program.

Congressman Owens came off as the white knight battling the bloated military budget. Where would he have stood if one of those plants had been in his district? His attempt to kill the program, whatever the merits, though, is rather typical do-it-yourself congressional micromanagement of defense policy. The question is, should an individual legislator decide whether a hardware program should be killed—in this case a program that the military felt it needed badly enough that it battled for it for over ten years? The services wanted the airplane so much that the air force took the rare step of awarding a contract for it to McDonnell Douglas even though Congress had not provided any funds. Congressman Owens's amendment is still another case of substituting the judgment of a relative outsider for that of those directly charged with the responsibility. Such off-the-wall, individual policymaking clearly is disrupting the U.S. defense acquisition system.

While Lockheed's C-5A is the most celebrated total-package procurement case, other contractors also ran into difficulties. Grumman, for example, was designing and building the F-14 Tomcat fighter for the navy under a total-package-type contract not long after the original C-5A program began. The late Lew Evans, who headed Grumman at the time, told friends in Washington about his enormous misgivings over the risk Grumman was taking in building a new military fighter on these terms. In the same inflationary spiral, Grumman lost hundreds of millions of dollars on the program, deeply wounding the company. In the middle of all this, Evans suffered a heart attack; his death soon afterward undoubtedly was hastened by the wracking his company took. On the other hand, the Maverick missile, a tactical weapon developed by the air force, is considered the most successful total-package procurement case—essentially because of a good program-management team and some hard-nosed contract decisions.

Obviously, total package is not inherently right or wrong, but more a two-edged sword. The buy-ins that the system tried to eliminate are bad—costly and risky for both government and industry. But preventing contractor buy-ins is difficult. The way total-package tried to introduce commercial risk into what has been coined a monopsonistic market (one with many sellers and a single customer) courted the frustration of a normal part of business: risk taking. Total-package procurement left no way open to recover in an all-or-nothing gamble. Total package also lessened control over development, not only for military program managers, but also for those in industry. While intending to put more problem-solving responsibility on the contractor, it backfired and left the developer a prisoner of the original requirement.

Total package and the C-5 uproar come down to this: There was outrage, breast beating, and a sincere, valiant attempt to make the military acquisition system work better. But acquisition's ailments simply cannot be cured by one wonder drug—in contracting, regulation, or anything else. Too much attention, too much hope, rides on procedure, and not enough on substance and judgment. Total-package procurement was not necessarily unworkable. But it was an acquisition method imposed by the Pentagon civilian hierarchy. The troops who had to carry it out had no rapport with it. They may not even have understood it. In the end, this attempt to improve the system—like so many others—cost the taxpayer more.

The TFX and Commonality

Competition, commercial practices, not to mention everything else in the way of nostrums for the hardware side of national security, are always graced with noblest intentions. Commonality fits into this mold as well. But like commercial techniques, common equipment may not work out so well in practice as it does in theory, or be as useful or cost-effective as its advocates believe it to be.

Prior to World War II, common aircraft were just that. The navy's Boeing F4B-4 and the army's P-12 basically were the same airplane. Both services operated a series of Curtiss airplanes. And during the war, the services bought each other's airplanes on occasion, as the Navy's PB4Y maritime patrol version of the army air force's B-24 Liberator bomber testifies. During World War II, the army and navy often used common trainer aircraft, but they have done so less since. The services usually used the same transport cargo aircraft then, and often (but not invariably) do so now—either aircraft developed by the military or off-the-shelf commercial aircraft bought by the services. The navy even adapted a commercially developed airliner, the Lockheed Electra, for long-range antisubmarine patrol. Trucks, personnel carriers, ships, and so on are often common equipment among the services.

In the postwar world, commonality came to be identified as a solution to interservice rivalry. The creation of the Defense Department itself was a form of mandate from Congress to the services to quit wrangling—or else.

Commonality takes different forms and is allied to, but distinct from, standardization. Richard P. Hallion, chief historian at the Air Force Flight Test Center at Edwards Air Force Base, divided aircraft commonality into four categories: (1) joint, simultaneous development of a common airframe; (2) subsequent adaptation of an airframe developed by one service for another; (3) development of different versions of airplanes for different services stemming from the same design configuration; and (4) common use of systems like engines, avionics, fuselages, wings, and the like. Only the last, Hallion rightly observes, has been more than sporadically successful.

Most of the issues in the ongoing debate about commonality came to a head in the TFX debacle in the early 1960s, in the attempt by then defense secretary McNamara to develop an all-purpose, all-service common fighter, attack, and just-about-anything airplane: Hallion's first category. Although, initially, it was to serve all the services, including the Marine Corps, as reality intruded into the program, it was narrowed to just the air force and the navy.

The navy resisted the McNamara concept from the beginning. Contrary to the usual stereotype of wasteful service jousting, however, the navy had valid technical grounds for its stand on the TFX. What the air force wanted in the airplane—a heavy, nuclear-capable strike fighter—turned out to be too big and too heavy to be operated aboard navy aircraft carriers. Besides, the navy had its own ideas about what it needed in a new fighter: an airplane, loaded with a complex long-range missile, capable of lurking at relatively long ranges from the battle group to knock down air attacks well before nuclear-weapons cargoes could get within lethal distance of the vulnerable surface ships. Because of the compromises involved, the air force had no enthusiasm for joint development of a common airplane either.

Service turf issues further complicated the situation. Navy stalwarts wanted to preserve the sanctity of the aircraft carrier, around which its battle groups and their claim to a share of the defense budget were built. Air Force Tactical Air Command officers wanted a nuclear-armed strike fighter to maintain its conventional forces, which were in danger of slipping into limbo with the ascendancy of the Strategic Air Command and nuclear intercontinental ballistic missiles.

The TFX controversy escalated into congressional hearings and an investigation. Political influence was suspected in the award of the program to General Dynamics in Texas instead of to Boeing in Seattle, as a biservice source selection panel had recommended. Without going into a blow-by-blow account, after all the uproar in Congress and in the press, the TFX program finally produced a workhorse fighter-bomber—the F-111—that still functions as a long-range strike aircraft for the Air Force Tactical Air Command and as a light strategic bomber for the Air Force Strategic Air Command.

While the F-111 got bales of newsprint notoriety, there have been other common programs wished on the services by the Department of Defense—the most recent being the navy adoption of the air force YF-17 lightweight fighter and its development into the F/A-18. Another example is the F-4 fighter. But neither was a joint development like the TFX; rather, these were adaptations and separate development (Hallion's second and third categories). After the navy put the F-4 into operation, for example, the air force bought the airplane but modified it to include a gun in the nose and rear seat flight controls.

The Office of the Secretary of Defense also pushed for multiservice use of the A-7. Again, this would not be joint development, but adaptation of an existing navy attack airplane that the air force was "encouraged" to buy. (The navy's original A-7 itself was a derivative of its carrier-based F-8 fighter.) But the air force was cool to the A-7, even after navy combat proving in Vietnam. When the air force did go along, it insisted on improvements—twenty-six of them. Then the navy brought along its own improved version, following the lines of the air force's modified airplane. Ultimately, both services got better airplanes, with considerable commonality.

Commonality has not lost its political appeal. Congress had urged the air force and the navy to get together in programs now under way for the air force Advanced Tactical Fighter and the navy Advanced Tactical Aircraft. These new airplanes have little in common except their stealth-design features. Yet the two services have signed agreements to study jointly the technologies entailed. Former navy secretary John Lehman accepted a move toward commonality before he left office in order to save the navy program from congressional axes.

Even in successful adaptation by one service of another's hardware, cost savings are illusory. Modifications usually offset lower prices found in using the same basic airframe or components. Because avionics and subsystems now sop up so much of the total cost of an aircraft—or missile, spacecraft, capital ship, tank, or whatever—the savings to be gained with a common airframe or any kind of frame are just not there any longer. While common avionics packages—if they can be put together—can save money, even their components can run into the thicket of differing needs for different missions.

As a landmark in the evolution of the U.S. defense acquisition process, the TFX laid the foundation for the way programs are structured today and for the associated hierarchical review and micromanagement. It also was a celebrated case of the influence of politics in Pentagon buying. It was never proved that McNamara, any of his deputies, or the service secretaries (one of whom was from Fort Worth, Texas, where the winning contractor's plant was located) were guilty of any wrongdoing. But clearly more than old-fashioned courthouse favor-swapping or congressional pork barreling was entailed. The president McNamara worked for, John F. Kennedy, owed his election victory in part to Texas and the forces of then-senator and later, under Kennedy, vice president Lyndon Johnson. Surely McNamara was not oblivious to all that. That it was the sole consideration is doubtful; that it figured in some fashion is likely. Few defense programs are ever divorced completely from politics.

A more important legacy of the TFX is the overruling of the service selection boards' choice of contractor by McNamara and his political deputies. They believed that Boeing's proposal contained too much risk for a program of this financial magnitude. And their reversal established a precedent for the substitution of political appointees' judgment—based on business, legal, or just plain political experience—for that of professionals with engineering and military backgrounds. Undoing the mischief that that precedent brought will be no easy task.

The TFX fiasco may be summed up by the Senate Committee on Governmental Operations report published in 1970, which concluded: "The history of the TFX program is one of a series of management blunders, a series of poor decisions at the highest levels of the Department of Defense." The phrase, "highest levels of the Department of Defense" should be emphasized, for the report singled out the political appointees running the military, not the program managers in industry or the military. TFX was a benchmark on the road to micromanagement as a way of life and the submersion not only of the program manager but also of the service chiefs. It was a clear signal of the fundamental shift coming in high-technology military hardware: from a performance-based approach to a cost-based approach.

Policy from the top can succeed if the acquisition and operating forces are left to work out the details. Even the best ideas will not work if they are forced onto an organization that does not understand—or distrusts—them or fails to recognize that shortcomings are being overlooked by decisionmakers. Both Congress and senior defense secretaries are obliged to consider potential efficiencies like commonality or commercial techniques. But they must not be blind to their side effects. And they must not substitute their judgment willy-nilly for that of the professionals. Micromanagement substituted for policy will not only compound confusion, but lengthen the development cycle and raise costs.

The International Dimension

Fifteen years after the TFX battle, William Perry, director of research and engineering in the Carter administration Defense Department, made NATO standardization and interoperability a centerpiece of U.S. international security policy. The point was to develop weapons, ammunition, and equipment that could be used by any NATO nation in case the alliance fought a common war.

The decisions of Belgium, Holland, and Norway to buy the American-developed F-16, but to produce it in Europe, followed this reasoning. Should these countries be involved in the same combat zone, each could draw on the other's spare engines, ammunition, ground-support equipment, and the like for their F-16 squadrons. More recently, the United States embarked on a mission to convince its European allies to join it in developing an advanced version of the F-18 for common use, displacing a joint European fighter effort under way. But they are unlikely to snap up the offer. Despite the appeal of standardization and shared investment with the United States, Europe is well aware of the relationship between defense employment and economic health. Further, it fears U.S. domination in weapons production.

As mentioned before, standardization is not synonymous with common equipment and is somewhat easier to bring off technically. An infantryman's rifle that used the same size cartridge would be a great asset in a NATO war, even if the rifles themselves were made by different nations. Aircraft or ground-vehicle fuels refined to the same specification and usable by varied kinds of equipment would ease logistics and supply problems. Standardized communications gear is another opportunity.

Nonetheless, across-the-board standardization is enormously difficult to bring about politically. No one is against it, but the economic and political interests of the various NATO countries— that is, concern with domestic jobs and domestic revenues— militate against buying foreign hardware for commonality's sake. Standardization is also an awesome and unwelcome administrative task. For this reason, neither Britain, West Germany, nor Italy, the larger NATO nations, nor France, which cooperates with the alliance, bought the F-16. France had its own Mirage fighter that was the primary competitor for what became the Belgian, Dutch, and Norwegian F-16s.

Shared weapons development on an international scale could reduce the defense costs of the United States and its allies. Joint research and development of a standard NATO artillery piece, tank, or missile, for example, would mean less cost to each nation, and the higher manufacturing volume also would result in lower production prices. Although this so-called NATO two-way-street concept was a centerpiece in the Carter administration, it never got enthusiastic support from the Reagan administration. But neither was it revoked, and acquisition directives now mandate a review of available allied equipment before U.S. development is started.

There has been some successful transatlantic traffic in military equipment. A new army antiaircraft weapon, for example, is part of an international joint venture. The U.S. Navy bought a British training aircraft—the Hawk—for less than it would have spent for a brand new custom design. But while buying the already developed British Hawk—rechristened the Goshawk for U.S. Navy service—did save money, a navy admiral told me, it was not a free ride. The navy spent millions adapting it for aircraft-carrier operations. Most important, though, it demonstrated to the Europeans that a two-way street was possible. Besides, saving money is not necessarily the last word. For example, to save more money, the cockpit displays in the original British version were left untouched. Now, the admiral explained, the navy wished it had a so-called glass cockpit—modern electronic and TV tube instruments—but it is too late to change; students will have to live with steam-boiler-type gauges.

But overall commonality in equipment on an international scale founders. First of all, there is the difference between European and American measuring standards. Conversion between the metric system and the U.S. equivalent is a horrendous chore. Thus co-production is tricky. And the United States, wary that enemy forces could cut off sea or air routes, would demand that an American manufacturer be qualified to produce overseas-designed hardware. Even if a sole U.S. or European manufacturer were chosen to build a standard vehicle, different metric and U.S. tool sizes make it extremely difficult to deal with the nuts and bolts of field maintenance.

These obstacles, along with all the usual parochial economic interests, make international commonality and standardization a distant, though worthy, goal. Similar problems make commonality of equipment among the services in the United States an equally difficult goal. Commonality cannot be attained by edict.

The Costs of "Better Business Practices"

The implications of the TFX fiasco reach beyond commonality to the radical changes McNamara was wreaking in the way the military bought its equipment. Cost-effectiveness as a prime test for military requirements has already been mentioned. The question was no longer just whether a weapon could do the job, but also whether it could do it at less cost than alternative approaches. Finding alternative approaches to what one or another of the services wanted to do became a cottage industry in the Pentagon. And since alternative approaches encompassed the idea of an alternative service, it raised the sensitive issue of service roles and missions—that is, military turf. Economic considerations certainly are valid in a peacetime military establishment that must live within a budget. Still, McNamara's enshrinement of economics left the professional military corps aghast that economics might become the driver for weapons development, not operational mission requirements. In the cutbacks after Vietnam, that shadow grew ever deeper, as it will again as the Reagan defense buildup peters out.

The whole McNamara thrust, culminating in total-package procurement, was for codified cradle-to-grave contracting. The solution to breaking the lock the contractor had on a program was perceived as locking in the contractor from the beginning. It became clear that there would be a few big winners in defense contracting and a large number of losers. (For "winners" read "survivors"). Defense contracting would become an all-or-nothing proposition. If, for example, the government committed to a two-service F-111 program, as McNamara's Defense Department planned to do, General Dynamics would have the program buttoned up and the F-14 program that kept Grumman in fighter development and manufacture would have vanished. In a sense, competition would be discouraged, almost in the name of competition. There would be less chance for a contractor to get a hearing for its alternate solution to a defense problem since that role had been preempted by systems analysts in the Pentagon. Bright ideas germinating from the research and development process would have less chance to flower.

The significance of this change should not be underestimated. It underlies many of the strains in defense hardware buying that followed, those that are with us yet today. In the name of introducing better business practices into the Pentagon, McNamara made the system less flexible and, in some respects, less competitive than it had been in the era of cost-plus contracting. True, there would be intense competition for the fewer, bigger programs. But only the largest corporations need apply. Once these enormous programs were awarded, once they were imbedded in the budget, the juggernaut would be rolling. Those who lost the big program would face a future of doing something else. The list of heretofore prime aircraft developers who have survived only with subcontract work (building sections of airframes) is a sign that such has come to pass. Now, of course, the wheel has come round 360 degrees and the game is to inject competition back into every phase of the process.

Pressure of this kind added to, rather than subtracted from, the possibility of an always-lurking overrun. With fewer, bigger programs, the contractor's incentive for unwarranted optimism about program costs mounted. Contractors shaved bids to levels they knew they could never bring in to buy the program—because it was the only game in town.

Entwined with fewer, bigger programs was the five-year programming and budgeting system that air force think-tank economist Charles Hitch brought to the Pentagon, making estimates of long-term, total program costs visible to Congress and the public for the first time. Few would argue that Congress and the public should be shown long-term military hardware costs. The late Harper Woodward, an adviser to oil-heir Laurence Rockefeller in his venture-capital investments in defense and technology start-up companies, told me, "My God, if we tell everybody what some of these things we need are going to cost, the taxpayer will never buy them." According to Woodward, the military requirements necessitated by growing Soviet nuclear as well as conventional power would be washed aside by public revolt, to the detriment of the security of the country. His vision took time in coming, but it did.

Long-range budgeting had various side effects. It left the Pentagon trying to predict what Congress might approve in the way of a military budget far down the road, alternating between realism and optimism. Too much optimism would mean the Pentagon gearing up for programs that eventually would fail to get through Congress. Too much realism would put the services in the position of not asking for programs Congress eventually might have agreed to. And, while it did not start the tendency of approved programs becoming embedded in future-year budgets like barnacles—irrespective of changing conditions—it created a climate more favorable for that tendency.

Long-term budgeting was designed to avoid the squeeze of too many program starts—programs sure to bloat in terms of required funding as they reached production stages—on too few dollars. Yet just as late president Dwight D. Eisenhower found out in the pre-McNamara days of 1957 that there was more on the military's plate than his prospective budget could pay for, the Reagan administration, in its defense buildup, is only the latest to confront exactly the same kind of overflow.

Another side effect of formal, long-term budgeting is that it discourages experimentation. In the pre-McNamara days, it was easier to build a prototype, a test version, of some new hardware idea—shades of fly-before-buy—and kill it if it turned out to be a flop. Its ultimate cost was not emblazoned in long-term planning and in massive contracts. Under long-term programming, and with McNamara's system of full-program commitment to a contractor early on, there is no way to sweep an unsuccessful idea under the rug and go on to something else.

The TFX put McNamara in a corner. He had battled the services, had almost forced a common airplane on the air force and the navy. His reputation was at stake at an early phase of the then-new Kennedy administration. His new approach to military buying promised scientific management and efficiency in place of military profligacy. There was no way McNamara could back away from the TFX, for if he did his reputation and his effectiveness in the Pentagon and with Congress would be ruined. The TFX program would be in the budget as long as McNamara was in office, regardless of whether something better might come along. Only an aroused Congress allowed the navy to wriggle out of the program that it had grave doubts about getting into in the first place. The contract, worth billions in the days when a billion dollars was a lot more money than it is now, also put the contractor on the spot. It was not the sort of environment in which objective research and development could determine that something was wrong, if such had been the case.

Perhaps more ominous in the purely pragmatic sense for both the military and industry was a hint of a kind of Gresham's law. Like the adage that bad money will crowd out good, would big money crowd out small? With emphasis on vast and total commitments for ships, tanks, and airplanes—rechristened weapons systems—small research and demonstration programs that were not included in big development could face rough sledding.

The fundamental issue is whether the small, off-the-wall research program—that is, exploratory development with no systems home—is being squeezed too hard. In the 1970s, Congress tightened the straitjacket that McNamara put on small research by mandating that basic university kinds of research must be mission-related. The move cut short university research funds and sent the message that speculative research was not a priority. Although funding has become less restrictive since, a legacy of the McNamara era is suspicion that research has been turned upside down, following hardware requirements rather than leading them.

McNamara did not invent the systems concept, which emerged in the Eisenhower era, but he put the weight of the Defense Department behind its elaboration into avenues its originators might not have expected. With the systems approach came concurrency. This meant that some, if not all, components and subsystems for a new vehicle, such as engines and electronics, would be developed simultaneously. If the invention entailed in one component was late, the whole project stalled and costs spurted upward. While tricky to manage, if the technical challenges are appraised accurately, concurrency pays off in faster development.

The TFX program was the most visible instance of a defense secretary attempting to overrule the services in a major acquisition program since Eisenhower began to centralize authority in the Defense Department. Besides dictating joint requirements for the TFX, McNamara overruled the source-selection board on the choice of contractor. And McNamara's assertion of power over the military commanders did not stop with weapons acquisition. There was an incident reported during the Cuban missile crisis when McNamara seized the telephone from a service chief in the Pentagon battle-command center to give orders directly to a commander at sea. No military officer missed the precedent established in the violation of what were then sanctified military channels, the inviolable chain of command. This incident and others like it, the TFX program, the increased authority of Defense Department systems analysts in acquisition decisions, each was a clear signal that the management of the U.S. military was taking what the military professionals considered an ominous turn.

Further centralization of authority in the Defense Department proceeded apace, until the Reagan administration set out to reverse the trend. But by then it was too late, the process had gone too far to permit much to be done. By that time Congress, in its rush to micromanage defense, had developed a full head of superheated steam. Decisionmaking was passing beyond the Defense Department to Capitol Hill. Now it is a guessing game as to who is in charge. And micromanagement of operations parallels that of acquisition. For example, a less-than-decisive navy carrier aircraft strike in Lebanon, after the bombing of a U.S. Marine barracks there, was run from Washington, D.C. And the marines were in Lebanon in the first place at the behest of the State Department—over opposition from the Defense Department. While the effects of centralization are difficult to measure, centralization certainly has contributed to the problems of weapons acquisition. The hours spent by program managers briefing those on up the chain of command, to the detriment of program management itself, are only part of the fallout.

As influential as McNamara's innovations were, they also followed a Newtonian law: They produced an equal and opposite reaction in the form of a return to prototyping, with the F-16, a decade later. Prototyping expressed outrage against the whole approach of engineering concept definition-to-death on paper.

To be fair, McNamara's idea of commonality has not always been wrong. It was just misdirected in the TFX decision. The air force adopted the navy's F-4 Phantom fighter without the rancor and accusations that marked the TFX debacle. It was an airplane that served well in Vietnam and was also bought by the British, West Germans, and Japanese. For that matter, the F-111 that emerged from the TFX battle was a good airplane as well—although it served a narrower mission than McNamara had envisioned.

An important distinction exists between the F-111 enmeshed in Capitol Hill charges of political influence in awarding the contract and the airplane itself—the political airplane versus the real airplane. Every defense equipment controversy aired in Congress and the press since then has had that element of political versus real hardware. They are not the same. Military professionals in general still resent what Washington has done, starting with the TFX, to the technical development and acquisition process.

8

Uncertainty: Technical and Financial

MILITARY buying has become fixed in the public mind as spending billions and, often as not, producing a turkey, not an eagle. As a way to escape military-equipment lemons, the Packard Commission revived an approach called fly-before-buy. The problem with flying-before-buying is that it costs more up front, in initial investment. That, in turn, leads to budget bloating and another trauma in military hardware buying: funding instability.

While fly-before-buy kinds of programs entail a long-term financial commitment—and money up front—this does not jibe with the one-year appropriations system under which the federal government generally operates. In fact, a program manager rarely knows for sure what kind of financing he will have for the life of the project—or even for the next year. He can plan all he wants to, he can include a reserve for unexpected technical problems, he can lean on the contractor to cut costs. But all this goes out the window if the Pentagon rejiggers its budget plans or if Congress does so for the Pentagon.

Both Congress and the Pentagon change their minds frequently. Then the contractors' work forces bob up and down in a costly dance. Pricing from subcontractors and vendors, which depends on quantity and timing, is disrupted. If technical problems follow, as they habitually do, there is no cushion to deal with them, and other phases of the work are upset. Not that these are excuses for every failure—for turkeys happen for a variety of reasons.

As a rule, though, there are rarely unmitigated, unredeemable turkeys in defense hardware. The hopeless cases get cancelled and the marginal ones are made to work, at the investment of extra time and dollars—it is something the acquisition system is designed to do.

Technology is not a sure thing. Old-fashioned cut-and-try will always be with us, something engineers understand—but taxpayers do not. A turkey may be necessary the first time to produce an eagle the second. One of the great mysteries of technical management, which puzzles military and industry alike, is that experienced, high-paid engineers with roomsful of expensive equipment can do it right the first time in one program but not in another. This fact of technical life is the premise for fly-before-buy, whose expansion, urged by the Packard Commission, is now written into Defense Department directives.

Prototyping: A Fix for Technical Uncertainty?

Fly-before-buy means to build a prototype; it does not have to be a flying machine. A prototype is simply the first version of a new piece of hardware and it is not expected to look exactly like the final product. It may be the first engine, the one manufacturers put into the test cell—specially constructed, insulated, and reinforced buildings where an engine can be operated at full power without undue racket and without spraying parts around the neighborhood if the engine blows up—to see how well it runs. It is the first laboratory-wired set of circuits and chips, the so-called breadboard model, to see if an electronic system will work. Because of their critical weight tolerances and the sensitivity of their design to small aerodynamic changes, aircraft can benefit more from prototype building than ground-based vehicles such as ships or tanks.

Prototypes serve diverse and useful functions. They are usually built with what is called soft tooling—that is, without the expensive jigs and fixtures that assembly-line production requires for fast and efficient manufacture. In that sense, they not only prove out the equipment—to ensure that the dimensions are right, that parts all fit—but also the tooling used to build it. If prototype aircraft demands redesign, tooling can be changed with relative ease. More important, a prototype aircraft can be test flown to prove out whether it is an eagle or a turkey, whether it meets the basic performance requirements the customer laid down.

Not everyone embraces prototyping, even for aircraft. Both military and industry developers believe that it is just not cost-effective to build throw-away prototypes of every piece of complex equipment—especially in light of the sophisticated tools now available to engineers. Computers used in complex and elaborate simulations are making cut-and-try a less standard operating procedure in developing new equipment, both for commercial markets and the military.
    Electronic gear, on the other hand, is a natural for prototyping because of its table-top, laboratory size, and generally lower costs. Breadboards and brassboards—that is, a more refined and production-ready breadboard—are fixtures in this area of technology. Missiles are something of the same story. A whole series of what amounts to prototypes are fired or launched to prove out a design and manufacturing process. The Soviets test missiles as if they were artillery—firing rounds before fielding weapons.
    Early on, at least from the 1930s, aircraft engines were commonly started as prototypes or test engines. Once a new engine was designed, the developers built one and ran it to see how long it took to break, and where. Then, back they trooped to the drawing board, wrestled with the problem, ran the engine some more, perhaps broke it again. Eventually, the engine either worked and went into production or it wound up on the cutting-room floor.
    This process has become expensive, unnecessarily so perhaps. As computers and their software have grown more versatile and sophisticated, engineers can design an engine, run it on a computer instead of in a test cell, and try to break it on a terminal screen—the easy way. Designers do more and more of their cut-and-try in what is called a preliminary design phase, trying to smoke out all kinds of specters and what-ifs on paper. Still, just like electronic breadboards, preproduction or test engines, even if not formally designated as prototypes, are development program standbys.
    Preliminary design phases are nothing new in technical development, military or otherwise. They are drawing more attention now simply because of the booming, almost prohibitive, costs of any large-scale project—particularly aircraft, which involve multi-billion-dollar investment. Anything to reduce margin of error helps. Commercial aircraft builders have reached the point where they are reluctant to design and build what is called a clean-sheet-

of-paper aircraft, one designed from scratch. Increasingly these manufacturers are adding new wrinkles to their existing stuff—modernizing their electronics, enlarging passenger cabins, converting to newer engines, improving wing profiles, and the like. Military developers have been forced into a similar course of action. Whole families of modernized versions of existing stables testify to the fact that the services found clean-sheet-of-paper aircraft unaffordable. Brand new military aircraft are scarce.

This was not the way development was handled in the technical flush that followed World War II. Both the navy and the air force had replacements in the works long before existing first-line aircraft had reached the end of their life spans. By the Korean War in the early 1950s, the air force had the superb F-86 fighter with its then-revolutionary swept-back wing. By the end of that decade, this still young aircraft was being superseded by the F-100, the first of the so-called Century series because their designations took three digits. Besides the F-100, there were four other brand new, very advanced aircraft being delivered to the air force. The F-100 soldiered on in Vietnam, but was soon superseded by the ubiquitous F-4, originally laid down by the navy.

The fact that the air force was willing to buy a first-line fighter developed by another service reflected a fundamental change: The pace of new U.S. military aircraft development was slowing down. In the F-4, the air force got a new fighter without the burgeoning cost of custom designing a clean-sheet-of-paper aircraft. By the late 1960s and early 1970s, only the appearance of a maturing generation of advanced Soviet fighters enabled the air force to start even one new fighter. This was the F-15, designed to deal with the Soviet covey. The navy, passing through the same shake-out, managed to start the F-14, a counterpart for standoff defense of aircraft carriers. These meant one aircraft for each service, not the stable of new ones of a decade or so before.

Later in the 1970s, the air force F-16 and the navy F-18 were designed and built; these aircraft, along with the F-14 and F-15, remain the first-line combat aircraft for each service today. Both the F-16 and F-18 are landmark aircraft in the acquisition sense, for both stemmed from the revitalized prototyping concept, aimed at curbing the increasingly risky process of going directly from paper design to production with no proving-out step.

Before World War II, company-built prototypes, which could be produced on a shoestring, were the way most aircraft were sold to the military. Vice Admiral J. T. Hayward, a naval aviator and aircraft-development manager, stumped for a return to that system in the late 1960s, despite the radical increase in costs that had taken place in the interim. He argued there was no better proof of concept than testing a flying machine, that paper programs cost more in the long run. David Packard, who had sponsored fly-before-buy as deputy secretary in the Defense Department and later expounded it from the platform of the presidential commission that bears his name, had the wisdom and the drive to put it into practice in the Pentagon.

More than just experimentation was involved in fly-before-buy. Experience with the F-14 and F-15 made it clear that, what with rampaging inflation in the early 1970s and the complex electronics going into them, high performance was coming at a high price. The F-14 and F-15 became the first fighters in the U.S. inventory to cross the $20 million plus per aircraft line. By contrast, the F4U used in World War II cost about $100,000—so prices for fighters rose more than two orders of magnitude in thirty years.

The Battle over Cost versus Numbers

Requirements, economics, and micromanagement combined in the early 1970s to make for a debate in the Pentagon and in the field that still is not resolved. Its crux was cost versus numbers, but the outcome spilled over into technical complexity in an attempt to produce lightness and cheapness in fighter aircraft. Numbers means how many troops, how many ships, tanks, and aircraft—the preponderance of forces in other words. "Fustest with the mostest," the classic slang dictum credited to Confederate general Nathan Bedford Forrest, has long been a tenet of military strategy and tactics. It is at the core of the confrontation with the Soviet Union, which has shabby technology and manufacturing, but numbers galore. This is a basic and important question about what wins in combat: high technology or numbers—or both.

For example, the F-4 became one of the world's most successful fighters on the premise that two engines, rather than one, were more likely to bring aircraft and crew home from combat—albeit at added cost, weight, and complexity. It also meant savings in peacetime, since a second engine could get a fighter back if the first engine failed simply for mechanical reasons, not gunshot holes. A similar argument for increased numbers—even at increased cost—is for two crewmen rather than one in the demanding split-second, electronic-eye combat now made possible by advanced technology.

These questions of numbers and costs are raised about ships, tanks, missiles, ground radars—every high-technology piece of equipment. All concern cost-performance tradeoffs—the kind that cannot be demonstrated until test and operating flight hours accumulate. What these questions boil down to is exactly what a fighter is supposed to be able to do in combat for what kind of investment.

For instance, do fighter aircraft have to be able to dogfight it out with opposing fighters, one-on-one, eyeball-to-eyeball, the white-scarf-and-goggles, personal combat of World War I? Or does a fighter just need to cruise along with its own powerful radar and a vast array of supporting sensors and computers on the ground, launching long-range missiles at targets its crew never sees? Or do fighters fight in gangs, one supporting and protecting another, using less complex ordnance and electronics? Do fighters have to fight in rain, sleet, snow, and fog, or is aerial combat a see-and-be-seen game? The answers have considerable implications for fighter design and cost, for one answer will be more technically complex and expensive than another. Agility and quickness, for example, bulk larger in the dogfight game, where range, endurance, and the ability to carry a heavy avionic and armament load count more. Analogous questions are debated over ship and surface-weapon design.

In the F-14, the navy sought an aircraft fit for electronic battle—one that could stand off from a battle group and fire a long-range missile at an attacker. The navy wanted to knock down enemy aircraft as far from the ships of its battle groups as possible. Hence came the F-14 with two engines, two crew members, and a relatively heavy and complex long-range missile, the Phoenix. In the F-15, the air force tilted more toward the dogfight concept and went with a single-pilot—though two engine—aircraft with shorter range and less complex missiles. But it was still a relatively big and heavy all-weather fighter.

Basically, despite all the transformations in technology over decades—despite all the electronic additions to aircraft, the advent of the powerful jet engine and exotic composite materials—the cost of aircraft still tracks with pounds of airframe weight, as Grumman aircraft designer Mike Pelehach has pointed out. The heavier the airframe, the more cost. Thus analysts in the Defense Department argued that, in light of constrained future budgets, the only way the air force was going to get its full projected strength in fighter wings was to find a lighter and cheaper aircraft than the F-15. While there were those in the air force who resisted this idea and battled for more F-15s, there also was an underground that supported lightweight fighters, that agreed with the numbers rationale, and that may well have been decisive in the decision. Thus the battle over cost versus numbers led eventually to the development of both the air force F-16 and, later on, the navy F-18. In the process, fly-before-buy got its testing.

The Lightweight Fighter Fly-Off Competition: Testing Fly-before-Buy

At the inception of the F-16/F-18 saga, there was no formal commitment on the part of the Defense Department or the air force to buy a weapons system; the idea was to finance, at least in part, the building of a couple of technology demonstrators. These were to be experimental lightweight fighters with new aerodynamic lines and new avionics. A simultaneous fly-off at the air force's test center north of Los Angeles would determine how each stacked up against the other. The fact that this was sold as only a technology demonstration program deflected opposition that might have erupted in a Congress already financing two multibillion-dollar fighter programs—the F-14 and the F-15.

The lightweight fighter competition injected a bit of life into what was becoming an acquisition system constipated with paper, reviews, briefings, and an endless decision hierarchy. Further, it allowed the prototype manufacturers and government program managers to take a fling at embryonic new technology without having to meet a production timetable. And the program was a remarkable achievement: The technology incorporated into both aircraft set the mold for fighter design all over the world for the decades to follow. Fly-by-wire control systems using electronic signals, rather than mechanical or hydraulic linkages, was one of these technologies.

When the two contractors for the lightweight-fighter demonstration built their prototypes, General Dynamics went the lightest weight route in what was then called the YF-16. (The Y in the designation simply meant prototype.) The company chose a single-engine, single-seat layout, one that broke with the trend of larger and fatter fighters. It had the rakish lines of a sports car and was one of the sexier-looking aircraft to come off the drawing boards in many a year. The pilot half-reclined instead of sitting upright as he flew the aircraft with a small pistol-grip controller at his right side; in front of him were cathode-ray tube display screens that would pale *Star Trek*. Because a single-engine aircraft carried more risk, General Dynamics picked the Pratt & Whitney F100 that had been through its teething troubles on the air force's F-15 fighter. Presumably it was a mature engine, and the air force welcomed wider utilization of a power plant into which it had poured large sums.

Northrop, the other lightweight-fighter competitor, went the heavier route in its YF-17 by using two engines. But it also stuck with a single pilot, and counted on equally awesome cockpit electronic automation. While Northrop picked a relatively new and untried engine from General Electric, it had been in gestation for years. The engine stemmed from one General Electric had produced for the T-38, a standard supersonic trainer for the air force. Over the years, it burgeoned in power and size, and Northrop had been using it for an aircraft it was designing to sell to Third World countries as a low-cost fighter.

The design and building of various prototype versions of the General Electric engine for the YF-17 had been financed with independent research and development money. While independent research and development has been attacked in Congress as a gift to contractors, and by antidefense groups as a system whereby the government finances contractors to develop hardware that they then sell to the military at fat prices, defenders can point to this case.

Independent research financed General Electric's development of what later emerged as the 404 engine in the Northrop YF-17, a valuable addition to the U.S. defense arsenal and one that became a highly sought after power plant by overseas aircraft builders, to the benefit of the U.S. balance of trade. Further, if this evolutionary research, build-and-try process had not been going on, the lightweight-fighter competition could not have been completed on short notice. For both financial and technical reasons, new hardware must evolve, and it is a long, trying process.

A bit larger with its two engines, and with a twin-tail instead of the YF-16's single fin, the YF-17 did not have all the hot-rod, high-performance trimness of the prototype F-16. The YF-17 was just not quite as sporty. Though looks are not the whole story, at air shows the F-16 later seemed to fly circles around anything on the field, and it became every fighter pilot's goal to get his hands on it.

How an aircraft looks is not a frivolous subject. While an aircraft that looks sleek and sexy will not necessarily fly that way—Curtiss built some slick-looking aircraft in the 1930s, whose performance led to Curtiss's disappearance from the aircraft market—aircraft designers will tell you that an aircraft that looks right usually flies right. The distinction is between looking good aesthetically and looking right from the standpoint of utility. For example, take the case of the F-4, with its thick body, bent-up wing tips, and drooping tail. Some consider it one of the uglier aircraft ever built. But it had a down-to-earth, I-mean-business look that fit exactly with its becoming one of the premier and most sought-after fighters in the free world. George Spangenberg, the civilian Mr. Fighter Design in the navy for years, told me that the competitor aircraft to the F-4 was a far better one in terms of pure flying qualities. As a single-engine aircraft, it was lighter and more agile than the twin-engine F-4. But, Spangenberg said, when the time came to look at doing the mission, at carrying a weapons load, the F-4 won the marbles.

An echo of this linkage between looks and performance came to pass in the aftermath of the lightweight-fighter fly-off. Both prototypes looked right and turned out to be fine aircraft—not perfect, but very good. They were good enough that the Pentagon made a case with Congress to turn the demonstration program into a development program. But problems developed.

The air force decided to go ahead with the YF-16, but not

without heartburn over the single-engine issue and not without complaint about pressure from the Defense Department hierarchy. Once the air force bowed to the cheaper-but-more-aircraft theory, to the dictates of the Defense Department that it would get its full tactical wing strength only with something less expensive than the F-15, the Pentagon civilians knew they had a good thing in the cost-versus-numbers game.

Before long the navy got the same word: It could buy something cheaper than the F-14 for a common fighter/attack aircraft—that is, one of the new fighter demonstrators in the fly-off program—or it would get nothing. The navy balked at the F-16, some said because it was an air force baby. There were more tangible objections, too. The F-16 might face problems in landing aboard carriers—a landing that puts bigger loads than concrete runways do on landing gear and support members. Besides, it had only one engine. And while lots of navy carrier aircraft have only a single engine, two make for a nice security blanket for overwater operations.

Even the navy, always recalcitrant to dictation from the Defense Department, saw the inevitable. It opted for the YF-17, but redesignated as the F-18 with a slew of modifications for sea duty. (Strictly speaking, the navy designation is F/A-18, for the aircraft is a combination fighter and ground-attack aircraft, a strike fighter rather than an air superiority fighter.) The navy also insisted on a contractor with long experience in building carrier aircraft, which Northrop lacked. McDonnell Douglas became the prime contractor, Northrop a principal supplier for fuselage sections. Northrop also retained the rights to an export version that did not go beyond the brochure stage—the F-18L—which became the source of a lawsuit brought by Northrop against McDonnell Douglas over who owned what.

Despite prototyping, despite fly-before-buy, both the F-16 and the F-18 had problems of one kind or another—not necessarily critical but sometimes embarrassing. Congress was drawn into the F-18 sharpshooting, which was magnified by old navy loyalties, by its resistance to Defense Department dictates, and by well-aimed zingers from competing contractors. Cracks in the tail section brought flight restrictions early in the F-18's flight test days. Then there were landing gear failures, doubly embarrassing given the switch to McDonnell Douglas. After the F-18 entered service with the U.S. Navy and in Canada, there were recurring skin cracks in the fuselage section and a fire hazard from failures of the titanium compressor blades in the aircraft's General Electric 404 engine.

Why did these things happen, despite years of experience and powerful new computer tools to aid in design? An impatient public is tired of hearing that humans are fallible and make mistakes or cannot be omniscient. In the case of the titanium compressor blades, history repeated itself. Rolls Royce had tried to use them in its commercial engine for the Lockheed L-1011 transport in the early 1970s. They failed to stand up structurally, and Rolls had to make an expensive switch to another alloy that reduced engine performance. Perhaps improvements in titanium technology justified its use in the 404 engine, and General Electric has been more willing than its arch competitor, Pratt & Whitney, to take technical risks to shave weight, improve performance, and win competitions. But grueling hours in service exposed what testbed and flight test running did not. General Electric's profits will shrink to foot the bill for fixes.

In the broader, policy sense, the F-18 exposed a truth in defense hardware: the first version of advanced technology hardware probably will not work quite right. Past Defense Department policymakers tried to mandate that there would be no development in service—that is, that there would be only a first version of any equipment, no subsequent versions with letter suffixes appended to their designations to denote a progression of modifications. This is like trying to repeal the laws of physics. Pre-Planned Product Improvement (P^3I)—a Pentagon procedure for doing the doable first and accepting the need for later, modified versions based on results in service—is a pragmatic answer to an unpalatable but possibly immutable truth.

For its part, the F-16 had failures of its single engine, which lost aircraft. Further, the F-16 proved to be a fair-weather fighter. It did not have the load of electronics carried by the F-15 for night and all-weather operations. It performed brilliantly for the Israelis in desert combat in the Middle East. But in the fogs, drizzle, and low clouds of central Europe, it couldn't match the venerable F-4. To solve the problem, an auxiliary navigation and targeting system pod, called Lantirn, had to be developed—a drawn-out procedure that meant more dollars.

Another surprise had to do with costs. In the beginning, the

F-16 cost less than $10 million a copy. Unit costs then drifted up to about $13 million. This is not high for a fighter by today's standards, but it is definitely not cheap. While it is half what the F-15 goes for, the F-15 can do more. The cost of the YF-17, designed as a land-based fighter and then modified into the F-18 to operate aboard carriers, escalated with the changes. The F-18 soon became a $20-million-a-copy attack fighter. Although the F-18, and especially its engine, is proving itself in service as a low-maintenance aircraft, it is by no means a cheap fighter either.

Evaluating Fly-before-Buy

All these considerations support the claims of opponents to fly-before-buy. They argue—not loudly, given that fly-before-buy is Pentagon policy—that prototyping is no guarantee against subsequent modifications and fixes. Aircraft design, they claim, has reached the point where a pure prototype is superfluous; designers can do it right the first time. While prototypes are useful for proof testing and manufacturing set-up, they contend, fly-before-buy can waste time and money by delaying entry into production.

In fact, however, unknowns are going to sneak up on prototypes as well as computer-design artists. While a case can be made that both the F-16 and F-18 could have been developed the same way without the political window dressing of the lightweight-fighter competition, it is difficult to quarrel with success. There is no question that the competition produced what became two first-line U.S. fighters. In the critical area of quality, both have sold well to overseas customers, who could have bought European or even Russian aircraft. Both had better reliability and maintainability than earlier aircraft. And even if fly-before-buy did not put a stop to rising unit costs, it flattened the upward spiral in program costs for fighter aircraft.

That being said, it is also necessary to concede that neither the cost dilemma nor the need to produce successive versions of the aircraft—to improve or fix the first one—was completely removed by this concept. And prototyping can be unnecessarily expensive if the technology involved in a program is well understood and if the buyer knows exactly what he wants. In such cases, it may be cheaper just to go ahead, the way commercial aircraft builders do, using the first aircraft as a demonstrator and making fixes, if necessary, as production goes along.

What fly-before-buy does for program management is to knock off the nonsense of paper-cost estimates, of paper-performance estimates, and get real hardware into the sky to get hard data. Fly-before-buy gives some real indications of manufacturing costs. A prototype injects hard-nosed experience and realism into a system filled with computer runs and marketing optimism. Flight testing demonstrates how accurate fuel-consumption projections are; it gives a preliminary idea of reliability, of maintenance man-hours; it shows whether the prototype will deliver on maneuverability, speed, and the rest of the performance its designers promised.

While fly-before-buy was a solution fostered by the Pentagon's civilian hierarchy, in this case (unlike the C-5 and total-package procurement), the managers who had to carry it out understood and empathized with it, and the idea proved successful in practice.

The air force used fly-before-buy to great advantage to get its drifting program for a new tactical fighter—the Advanced Tactical Fighter (ATF)—moving into development. The operational date for the new fighter had been slipping farther and farther back into the 1990s. When the Packard Commission report emphasized the fly-before-buy concept, the air force, almost overnight, rewrote the rules for bidding on the ATF program, which up to that point had called for another set of paper studies. Instead, there would be prototypes, since designated the YF-22A and YF-23A. Further, the two contractor teams selected to compete for the final award would be given a fixed amount of money to build those prototypes. By design, it would not be enough to cover their costs; one contractor estimated it would take about $300 million of his own money to do the work—and with no assurance that his company would ever produce anything to recover its investment. But the air force had laid the groundwork to sell the program to Congress, on the basis of flying hardware, early in the next decade. Though not much of a gain in delivery schedule, the program was at least moving ahead. And that is no small accomplishment.

As the saying goes, the jury is still out on the ultimate contribution of the fly-before-buy concept to military buying. Prototyping, fly-before-buy has won a niche in acquisition strategy. But like most such techniques, judgment and flexibility must be exercised in how and where it is used.

Funding Instability and the F-15

While the lightweight fighter was coming to pass, the aircraft whose purported high cost started the whole thing—the F-15—was sinking deeper into a cost quagmire due to vacillating budget numbers. Not that the F-15 was the first military program—nor will it be the last—where funding changes upset cost estimates and tooling investments; such is more often the rule than the exception. As early as twenty-five years ago, funding instability was recognized as producing significant uncertainty in the military acquisition realm, which was already buffeted by changes in the direction of government policy and strategic doctrine. According to a 1962 Harvard Business School study, entitled *The Weapons Acquisition Process*, which was influential in the fixes attempted in the McNamara Pentagon, "financial crises continually arise, to be met by shifting funds from one program to another . . . it is not surprising that the financial plans may have been overtaken by events."

A decade and a half later, events certainly overtook financial planning with reference to the F-15 program. Development of the F-15 began in the wake of the C-5A fiasco. It was to heal the wounds the reputation of the military-acquisition system had suffered in the C-5A case, through a higher degree of military involvement in contractor management. As a showcase for more intense air force management, the F-15 would mark a new degree of control over the contractor by the System Program Office (SPO) that the program manager runs. Control was fundamentally simple with the F-15: The contractor in St. Louis was not to make a move without checking with the program office through a special tie-line set up for quick-and-ready communication. A handpicked air force team of fast burners—the high achievers on a fast track—was assigned to the program.

The star program manager that the air force picked to run the F-15 was Ben Bellis, whom I met when he was a junior lieutenant colonel. At the time, he was on his way to deliver a paper on configuration control at a watershed meeting to which the air force had summoned its large contractors to tell them how life would be under the new McNamara regime. Configuration control was a hot subject then; even today, it is an important part of systems integration and logistics. It was a significant reform to both customer and contractor. Simply put, configuration control means keeping close tabs on the status of design in a complicated piece of hardware so that all the bits and pieces fit together at assembly—and later in the field when maintenance and replacement with spare parts come into play. Applied to electronics, it means that all components fit and play together compatibly. Configuration control was a mental training ground for Bellis in his later management of the F-15 program.

The navy, which had gone through the kinds of overruns on shipbuilding that the air force had with the C-5A—complete with government claims for refunds from the contractor and contractor claims for payment from the navy—also turned toward stricter program office control. What had happened, one naval officer told me at the time, was that the navy had allowed future ship users into contractor yards to see how vessels were coming along. Most of the visitors had ideas on how to improve the ship's layout. The contractor, most likely on a cost-type contract, would have a man on hand with the clipboard, taking notes. Hordes of change orders followed the hordes of visitors. When the program director got the bill, there was hell to pay about who had ordered all the revisions. The military customer obviously bore a share of the blame, but contractors were naive to conjoin in the process. Shipbuilding was no isolated instance of too many cooks and too little control over engineering changes.

Intensification of control over programs at higher and higher levels of authority spread with little restraint; it now pervades the whole Defense Department's and Congress's approach to military buying. There was a difference, however, in the F-15 program. Its program office had both responsibility and authority. As the process evolved, micromanagers in the Defense Department and Congress only have the authority; they do not share the responsibility. An early 1980s Air Force Systems Command study, entitled Affordable Acquisition Approach (A^3 for short) revealed the impact of what was called external management—a euphemism for micromanagement. Of the fifty-five programs spanning thirty years that it studied, external management affected 55 percent—41 percent of the pre-1970s programs, 68 percent of the later ones. In each case where micromanagement inserted itself, funding stability eroded. The final chapter is cost growth and schedule slippage. As the study pointed out, micromanagement may not always be the cause of cost growth in itself, but it comes as part of the package.

Should a program run into more than its share of intractable and expensive-to-solve technical problems, the sponsors may scale back the requirement. Then the Pentagon hierarchy and Congress sniff trouble, suspecting that the requirement was too ambitious to begin with. Their support wanes. Funding starts to gyrate, leaving technical problems to persist; program reviews proliferate, delays ensue, and costs run further out of control. By now the program is skidding down a slippery slope toward fiasco or disintegration.

In exchange for the intensified supervision in the F-15 program, production stability was offered as a goodie to the contractor. The initial number of aircraft was fixed at 729. Production rates were to build up over a couple of years to 144 aircraft annually by the 1976 federal fiscal year; this would allow for some early low production numbers to make sure the aircraft was going to meet its specifications without big fixes and for normal production-line learning processes. In the event, that assembly-line rate of 144 annually, a scale on which the production tooling had been built and bought, only held for one year. After a peak in 1976, the rate moved down; by fiscal 1978, annual production had dropped to less than 100 a year, and by fiscal 1982 it hit bottom at 36 a year.

At peak production in 1976, the program cost of an F-15—that is, total cost, with development or support expenses apportioned to it—was about $20.5 million. When production dropped to nine F-15s a month, the program cost of an F-15 rose to more than $23 million. Computing the unit price using flyaway costs—that is, the bare manufacturing costs of building the aircraft—reveals the same increase in cost. By fiscal 1981, the flyaway cost of the F-15 had risen to $18.4 million a copy; the following year, when production bottomed at thirty-six aircraft, the cost rose to $23.8 million. The reason for that big a shift in just one year is that in 1981 forty F-15s were built for overseas customers in addition to the forty-five built for the United States Air Force. So the cost comparison is actually $18.4 million per F-15 when eighty-five aircraft were built versus $23.8 million when fewer than forty F-15s were built.

Inflation also figured into these price increases. Inflation was rampaging in the 1970s—at an average rate of 11 percent a year—and the defense budget was not coping with it. Military planners were consistently underestimating inflation in their budgets. In the fiscal and monetary giddiness of the mid-1970s, with wild escalations in prices, the estimated total program cost for the F-15 rose by a billion dollars in one six-month period. But even if there had been no inflation at all, the cost per F-15 would escalate simply because of the lower production numbers.

Stretch-Outs

Stretching out production—that is, producing fewer aircraft per year, for example, as was done with the F-15s—is a typical Pentagon response when the budget for the upcoming fiscal year is smaller than anticipated. When acquisition managers and planners are backed into a corner, stretch-outs are the classic response. Stretch-out is one of the less painful ways to cut: buy fewer quantities each year; spread the original total over more years; less cost per year, more overall. Uneconomic as stretch-outs are, cancellations are worse—not only costly in terms of termination charges, but also upsetting local employment markets and failing to deliver the military equipment called for.

When Ronald Reagan's new defense team entered office, it resolved to do something about uneconomic production rates. Part of the Reagan defense budget increase was for front-end money to build more units immediately and, by quicker completion of programs, save funds later. This worked in the case of the F-16. But the F-15 was still bumping along at thirty-six aircraft a year in 1984. The F-15 total crept up slightly the following year to forty-two, and edged up a bit more in 1986 to forty-eight. With those forty-eight aircraft, the F-15 program reached its original target production figure of 729, but it took fourteen years to get there. If the government had stuck with its planned production rate of 144 F-15s each year, the program could have been bought out (that is, funded and contracted out to completion) in seven years—by the end of 1979—at a savings of at least $2 billion. Budgetary stretch-outs moved the production of 200 F-15s from the 1970s into the early 1980s. Double-digit annual inflation then added double-digit increases to the cost. Thus stretching out the F-15 program for budgetary reasons did not save money—other than to keep the military-spending tab under whatever lid was favored from year to year.

Low-production quantities figured in more recent whistle-blowing in the MX intercontinental ballistic missile program. Northrop, the contractor for the inertial measurement unit for the precision targeting guidance system, could not meet delivery schedules. There also were complaints of quality shortcomings. One of the reasons Northrop cited for the delivery problem was that quantities were so low that it never had the opportunity to come down a proper learning curve.

Congress, not surprisingly, was involved in these quantity limits. Representative Les Aspin of Wisconsin, as chairman of the House Armed Services Committee, may have saved MX by proclaiming skepticism and holding the numbers low enough for a reluctant Congress to accept the program. Congress had been baffled by the conflicting claims of two administrations: Carter asserting that MX had to be dispersed on mobile launchers, shuttled between shelters to escape a Soviet nuclear strike; Reagan insisting that the missiles had to be packed densely together in underground silos to survive. So Capitol Hill cannot be blamed for making its own technical judgment, going off on a tangent by supporting a small mobile missile that, in larger numbers, would be a successor for MX but without MX's ability to take out the massively shielded Soviet silos then under construction. Salvaged as it was, the low quantities for MX were a Pyrrhic victory in terms of the weapon's economics and its deployment schedule.

Spiraling Costs

The air force A^3 study put funding instability at the top of the list of reasons why development programs take longer and cost more—surprisingly ahead of technical problems. Sometimes, it noted, funding cuts cause technical problems. Of the twenty-seven pre-1970s programs that were studied, technical problems contributed to cost growth in 70 percent, as compared to only 36 percent in the twenty-eight post-1970 programs. Technical complexity, however—defined as large numbers of equipment interfaces, components, or subsystems—ranked with funding instability as a reason for cost growth in the more recent programs the study analyzed.

Other studies, by the Defense Science Board and the Rand Corporation among them, were equally concerned about the role of funding instability and program stretch-outs in the growth in cost of military hardware. No one has produced a cure-all, but the air force A³ study had some tough advice: Get realistic. That means estimating costs so that low-ball forecasts that fail do not chill program support and excite micromanagers. It means budgeting for risk and for unknowns. And it means casting a hard eye before committing to full-scale development of new programs, and thinking seriously about putting marginal programs to sleep early, so that they do not destabilize future planning. The implication is that too many programs are getting too far into development under a total budget that cannot accommodate them all. As the study cautioned, by the time a program reaches Milestone 2—the start of full-scale development—over 80 percent of its life-cycle costs are locked in, and the opportunity for cost reductions is very limited.

Funding instability was a special concern of the Packard Commission report. In its interim report to the president, it recommended biennial budgeting:

> Congressional approval of the budget on a year-to-year basis contributes to and reinforces the (Defense) Department's own historical penchant for defense management by fits and starts. Anticipated defense dollars are always in flux. Individual programs must be hastily and repeatedly accommodated to shifting over-all budgets, irrespective of military strategy and planning. The net effect of this living day-to-day is less defense and more cost. Although often hidden, this effect is significant—and it can be avoided (page 6).

It also favored multiyear funding for individual programs, to escape the usual pop-ups and dips in annual congressional budget massaging. Funding is thus committed for several years—committed, that is, as much as the federal budgeting system ever is. Still another significant Packard Commission recommendation to stabilize funding was to institutionalize baselining—that is, specification of design, cost, and scheduling that the program is supposed to hew to—for major weapons systems at the outset of full-scale engineering development. A baseline agreement is analogous to the agreement a commercial program manager has with his company's chief executive officer: As long as the project stays on its baseline track, the chief executive lets the program manager run it unhindered.

What the Packard Commission was getting at, in the tradition of the failed McNamara revolution, was introducing more commercial business practices into the Pentagon. If military development were run like commercial development, the commission believed, it would introduce more stability into the whole process. In a sense, the commission was supporting expansion of procedures that were more or less already in place. Biennial budgeting, multiyear funding, and baselining for major weapons systems were ideas that had already made some headway in the Pentagon and Congress. The B-1B, for example, was a multiyear-funded baselined program. But while these recommendations make sense, the way things ought to be often collides with actual practice. In the case of the B-1B, multiyear funding and baselining did not prevent the disappearance of its contingency cushion. Also, it is not yet certain that multiyear funding will be immune to meddling, changes of mind, or simple estimate errors.

While Congress can be a spoiler for funding stability, it is not the only one. Vacillation in the Pentagon—a decay in internal support—also disrupts programs. Sometimes change is unavoidable, such as when new intelligence upsets a requirement; sometimes a change of the guard in the service or Defense Department brings different ideas; sometimes an analyst raises an issue that can't be argued away.

Funding instability also stems from the Pentagon's predilection to do five-year planning and budgeting based on chronically unrealistic estimates of what funding Congress eventually will approve. Then every year comes the drastic overhaul as the budget is carved to fit what Congress gives. Further, with Congress insisting on a single-year budget approval system, five-year planning takes on an air of never-never land. Even a two-year budget doesn't work. Congress can, and often does, change its mind on program-funding levels or on over-all budget policy. Five-year budget planning is an exercise in futility more often than not. Private industry, for that matter, has cooled to five- or ten-year budget-planning exercises; instead it settles for a plan for the next quarter.

The Maverick: An Almost Successful Escape from Funding Instability

Relatively few programs are immune to funding uncertainties over their lifetimes. Even programs that ought to be on a clear, smooth track like the Maverick missile, now in its peak production phases, are afflicted. Maverick, a missile for attacking ground targets from the air, its design based on hard lessons learned in combat in Vietnam, is a uniquely successful application of total-package procurement. Thomas M. McMillin, now the Maverick program manager, ascribes its on-track schedule and cost performance in part to a top-flight government-industry management team formed at the program's inception. McMillin also cites the insistence of the original contractor, Hughes Aircraft, on an abnormally high escalation clause, which protected the program when inflation boiled over in the mid-1970s.

In addition, Hughes created a very good value-engineering team, whose performance was related to profit sharing under the terms of the incentive contract. Value engineering is a kind of design review by an independent group seeking changes to reduce costs. For example, value engineering may mean alterations in piece parts that preserve the integrity of the hardware but make for easier and cheaper manufacture. In other words, the engineering team is given latitude to use its judgment, and, given the room to maneuver, can do a better, less expensive job.

In the initial stages of the contract, Arthur L. Zussman, a Hughes group vice president, related, a tough program manager at Hughes insisted on sticking to the letter of the contract. That meant no product improvement, no performance enhancements—just giving the customer exactly what he asked for, no more, no less. In that sense, Maverick was a signpost on the road toward cost-based, not performance-based, military weapons development in the United States.

Maverick has since gone through several versions. Currently, the Pentagon is trying once more to do something good in contracting through expansion of a system called second sourcing. Although the navy rushed into second sourcing in an unprecedented way, the air force had reservations about the idea because it required the government to spend money to run a competition, familiarize another source with the task, and then set up for an alternate production line.

Second sourcing was common during World War II, when the Fords and the General Motors were pressed into building aircraft, but it fell into relative disuse after the Korean War. Whereas wartime demands for equipment in a hurry warrant the added expense of establishing a second production source, in peacetime, it is usually necessary to wait out slower delivery schedules from a single assembly line to save money. Further, peacetime production-run quantities are often too small to justify the investment in a second source by the government, the contractor, or both. Also working against the use of second sources is the complexity of weapons, unstable funding (if the Pentagon or Congress change their minds about supporting a program, a prudent investment in tooling and teaching can go sour), and contractors' claims to the design and manufacturing processes of systems they develop, which may block second sourcing or add to its costs if their processes or ideas must be licensed.

Production quantities and funding instability threatened to undermine the Maverick second-source program before it had a chance to return any benefits to the government. The 1983 projection for a production run of 60,000 through fiscal 1990 made for large enough annual increments to support a dual-assembly operation. Besides, Hughes was having its troubles with the navy over quality control and contract specification compliance. A little insurance, a little more competitive pressure, could not hurt.

Raytheon, a company that has turned winning second-source programs into an art, added Maverick to its string. Raytheon was not the lowest second-source bidder, but it convinced the air force that it could deliver the product with a minimum of fuss and feathers—at minimum risk, not minimum dollars. In any event, minimum risk, over the long run, is likely to be the minimum cost.

Second sourcing, done right, is not a free ride into a program. If the second-source contractor accepts the drawings and data it gets from the prime source as Holy Writ, it lays itself open to unpleasant, perhaps financially devastating, surprises. Hence Raytheon did a careful production-engineering analysis of the data package for Maverick, in effect walking through the basic design itself. Once it won the Maverick second-source contract, Raytheon faced a thirty-month qualification effort to demonstrate it could build the missile to Pentagon standards. The Raytheon missile had to fit and work the same as the Hughes missile; it had to be interchangeable.

No sooner had Raytheon built missile-checkout facilities and geared up for production than the Gramm-Rudman-Hollings budget-ceiling amendment intruded. On top of that, the air force was having its own troubles trying to fit its ten pounds worth of programs into the traditional five-pound annual budget bag. The budget figures for the Maverick began to roll backward.

By mid-1986, it began to look as if the projected 12,000-a-year Maverick production for 1987 would drop drastically. Instead of building 60,000 missiles by 1991, production would continue through 1998—at a peak-year quantity of around 7,000 and, for near-term years like 1987, something closer to 2,000. At that level, the economies of scale for two contractors deteriorate; one can handle the job efficiently. With stretch-out in the wind, the air force studied the effect of a cutback in production from 9,600 annually to 7,200 and found that, without any engineering changes, unit costs were driven up 10 percent.

Both Hughes and Raytheon were nonplussed at the drop in projected annual production numbers. Hughes, having assumed a 50-50 split of a 12,000-missile annual production rate, had decided to invest $40 million in a new, nonunion plant in Georgia to compete with Raytheon's Tennessee plant. Such low-cost plants benefited the government in terms of lower prices for the Maverick. When the bids came in for contracts, prices were low enough that the air force got 3,200 missiles for its limited funds, not the 2,000 it expected. So second sourcing did help. "We're caught in a box," McMillin said of the pricing windfall. "We can't be too optimistic on price or we will be accused of being overoptimistic. We can't be too conservative or we will be accused of overconservatism." Price concessions of that magnitude, however, are not likely for future contracts. And while Hughes has a long way to go to recover its Georgia investment, second sourcing, curiously enough, was one of the reasons for its earlier success with total-package procurement. Hughes had two sources for Maverick components and, as a result, did not suffer expensive schedule delays because of development snags.

While Maverick is a successful program, it only narrowly escaped disintegration due to funding instability in its early years. In the rigors of the 1970s economic climate, before the program could build up to its early production targets, its funding got a year out of sequence. Even with its inflation-escalation clause, it was only the fact that the air force had given Hughes risk funding—a sort of convoluted advance payment—that enabled Hughes to keep its Maverick work force together and keep its vendors in the program until early production rates built to projected levels.

Solving the Problem

Funding instability and what it has done—because of program delays—to costs is a sorry story. To attack this problem, Congress, the White House, and the Pentagon must synchronize their financial and strategic planning and review. Cost control starts with policy stability. Then there is the matter of low quantities and, by commercial standards, ludicrous production rates for defense equipment. Low quantities and production rates make normal overhead, not to mention facilities investment, a disproportionate burden in military acquisition. The solution that neither the Pentagon, the administration, nor Congress wants to embrace is to buy out programs faster, to use restraint in starting new programs, and to take the budget money available to support production levels that make better economic sense.

Stable funding, as in the case of the F-16 program, provides a foundation for success. It is not the sole determinant, but it clearly is a prerequisite. Requirements also are enormously influential in shaping success or failure—but stable funding is essential. Consider both the F-14 and F-15, for example, which evolved from differing but well-conceived requirements. Both earned a respected place in the U.S. arsenal. Yet funding instability—which resulted in smaller production runs and schedule stretch-outs—drove up costs for both.

Also critical to program success or failure, and to cost control, is the handling of engineering change proposals (ECPs)—that is, the rigidly formalized, documented procedures to prevent needless engineering and design changes from running up the price tag. Engineering changes are an invitation to success or failure for a military project. They can be cost savers—as they were for Maverick's value-engineering team. But if they are unnecessary, such changes mean goldplating and technical complexity. Codified procedures and reams of regulations will not fail-safe the process.

Fly-before-buy also can be a useful tool, but, again, it is not as critical to the success of a program as well-drawn requirements and stable funding. It is cut-and-try on a planned basis, and hence a gauge of the soundness of the requirement for which hardware is built; a measure of whether there is too little or too much technical complexity entailed, whether engineering changes are essential or just tinkering. But the principal value of prototyping is in confidence building—confidence for the program manager in terms of proven performance, confidence for the Pentagon and Congress that hardware will work in the field, that a turkey is not simmering away in the oven. In an era of waste, fraud, and abuse, such is by no means to be taken lightly.

9

Evading the System

THERE is a kind of military buying that circumvents the bureaucratic system of regulations, paperwork, quality control, and congressional micromanagement, and, evidently, does so to its advantage. The process is so secret, though, that it is almost impossible for anyone on the outside to find out with certainty whether the programs produced this way really are delivered better and faster than the ones produced in the open.

These are the black programs, some so closely held that military officers and contractors involved cannot even admit to their names in public. Black programs may be left out of budget documents entirely, though some are included by obscure code name, with or without a dollar figure that would provide a clue to their size. These projects are so characteristic of reconnaissance and intelligence operations that they have become synonymous.

Supersecret weapons development is not new. Witness the atomic bomb. And people both in and out of Washington claim that the best run black programs have accomplished more for less. On the other hand, the Advanced Technology Bomber, the secret Stealth bomber under development by Northrop, is exceeding its cost estimates. By summer 1987, Northrop had written off more than $200 million on unidentified programs—most of which had to be on the Stealth bomber—excess costs that it rather than the government had to absorb. This is something that advocates for the air force B-1 Bomber—a competitor of a sort—had predicted was sure to happen.

The two programs offer a comparison of the workings of the formal, open acquisition system (the B-1) and the secret realm (the Stealth bomber). Ronald Reagan revived the B-1, which had been cancelled by former president Jimmy Carter, with the commitment to produce 100 airplanes. Naturally, B-1 supporters in the mid-1980s campaigned to pierce that ceiling. So continuation of the B-1, a known quantity, and development of the Stealth bomber, with technical uncertainties and unknowns still ahead, were aiming at the same pot of money for their long-term existence, even though each was on the approved program list for the immediate future.

The B-1 Bomber: Shortcomings Exposed

For a time after it was revived, the air force pointed to the B-1 with pride and joy. The revived B-1 started out as a showcase program, complete with a management tracking system that included red devils—a catch phrase for the red flagging of problem areas that might cause the program to run over schedule or cost. None of this hot-shot management science prevented the B-1 from turning into a flap after the first deliveries to the Strategic Air Command.

First, there were complaints over fuel leaks, a continual plague for big airplanes with tons of what amounts to kerosene stored in tanks in the wing structure itself. Sealant is difficult to install with surety in cramped nooks and bays to begin with, and temperature changes and flexing of the long, thin wings in flight ruthlessly expose any flaws. Rockwell, the contractor for the B-1, had not built a big airplane since the cancelled B-70 bomber a decade earlier, and it had fuel leaks, too.

A far more serious shortcoming occurred in the airplane's electronic warfare gear, equipment that is vital for its successful penetration of enemy air defenses. Skepticism over the B-1's ability to survive the vaunted Soviet air-defense system—the Soviets are obsessive about inviolability of the motherland's defenses and give these top priority—led to the cancellation of the B-1 in the late 1970s. When Reagan revived the B-1, then designated the B-1B, the system was redesigned and considerably upgraded. The electronic warfare gear grew from 88 so-called black boxes stuffed with chips and boards to 118 black boxes. Although each of the B-1B's 118 black boxes checked out according to specification, they did not work so well when connected.

According to the air force, it was a typical integration problem, which it was—in spades. In military electronics manufacturing, it is common for individual chips or components to perform as the paperwork says they should, meeting the required tests, and yet not work exactly right when wired together in a black box. Voluminous tests may satisfy the inspectors but miss the basics. It is a measure of the endemic preoccupation in defense contracting with meeting paperwork specifications for each part and piece while losing sight of the most fundamental requirement of all: that they all play together in harmony for the user in the field.

In part, the shortcomings of the electronic countermeasures resulted from industrial complications—among them the difficulties of producing enough top-quality components within the designated time frame. In part, they stemmed from incorrect assumptions made—because of the lack of hard intelligence data—about Soviet defense hardware and practices. As a result, changes had to be made. And while these were doable, it would take time and, of course, money.

There is more to the countermeasures equipment story. Instead of using an integration contractor, as is common practice on complex electronics programs, the air force decided to act on its own. The air force could have hired Boeing as integration contractor on the B-1B at a cost of about $250 million. But in light of the fact that the air force felt Boeing was late with the same task on the earlier B-1A version, it decided to do the job itself. Further, it accelerated the delivery schedule for the equipment, something the contractor, AIL division of Eaton Corporation, was not ready for at that point. Integration is a critical step in technical development: making the thousands of pieces work together. Whether an integration contractor could have done better is an interesting academic question but moot at this point.

Concurrency was another stress point in B-1B development. Concurrency is the simultaneous development of subsystems in a program, including those subsystems that may be technically difficult—like engines or countermeasures. Under concurrency, if one or another subsystem runs into trouble, the entire program is delayed at potentially high cost. The lower-risk alternative would have been to crack the hard technical nuts first, and then, when they were up and running, proceed with the rest of the system. But General Lawrence A. Skantze, a successful program manager in his own right, who spent much of his career in acquisition before retiring in 1987 as commander of the air force Systems Command, defended concurrency in B-1B development in a speech to the Aviation and Space Writers Association in San Diego, California, in 1987: "We currently spend $500 million a month on production. . . . At that rate, a slip of even one month means big financial trouble. Had we elected to delay the production contract for one year past development start . . . we certainly would have reduced the over-all risk . . . but we also would have increased the cost $3 to $4 billion and delayed achievement of full operational capability by a year and seven months." With even less concurrency, the program could have cost as much as $8 billion extra. That is, $1.5 billion to $2 billion for each year the program was pushed back, keeping the whole infrastructure together, to await subsystem development—and without the discipline imposed by meeting a concurrent program schedule, delays could easily run to four years or more. So the air force made the decision to buy out the program as fast as possible.

It is no secret in defense hardware acquisition that time is money, exasperating amounts of money. Yet far too often, reforms intended to fix the system cause program cycles to lengthen, which runs costs up still further. Or budget makers, in the Pentagon or Congress, cut back production schedules to meet annual budget ceilings and stretch out programs, with the result that total costs burgeon.

Meanwhile, Eaton's B-1B problems, and the investment it projected would be necessary to stay in the electronic warfare business, led it to put its AIL division on the block. It was still on the block a year later, and how saleable the division might be was unclear—especially after mid-1988, when the air force, nettled by late deliveries, cancelled a $153 million contract with Eaton for radar-jamming equipment for the EF-111 attack aircraft.

Yet more troubles lay ahead for the B-1B. On a low-altitude training flight in Colorado in 1987, a B-1B struck a flock of birds, ingesting some in its engines. A fire followed and the airplane crashed; two crewmen were unable to escape. When a piece of equipment worth a couple of hundred million dollars is destroyed in an accident of any kind, and when servicemen die, questions follow. Two more have crashed since.

Fixing the B-1B's countermeasures equipment, its fuel leaks, and perhaps what comes out of crash investigations will cost money—both the government's and the contractor's, perhaps as much as $8 billion, according to John J. Welch, assistant secretary of the air force for research and development.

Because of the initial successes in the B-1B program, Congress virtually declared victory before flight testing was under way. In enacting the fiscal 1986 budget Congress took $1.2 billion out of the B-1B program—much to the consternation of program managers. (Another example of funding instability.) As Skantze put it: "Congress dismissed our pleas and took the money. They said if we needed any more later, to just come back and ask." When the air force did, when the technical shortcomings appeared, when it asked for $600 million back for fixes, Congress reacted with charges of budget busting.

The Politics of the B-1B

Whether the B-1 should have been cancelled in the first place—either because of Carter's defense budget targets or because of doubts over its ability to penetrate Soviet air space—is moot now. Ten years of woodshedding should have made for an aircraft better able to survive air defenses. Of course, if the earlier version had been produced, it would have had a decade of service under its belt by now. Why Ronald Reagan revived the B-1 also is moot. Experts differ on just how good Soviet air defenses really are, especially after a German pilot took a single-engine Cessna monoplane across the Finnish border and landed in the middle of Red Square.

One reason for building the B-1 was the geriatric B-52 force it was to supplant. The B-52 entered service with the air force in the 1950s; by the 1980s, even later versions were sometimes older than the pilots flying them. Electronic equipment aboard often dated back to the vacuum-tube era. As manufacturers dropped obsolete components from their catalogs, the air force was forced to have them custom made at ballooning cost. If replacement of an old fleet was the objective, though, why stop with a hundred airplanes? That short a production run barely takes advantage of learning-curve economies. And spreading the costs of designing the B-1B and putting it into production over such a small number of airplanes makes little economic sense.

Basically, the B-1 revival was a Reagan political statement, a poke in the eye to the Carter administration's MX intercontinental ballistic missile, with its convoluted hide-and-seek basing scheme scattered all over the western United States. But while Reagan came into office pro B-1 and anti MX (rechristened Peacekeeper in a later Reagan public-relations ploy), he wound up battling to retain both.

Skantze argues that, in the case of the B-1B, the air force was responding to a congressional mandate in the twilight of the Carter administration. The mandate was not specifically to get the B-1 but rather a new strategic bomber into service no later than 1987, to bolster the patriarchal B-52 leg of the strategic nuclear triad. Congress well knew that it had to look sharp on national security before Reagan, with his winning strong defense plank, took office.

After Reagan assumed office, Caspar Weinberger (his new secretary of defense), General Richard Ellis (who then commanded the Strategic Air Command), and Skantze (then the head of the System's Command division that developed new airplanes), sat down to figure out how to respond. All recognized the startling potential of the Stealth bomber, but all also recognized the severe technical risks that would come in designing and testing such a radical concept. "In the final analysis," Skantze related, "the only way to quickly modernize the manned bomber leg was to build a limited number of highly effective B-1Bs, deploy them as rapidly as possible, and, in effect, buy the time for Advanced Technology Bomber development. The B-1B alone could not provide the long-term enduring penetration capability that an Advanced Technology Bomber offered." But the Stealth bomber could not possibly be ready before the 1990s.

It was the congressional mandate, Skantze contends, that shaped the decision. There was no way the U.S. Air Force could have pushed a totally concurrent B-1B through the Pentagon and Congress without it. True, but would that sense of urgency have emerged in Congress if Reagan's campaign had not sandpapered the Carter administration for cancelling the B-1, for its whole handling of the U.S. strategic deterrent force? Hardly.

When I visited the headquarters of the Strategic Air Command, not long before the B-1B was to enter service, I was surprised at what could only be considered mild enthusiasm for the aircraft.

Certainly, the command was glad to have a new bomber coming on stream. But there was no critical role for the B-1B. The B-52 was still the cruise missile carrier—the truck that hauled unmanned weapons a few hundred miles off enemy shores, launched them, and ran for cover. The Strategic Air Command was more interested in the Stealth bomber, albeit still in early development, as the instrument to search out and attack such targets as mobile intercontinental ballistic missile sites. Further, the B-52 could be overhauled—fitted with modern electronics—for less than the $20 billion or so going into the B-1B program. Old as it was, the B-52, like most military airplanes, had not flown the thousands of hours that a commercial transport does in its lifetime. The hours it had were hard ones, but there still was life in the airframes if the avionics could be modernized sufficiently.

At that time, the B-1B was still enjoying its image as one of the better run military buying programs. In fact, the argument could be made that Carter's cancellation had been of value in terms of rethinking the airplane's design and getting a better fix on the kinds of defenses it would have to penetrate. But then the complaints arose, and critics had their chance to potshot at what had been a big success story. Much to its credit, the air force did not burrow underground, as often happens in defense brouhahas: Flight footage showed up on the evening news, along with interviews with pilots who stated what a swell airplane the B-1B really was, and a paper was issued, contrasting media myth and technical fact. Still, shotgun charges in the media and time-consuming responses are sorry ways to run a defense effort; the truth is far more complicated than either allow. One thing is clear: Such fussing simply adds more incentive for the services to resort to black programs so that, at a minimum, they can run their programs without a million questions interfering with the work schedule.

Aside from the question of black versus white programs, development of the B-1 also ties into another thread in the acquisition fabric: requirements. When the B-1 was originally conceived and the program started, it was in response to what this country knew about the state of Soviet air defenses. Although money was certainly a consideration in Carter's cancellation of the program, evaluation of the Soviet threat also had changed—and thus requirements changed.

Considering the way Reagan's election figured in the revival of the B-1 program, the implication is that intelligence estimates of the Soviet threat vacillated with the political climate—and, of course, so did requirements. Clearly, the professionals could not make the president look bad by dumping on the B-1 as no longer strategically necessary. Yet it was obvious that the Stealth bomber looked far better—at least on paper. But the B-1B was a good insurance policy—an airplane in production that could fill in if the Stealth bomber dropped out of the running because of technical upending. Still, the B-1B is an expensive insurance policy. The production line shut down, as intended, at a scanty production run of 100 airplanes, which is neither economical nor a very impressive operating-force number. By mid-1988 there were complaints of spare-parts shortages for the B-1, which is not surprising because of the relatively high costs of supporting and maintaining a low-production-run system. Nonetheless, the B-1 case is more compromise than scandal—a case of how politics and technology are pushed to ignore such practicalities as learning curves and economies of scale. The test is whether the country's national security interests are reasonably served in the process.

The role of politics—as in the impact of congressional pressure on good economic judgment in the B-1B program—cannot be overstated. The air force would have liked to buy more B-1Bs, but it well knew that if it tried, Congress would react as if an attempt had been made to derail the competing Stealth bomber. At the same time, the air force knew perfectly well that the schedule for delivery of the technically complex Stealth bomber was unrealistic. Secretary Weinberger, himself, had swallowed the contractor's optimism that the Stealth aircraft would be flying in 1987. Though air force leaders tried to soft pedal such salesmanship, they knew any rowback from schedule targets would be interpreted, again, in the Defense Department and on Capitol Hill, as a ruse to buy more B-1Bs. Rather than risk the wrath of Congress, and that of the Pentagon brass as well, the air force held its peace.

One truism, a common one, the B-1 leaves to acquisition policy is that the best way to run a program is quickly. There are some, in and out of the military, who contend that they also should be run in secrecy. If by secrecy is meant without meddlesome interference and oversight, if by secrecy is meant expeditiously, then amen. If secrecy means without any public scrutiny whatsoever, that is a very different matter—a difficult, if not unwise, way of doing business in a democracy. Yet that is exactly the risk in the way black programs are heading now.

Black Programs: The Secret Realm

Congressman John D. Dingell has taken a passing interest in the proliferation of black programs. He is not the only congressman to question the military's increasing invocation of secrecy. Inquiries have come from both sides of the political fence. In a letter to Defense Secretary Weinberger, Dingell questioned whether the Pentagon was using secrecy to cover up bungling or wrong-doing or to escape accountability—that is, to his subcommittee—in military-buying practices. This kind of scandal-sheet rummaging for fraud does not touch on the vital policy questions entailed in black programs, however.

The critical policy issues are these: How much secrecy is necessary or permissible in nominal peacetime in a democracy in which the voters and their representatives are called on to make decisions on spending for military equipment? Does secrecy remove discipline over program management or spending or, to the contrary, enhance efficiency? To what extent is the proliferation of black programs a symptom of the ills of the military acquisition system—that is, bureaucracy, overmanagement, and unnecessary paperwork?

There are arguments on both sides. In any case, there are practical limits to technical secrecy. Commercial companies try to keep trade secrets as tightly as the military does state secrets, but they know they won't be kept for long. More important, in the commercial view, is to stay one step ahead technically. Synergism from technical exchange tends to outweigh the benefits of secrecy.

But in the case of Stealth technology, which became a tent under which a covey of military programs were assigned to the black budget, developers felt strongly about the need for secrecy. Stealth must remain black, they argued, because every month it stayed out of Soviet hands meant a vital edge in U.S. ability to outfox Soviet air defenses—and that lead, that amount of time, was something money and effort could not buy. Once the Soviets knew what

Stealth aircraft looked like—and a part of the secret was in shape—then they could begin to design radars or other detectors to cope with the new technology.

Stealth technology has remained amazingly secret in the 1980s, considering that airplanes designed with its methods began flying around the country much earlier. For example, the SR-71 reconnaissance aircraft, the Blackbird, had been flown at air shows and photographed ten years before stealth came along. While Stealth technology has evolved since the SR-71, this aerodynamic and stealthy airplane, with its compound curved, black-coated surfaces, was its granddaddy. And the Blackbird was the three-times-the-speed-of-sound successor to an early black program, the subsonic U-2 that was shot down snooping over Russia on May Day 1960. The air force finally published a sanitized drawing of the Stealth bomber in spring 1988, on the grounds that, by fall, the aircraft—by then publicly designated the B-2—would roll out of the factory for any passerby to see.

Stealth is a matter of degree. Israel flew stealthy small, pilotless reconnaissance aircraft in the invasion of Lebanon. Nothing about them was exotic. They were made mostly of glass fiber that provides a weak radar echo and their tiny size compounded the difficulties the Syrians had in finding them. The B-1B itself was redesigned to be more stealthy than the earlier version, the air force says, though there are designers who say Stealth has to be incorporated from scratch.

Stealth is not a single technology but a bundle of techniques that trade off some aspect of performance for lower detectability. These tradeoffs in performance have led to the suspicion that the insistence on secrecy may stem from the desire to downplay shortcomings in the technology. For example, a couple of squadrons of Lockheed's air force Stealth fighters, with an out-of-sequence F-117A designation, have been flying out of a closed base in Nevada. At least three crashes have occurred, and gossip has it that these were related to structural complications and constraints.

Questions also have been raised about whether the secrecy over the Stealth bomber that Northrop is developing is to hide its stealthy shape or to conceal technical thorns. Supporters for piercing the 100-airplane ceiling for the B-1 bomber used the Washington gossip mills to circulate the story that the air force had to bring

Boeing, with its knowledge of composite materials, into the program to help it along. They scoffed at the cost estimates for the advanced bomber—a safe bet on any program—and events are bearing out their predictions.

By late 1988, the budget estimate had doubled to about $68 billion or $500 million a copy. If the B-1B had its turn in the barrel in 1986 and 1987, the B-2 Stealth bomber was rolling merrily around there before 1988 had reached middle age—secrecy or no. Congress was threatening competition, a dubious economic proposition for the number of aircraft projected. The Pentagon's acquisition czar, Robert B. Costello, was denouncing Northrop for poor quality control and grumbling about its cost per copy rising toward the half-billion level. But as one air force officer put it, alluding to Costello's General Motors background: "He thinks Northrop can pop them out like Chevrolets." In this air force officer's view, the pendulum had swung, as it typically does in defense development, from unwarranted optimism to excess pessimism.

Without knowing the secrets that black programs hide, it is difficult to say whether their secrecy is warranted. As the foregoing suggests, there is always the temptation to classify to cover up abuses, shortcomings, or failures—or even for the sake of convenience. I suspect that to a large degree, black programs represent escape from the excessive paperwork and micromanagement of the acquisition system.

Sheltering without Secrecy

A program can be sequestered from the system without secrecy. General William J. Evans, a top-notch acquisition manager in the air force, for example, created a special task force to improve air force electronics. Do the technical job, Evans told the team, and he would run interference—sheltering money for projects and keeping meddlesome bureaucrats at bay. The results were something a young colonel on the team who told me the story was proud of. Among the innovations were an advanced microchip and the ADA computer-program language that is now specified for new defense computer or communications systems as the long-sought defense standard language. Eventually Evans was reassigned as usual with the military, his technology team lost its immunity from the bureaucracy, the spark vanished, and the colonel left the service for a job in industry.

Sheltering, segregation, fencing off, whatever it is called, is one of the essentials prescribed for running a successful project by Lockheed's Kelly Johnson, the founder of the Skunk Works that epitomizes lean program management and noninterference by outsiders—that is, by anyone, inside or outside of the contractor's organization, who is not one of the handful involved in the program.

An achievement in program management that is still hallowed in the annals of aerospace was the development of the P-80, the first U.S. jet fighter to go into service with the air force, for which the Skunk Works was founded. Johnson had committed to what was then the army air corps to build a prototype for the airplane in 180 days, incorporating the then little-tested turbojet engine invented in Great Britain. To the surprise of skeptical Lockheed corporate officers, the prototype was accepted by the military buyer on day 143 and led not only to a first-line fighter but also to a trainer—the T-33—a veteran utility warhorse that served both the air force and the navy for years. Delivery in 143 days stands in stark contrast with today's decade-long development cycle. (The navy's Polaris missile, which had project-type management analogous to the Skunk Works in its sequestered-from-the-system, dedicated industry-government team structure is also considered a great weapons-management success story.)

In addition to strictly controlling access by outsiders, Johnson's Skunk Works management tenets, as set forth in his autobiography—*Kelly: More Than My Share of It All*—called for drastic curtailment of project-team size (both military and industry) and ceding almost complete control of the program to the manager. These concepts are the antithesis of defense program management today, where the project manager spends his days briefing Pentagon authorities on why the development is important, and where Congress second guesses what everybody is doing.

Johnson went on to run the development of the U-2 and the SR-71 Blackbird, each with military and CIA involvement and very black programs at the time. According to Johnson, with the U-2 "the government got a bargain on that contract when completed—about $2 million in refunds on contract costs, and six extra airplanes from spare parts we didn't need because the U-2 functioned so well." The U-2 had the advantage of being able to tap the CIA reserve fund, avoiding all the grief of funding instability, and so did the SR-71. According to William E. Burrows's *Deep Black*, a book about the secret reconnaissance universe, Ben R. Rich, Johnson's successor at the Skunk Works, claims "the U-2 and its successor, the SR-71, owe their existence to the fact that the air force's labyrinthine specifications, regulations and horde of 'blue light specialists and red light specialists' could be bypassed in favor of a small group working informally 'in a black, skunky way.'"

Johnson also favored project management—that is, a self-contained program with its own support functions such as accounting and purchasing. But project management does not work for every company—especially those used to working with centralizing accounting or engineering departments—or for every project within a company. Critics say that what good project management does for an individual program is lost in dislocation of other operations. Besides, so many company accountants and auditors are needed these days to cope with the army of government auditors (for every government auditor or inspector to visit a plant, a contractor must hire at least one employee to deal with him) that centralization of such functions becomes a matter of self-defense.

Another reason why Skunk Works operations don't work everywhere is that there are not enough Johnsons or Evans to go around. It takes a unique kind of manager to command the confidence and obtain willingness of a corporation—not to mention the government customer—to delegate the autonomy a Skunk Works must have. While industry may plead for freedom from government oversight so that it can get the job done, corporations are by no means immune to their own micromanagement proclivities. Skunk Works autonomy for program managers is in very short supply now.

Even Johnson didn't always win. During the fighter competitions of the 1970s, Johnson brougnt in a design for an airplane that had enough range to take off from the West Coast and strafe Washington, D.C., without refueling. But the air force wanted maneuverability, not long legs. Lockheed lost the competition, leaving it frozen out of fighter development for fifteen years. Johnson tells it differently. He says that the F-14 and F-15 were too big and expensive to compete with the Soviet stable, but that Missouri's senator at the time, Stuart Symington, wanted the F-15 contract for McDonnell in St. Louis. Lockheed's chairman finally had to tell Johnson to shut up about heavy, high-cost fighters. Johnson says his unsolicited proposal for a lightweight fighter eventually materialized as the F-16.

To their credit, top defense managers, aware of the steadily lengthening acquisition cycle and burgeoning management layers, would prefer to operate with some kind of Skunk Works principles. In new and revised acquisition directives, there are provisions for streamlined management and for reductions in the layers of authority between program manager and senior levels. But directives don't manage programs. And despite the fact that experience with the B-1, with the Stealth bomber, and with myriad defense programs over the years has shown that obsession with scientific management systems, clever contracting procedures, regulations, and specifications have not insured success, the Department of Defense continues to emphasize form, losing sight of the importance of finding good people and allowing them to manage.

Does Secrecy Work?

Did secrecy, in the sense of insulation from outside interference, make for the success of the U-2 and SR-71 programs? Or was their success the product of a brilliant designer and project manager? The answer is yes to both. Fencing out the micromanagers gave Johnson and his team the elbow room they needed to get the job done. Without the genius of the designer/manager, all the secrecy in the world would not help. With it, insulation let the top talent get the work done quickly and effectively.

Can the Skunk Works principles, if not the every detail, be applied to other defense programs? The answer is a qualified yes. Certainly, programs can profit from the best in the management practices of black programs—that is, management in the Skunk Works style: reasonable commensurate authority and reasonable freedom from interference for first-rate program managers and small project teams (at least in relative terms). That means pruning away the hordes of layers in the Pentagon, and of auditors, systems analysts, busybodies, congressional second guessers, and all the rest that are smothering program management. Skilled oversight, of course, is as necessary as skilled program management, but too many layers inhibit authority at the top from shielding program managers on the firing line. There also must be a path for appeal, in case even a good program manager becomes too autocratic. The critical principle is insulation from meddlers, not from reasonable oversight.

In the case of the B-1B bomber and the Stealth bomber programs, the question is whether the secrecy of stealth will bring about a better program, if not a better airplane. The answer is not necessarily, because it isn't clear at this point—because of that very secrecy—whether all the other ingredients are mixing well.

Despite the fact that the B-1B is under a media cloud, it cannot be written off as a bomb instead of a bomber. Its very openness, the public access to its problems—and all programs have them— makes it seem in worse trouble than it really is. Public performances are risky, governed by Murphy's law that the toast always will fall with the buttered side down, that the most critical component always will fail. Skantze argues that the B-1B program was a significant achievement in terms of the degree of redesign (including Stealth among other things), taking on the technical challenge of the upgraded countermeasures package, meeting a demanding schedule, and managing risk—specifically dealing with how much concurrency to accept, how much development time to schedule, how to balance speed with the hazards of new technology. It will be at least five years before the merits of these two bomber programs may be demonstrated with precision, and a judgment made as to how well the B-1B, developed in the open, behaves in service in comparison with the Stealth bomber, developed under the black cloak.

Both programs and their troubles are bound up in another truism of military development: Nothing is ever all black or all white. Few programs are as good in the beginning as their salesmen project, and few are as bad in the end as their critics aver. Far too much smoothness is expected in the development program. Far too little attention is paid to the rest of the life cycle, how well or how poorly hardware performs in the field over the long pull. Therein lies the essential measure.

10

Fraud Revisited: Criminalization in Acquisition

ENCRUSTED with barnacles—the accumulation of two decades of remedies and of management burgeoning to apply them—the nation's weapons-acquisition system staggered into the 1980s looking for surcease from Ronald Reagan. What it got instead was a boot from behind: the waste, fraud, and abuse scandals. Its convoluted and lame-sounding explanations did little to calm an indignant citizenry.

If the scandals had concerned only waste and abuse, the military and defense contractors might have served as scapegoats for the country's continuing frustration with the high cost of national security, and that might have been the sum of it. But something had to be done about fraud.

First there were indictments and a few cop-outs by contractors eager to get the ordeal over with as quickly and quietly as possible. Companies rarely defend themselves. Usually they crawl into their foxholes, saying, "Don't do anything to offend the customer." If the government decides to prosecute, as in the frequent disputes over billing, the contractors tend to plead guilty and pay up rather than fight with their only customer. Then, the government auditing and inspection machine ground on to the point where contracting has been criminalized. Contract disputes are settled by indictment, not as they had been in the past by negotiation or by appeals board. Indictment was not even a necessary formality in the thirst to investigate and prosecute in the twilight of the Reagan era. Just a leak to the media was enough for automatic conviction.

Wrongdoing, of course, should be rooted out. The trouble is that in the weapons-acquisition process, wrongdoing often is confused with contract disputes. Two kinds of situations are being mixed together in these accusations of fraud. At one extreme is the old-fashioned kind of payoff, where a contractor hands out money to someone—a government employee or another contractor—for business favors. These had been relatively rare in federal contracting in general. But that flavor tinges the investigation that erupted in print and on television (but, perhaps significantly, not in the courts) in mid-1988. Here the real shocker was that, unlike most past cases that involved rank-and-file, the tentacles seemed to reach into the top levels in the Pentagon. Obviously no one in the military or among contractors tries to justify out-and-out payoffs.

Accusations of fraud then extend to the gray areas—that is, entertainment, gifts (from trinkets to luxuries), and political conniving. At the other extreme, and not necessarily constituting fraud, are accusations related to contract compliance, which involve claims of improper charging of accounts for government contracts (an especially hot subject now), disagreements on what regulations mean, and disputes over contract terms and terminology.

According to the Packard Commission report, "the public is almost certainly mistaken about the extent of corruption in industry and waste in the Department [of Defense]. While fraud constitutes a serious problem, it is not as extensive or costly as many Americans believe. The nation's defense programs lose far more to inefficiency than to dishonesty." Further, the country spends far more trying to root out fraud than it loses from it. As important as oversight may be, the Packard report states, "no conceivable number of additional Federal auditors, inspectors, investigators and prosecutors can police it [the acquisition process] fully, much less make it work more effectively." Nonetheless, a great deal of effort—and money—has gone into efforts to root out evil in the acquisition system.

A Benchmark Case and the 1988 Scandals

A benchmark contract compliance case that erupted on the eve of the space shuttle *Challenger* disaster in 1986 should not be forgotten ten as new charges of fraud capture headlines. The case involved James M. Beggs, who headed the National Aeronautics and Space

Administration when his indictment for criminal fraud was handed down. Beggs had been a vice president of General Dynamics, and, along with three other managers there, was accused of mischarging to the government $7.5 million in labor and material costs during the competition for the army's Sergeant York antiaircraft gun.

Following the indictment, Beggs was forced to resign from NASA. His reputation remained under a cloud while prosecutors and defense lawyers skirmished over what the arcane contract really specified in terms of which costs could be charged to what account. Midway in the case, the General Dynamics legal team even convinced the presiding U.S. district judge to take the unusual step of asking for an outside interpretation—in this case from the Armed Services Board of Contract Appeals. Eighteen months after the indictment—too late to salvage Beggs's NASA career—Justice Department lawyers dismissed the charges, admitting that the contractor's interpretation had been right. Before he left office, former attorney general Edwin Meese apologized publicly to Beggs for the affair.

As far as contract disputes go, they used to be handled pretty much by the Armed Services Board of Contract Appeals—that is, if differences in interpretation could not be settled by negotiation between the contractor and the government contracting officer or his superiors. Spurred by the Civil False Claims Act, contract disputes now wind up in the hands of prosecutors or grand juries, who are expected to become instant authorities on scores of different kinds of defense contracts. Even experts differ on their terms. Justice Department lawyers in the Sergeant York case, who pored over millions of documents, overlooked the documents they needed to understand the issue, and Defense Department auditors and acquisition officials differed on the contract's meaning.

After his case was dismissed, Beggs termed it a witch hunt, inspired by congressional and media stories of waste, fraud, and abuse. Orchestrated leaks or ballyhooed indictments and quieter dismissals are not isolated instances in Pentagon criminal cases. One case, whose threads were picked up in the investigation that rocked the Pentagon in mid-1988, dealt with trafficking in confidential information. Justice Department prosecutors charged GTE's Government Systems Corporation as well as three employees or consultants with unauthorized possession of documents that might give them competitive advantages in winning military business. As is often the pattern in criminal prosecutions of contractors, the company decided not to fight and pleaded guilty. The employees did not. Eventually, charges against them were dropped.

While this case did not contain accusations of payoffs for information, as the 1988 investigation does, it puzzled defense circles at the time. Why, it was asked, was anyone surprised enough to prosecute over the way hot documents float around Washington? Had the prosecutors never heard of industrial espionage or just plain old aggressive marketing? Consternation surrounded the 1988 investigations for analogous reasons: that anybody would find it necessary to pay for documents so easily obtained. The uninitiated are in awe of secret stamps on documents. Players in the Washington defense game, with billions in contracts at stake, sometimes find it hard to take such restrictions seriously. They know that some third-level bureaucrat may have ordered a document classified out of rote, a document a contractor might really have a claim to for planning its engineering and business strategy in the government's interest. If contractors actually are paying for hot documents, it marks the ultimate in Reagan administration privatization: finding a commercial market for what used to be leaked for free.

For that matter, competitive documents sometimes are forced on contractors, and for hard-headed reasons. A decade or so ago, the air force made it a formal policy to give technical data from one contractor's proposal to other competitors to make all the bidders more competitive and more amenable to price cutting. Company protests ended the practice then, but that sort of thing arose as well in the 1988 investigations. General Electric's best and final offer in an engine competition turned up in rival Pratt & Whitney's hands. But it had been furnished by the government to stimulate a lower bid than the one Pratt & Whitney had submitted earlier. Pratt told the service there was no way it could meet General Electric's price and bowed out—only to have the government continue to negotiate. Eventually it gave Pratt a share of the program anyway—no doubt to keep General Electric on its toes.

Government steering of business to one contractor or another, especially if bribery is suspected, is in a far more lethal league than leaked documents. It is hardly a new issue, for it was at the core of the charges of political influence in the TFX contract award. Contractor protests or lawsuits over such issues are hardly rare. Yet such steering is done for policy reasons, too, to preserve a contractor's technical base or retain a competitor where bankruptcy looms otherwise.

Yet another consideration enters into the 1988 scandals—that of prosecutors finding themselves in the middle of contractor, intraservice, and just plain Pentagon personality wars. Both former navy secretary John Lehman and his research and development deputy, Melvyn Paisley, had broken a lot of service and contractor rice bowls while they were in office, and Pentagon memories are long. Their disregard for the system was one of the reasons for complaints in the Pentagon about the destruction of traditional checks and balances in acquisition in the Reagan era. Then, there were the lesser, but sometimes more unforgiving affairs, such as the former Defense Department official who lost a responsible job at Raytheon in 1986 because Lehman and Paisley complained about a skeptical speech he made on military budget levels.

Make no mistake about it, though, there was talk of sleaze in Paisley's background when he got his Pentagon job in the early days of the Reagan regime. I heard some of it then, but never any specifics to back up the whispers. In the initial leaks in the 1988 scandals, neither the FBI nor the Justice Department mentioned anything about background checks on Paisley—those they are supposed to run to clear prospective appointees before they even go on the short list for high-level government posts. Clearly, Paisley is the prime target of the 1988 investigations, which are taking the form of a huge fishing expedition into the dealings of any contractor or government official who turned up in wiretaps of his telephone conversations. Some of these conversations will indeed be damaging to contractors and individuals, but whether they are criminal matters has still to be proven.

Too many were quick to judge Paisley before a bill of particulars was issued. Both Paisley and his boss Lehman tilted at the system. As the tough talking arm of the team, Paisley's role was to beat up on contractors and bureaucrats to get the pachyderm of a system to move faster or cheaper or in the direction they wanted it to go. Paisley's departure from the Pentagon into the consulting world may eventually be judged as a descent into money-grubbing. Or it may simply have been circumvention of a glacial system to get things done by other means. Contractors will pay to evade the toils of the system; the crux of the 1988 scandals will be how much behind-the-scenes evasion is legitimate.

Increasing Oversight: External and Internal

Out and out indictments are fairly rare compared to visitations to contractors from auditors, review teams from individual services or defense agencies, and congressional staffers. Audits and reviews were nothing new, but the waste, fraud, and abuse era multiplied their number and frequency. Often, these are billed as investigations. These contract reviews can be beneficial. For example, recently, an air force assessment of a United Technologies rocket motor division on the West Coast revealed only marginal product integrity, quality assurance, and contract management, along with weak program management and late deliveries. This report card will get attention from the parent corporation's top management. Tough as such reviews are on the reviewees, they deal with a mushrooming problem in the world of big government and big conglomerates: With all the competing departments clamoring for notice, and with all the intermediate bureaucratic layers, it is hard to get a response from the top. Bad report cards break the bureaucracy barrier.

Besides the multiplication of review teams and audits, a pronounced adversarial, prosecutorial tone was introduced in their conduct. Eager auditors, investigators, and Justice Department lawyers, who were already plenty active, became more so. Instead of negotiation, there was accusation. Even when, for example, TRW's chairman informed Air Force Systems Command officers about a mischarging case in one of his company's divisions, his offer of redress was spurned by the Pentagon and the Justice Department, which decided to prosecute.

In addition to outsider reviews and investigations, contractors were urged in the Packard report to police themselves. If industry wants to get the auditors off its back, the commission's chairman advised, it had better take steps to show it is cleaning up its own act. Defense contractors were told to promulgate and vigilantly enforce codes of ethics and monitor them for strict contract compliance. "Contractors have a legal and moral obligation to disclose to government authorities misconduct discovered as a result of self-review," according to the Packard Commission's interim report. From that came a set of defense-industry initiatives on ethics and conduct, signed by more than thirty companies.

These initiatives created a whole industry substructure: formal codes of conduct, compliance officers, ombudsmen, ethics training programs, and hot lines for employees to report infractions. As a public-image exercise, the initiatives were one thing. As operating procedures, they were quite another.

Companies were uneasy about the hot lines, which put them in the role of police, but did not give them the powers of enforcement or the protection from liability afforded public agencies. Informants might be exposing wrongdoing; they also might be venting their anger at a coworker or a boss they want to get rid of, in the safety of anonymity. Meanwhile, the reputations of investigated employees would be tainted by the very act of an investigation—even if, in the end, it produced nothing. Another incentive to whistle-blowing was that whistle-blowers could share handsomely in the recovery of any money by the government. For example, a California lawyer has made a cottage industry out of encouraging confidences from Northrop employees about the company's troubles with the Stealth bomber program, offering them a share in rewards from the suit he has filed under a false-claims statute that encourages whistle-blowing.

These hot lines for whistle-blowers were not just an industry phenomenon. They extended to the military. General Skantze, for example, was confronted with anonymous charges that were later laid to rest by the Pentagon inspector general's staff. For such ranking military officers, whistle-blowing is as demeaning as the lie detector tests forced on them in the Reagan administration's hunt for security leaks. Both industry and the military liken the hot-line approach to McCarthyism—guilty until proved innocent—but without the public revulsion that subdued the late senator from Wisconsin.

As endorsed by the Department of Defense, voluntary disclosure gave little advantage to the company. Deputy Secretary of Defense William H. Taft IV promised contractors a speedy trial, but the Justice Department warned that it had a heavy workload and wasn't sure about that. Beggs and his colleagues waited eighteen months for the government to recognize it did not have a case to bring to trial. If voluntary disclosure was precipitated by a government audit or prospective investigation, the disclosure would not even be credited as voluntary, for whatever advantage that had. With voluntary disclosure, contractors were damned if they did and damned if they didn't. They were warned of prosecution based on voluntary disclosure and of prosecution if they tried to cover up violations. The policy question is whether prosecution—even civil litigation—is the route that the government should follow in maintaining its national security objectives.

Dealing with Noncompliance

One way in which the government has dealt with contractor sins of omission or commission is simply to terminate the contract. One example is the cancellation of Eaton's development of electronic warfare gear for the air force EF-111 attack fighter. This approach has its pluses and its minuses—as the following case, in which Fairchild fouled up an air force trainer program, illustrates. Similar lessons may be gained from looking at the B-1B electronic warfare program.

In the early 1980s, the air force decided to replace its Cessna T-37s, which had been soldiering along in the Training Command for thirty years and served as a light attack-aircraft in Vietnam. It ran a competition. Most of the entries were Americanized versions of European trainers, since European countries had spent more on, and built more, trainers than this country had. One U.S. company, Fairchild Republic, submitted an all-new all-American aircraft, and it went so far as to invest in building a small-scale prototype. Fairchild pursued the program with vigor and it won. It should be pointed out that Fairchild planned to build the airplane at a plant on Long Island, where its A-10 attack aircraft for the air force was reaching the end of its production life. New York, of course, is a big state with lots of congressmen, several of whom sit on the Armed Services or Appropriations Committee—all aware that jobs on Long Island were at stake.

By the mid-1980s, as the first airplane—designated the T-46—was ready to roll out, it was apparent that Fairchild was having problems on the assembly line. These problems could not have come at a worse time; the waste, fraud, and abuse hue-and-cry was peaking, and the services and Defense Department auditors were reacting. Foreshadowing the battle of auditor against auditor to see who could find the most wrong, the air force initiated an on-the-spot visitation to contractor facilities called the Contractor Operations Review (COR). According to the contractors who went through them, cored was the right word.

It is standard operating procedure for defense contractors to be placed under the cognizance of the services, or under the Defense Logistics Agency if their work is a mixed bag of components for different services or government agencies. A military plant representative is sent, by whichever service or agency has responsibility, to keep an eye on things. But the COR review elevated this process to another level altogether. When the aggressive COR teams hit the road (teams from a separate branch of the air force Systems Command called the Contract Management Division), the diligence and decisions of the targeted plant representative also were on the line. Not surprisingly, a game of one-upmanship resulted to see who was the toughest in finding error, waste, fraud, and abuse.

When the COR team hit Fairchild in one of its first sorties, it found plenty to crab about. Essentially because the T-46 program did not gear up as fast as the A-10 wound down, Fairchild had lost a cadre of experienced plant-floor supervisors. Trying to get the first T-46s built was a struggle that the COR review intimated the company was losing. Some responsible Fairchild managers lost their jobs in the wake of the review, but there were no grand juries or indictments then. The process of criminalization had not accelerated to the speed it reached later. Besides, a program foul-up usually is not an indictable offense. So far, the government thrust for prosecution has been in the handling or accounting of money, not performance shortcomings, though perhaps a criminal charge of sloppy program management is coming.

The air force, taking a businesslike approach, moved to terminate the program. Then politics intervened. The New York delegation screeched when the air force dropped the T-46 out of its budget. It got Congress to put money back in, whether the air force wanted it or not. Such situations are common enough, as in the persistent insertion by Representative Les Aspin, chairman of the House Armed Services Committee, of funds into the defense budget for trucks made in his home state, trucks the army does not want. Even Representative Thomas J. Downey, a frequent defense spending antagonist, was on the front lines calling for restoration of the program. After all, his district was affected. But two years later, the New York delegation lost, and the T-46 was finally terminated.

Contract termination, as apt as it may be, can be a costly business. Take the case of an army contract for radios in which a small New England company bought the business by underbidding a larger Midwest concern that had been producing the equipment. Stung by lack of delivery from the new contractor, program managers cancelled the contract after a fairly quick (by government contracting standards) investigation and report. Thereupon, the small company went into bankruptcy and sued the government. It offered to settle for $2 million—essentially to pay off its suppliers on the contract. Against legal advice, the program people and the Pentagon insisted on going to trial. There the fact came out that the original Midwest radio manufacturer had hung onto 200 to 300 key drawings, putting the new company in a hole not of its own making. The appeals board judge excoriated the government and awarded the company $7 million. So the service was stuck with no radios and a larger bill.

Termination also is harsh on the contractor employees who lose their jobs. But it may work to the advantage of the contractor, as in the Fairchild case. In the aftermath of the Contractor Operations Review, Fairchild's chairman saw advantages for the company if termination ensued. Termination would release the reserves Fairchild had put aside for losses on the T-46, clean the matter off the company's books, and let it concentrate where it was doing better. By summer 1987, the company was doing just that—preparing to sell off aircraft manufacturing operations in order to pursue its other aerospace and defense electronics work, where it was showing a profit.

A second government approach to contractor noncompliance is to initiate more direct intervention into the way the contractor runs his business. This approach, too, has its pluses and minuses—mostly minuses from the standpoint of managing a business—as the case of Material Requirements Planning, a computerized accounting system, reveals. Government has set standards for and has certificated contractor accounting systems since the 1970s. This is an area fraught with shin stickers, from contractor mischarging through sloppy or fraudulent accounting on one side to arbitrary cost definitions by the government that unfairly penalize the contractor on the other. Irrespective of the rights and wrongs, government control over contractor accounting is one of the steps toward de facto nationalization of defense companies.

Hypnotized by big defense bucks, industry has not put up much resistance to government auditors telling contractors how to run their businesses. Backing the auditors is a maze of Defense Department and service directives and acquisition regulations—especiall, the code of Cost Accounting Standards adopted by the Defense Department in the 1970s to try to bring some admittedly needed order in the way defense companies handle their government business books. In an enterprise as enormous and complex as defense hardware and research buying, some kind of common standard is necessary to keep accounts comparable and open to analysis. The policy question is whether these painfully detailed regulations are turning private industry into quasi-government agencies, and, on top of that, confusing everybody.

In the case in point, Textron's Bell Helicopter in Fort Worth, which builds aircraft predominantly for the army but also in quantity for the commercial market, was under investigation for its accounting practices using the computerized Material Requirements Planning system. Government auditors claimed that Bell Helicopter deliberately used the system to double bill the government. Bell agrees that the mingling of inventory from one military program with another, or with commercial work, is an invitation to accounting recriminations. So it settled the case on this basis: $46 million went to the government under terms of savings clauses in contracts back to 1984, and $22 million went to the government as a settlement of claims. The $46 million covered excess profits Bell had promised to give back to the army if use of the Material Requirements Planning system produced the kind of economies expected. There was an internal stalemate at Bell over the $22 million, between those who felt Bell did not owe the government another nickel and those who said legal costs, should the threat of government prosecution materialize, and customer ill-will were not worth the candle. In the end, the hold-outs capitulated and Bell paid the whole $68 million.

Disputes among auditors and the audited over inventory accounting are old hat, both in government and nongovernment business. But whereas in nongovernment business, these disagreements are relegated to the small-type footnotes or auditor's certificates in annual reports, in defense contracting they move to the front page and into the courts.

Inventory—the raw materials, subassemblies, and components that make up the final manufactured product—is what the Material Requirements Planning system is all about. This computerized system is used to manage a factory's or a company's entire production flow—both inventory and work orders. It is designed to be responsive to production and delivery schedule changes and to shifts in customer demand for products. Given projected manufacturing schedules—a constant challenge in defense work—Material Requirements Planning computers respond with what part is needed when and where it ought to be along the line. Japanese industry has developed inventory control to a degree disconcerting to its international competitors, who are scrambling to adopt sophisticated techniques like Material Requirements Planning and its offshoots and successors to keep pace.

Government auditors zeroed in on the Material Requirements Planning system because of its practice of allocating parts and material from a common stockpile to programs as needed—trying to avoid shortages and panic orders in meeting production changes, since emergency, fast-response orders are expensive—leaving accounting to catch up later with proper charge numbers for each piece. In a plant with various government programs, stocks ordered for one could be drawn down for another. If the plant has both commercial and government work, the common stockpile could be tapped for each, as needed. The auditors became concerned about how precise the accounting was for that inventory.

Further, government contractors work on the progress-payment system. Government pays for a percentage of inventory and work in process as the contractor goes along—avoiding bank loans, since, as a rule, interest charges are not an allowable expense under government contracts. Commercial manufacturers, in contrast, do borrow to finance inventory, but they recover the interest charges in their pricing. Government auditors contend that the specific government program involved owns any inventory covered by its progress payments. On that basis, their argument runs, the contractor may be playing games by diverting inventory from one government program to another—not to mention commercial work. That courts mischarging, in their book. So it boils down to a battle between the shop floor, which wants a part now without a lot of paperwork, and the auditors, who insist on a precise and detailed paper trail for each bit and piece the government pays for, with all the time and energy that entails.

As Robert B. Costello, then assistant secretary of defense (production and logistics) and since defense acquisition executive, told a House subcommittee at the time of the Bell Helicopter investigation, automated inventory control systems can provide improved productivity and lower costs—and, in general, government auditors do not have a problem with the concept. According to Costello, the government had ample authority to deal with discrepancies through, for one, reductions in progress payments. Figures of a billion dollars in overcharges tossed around in this investigation were misleading, for, Costello noted, they were for inventory value and did not necessarily represent overcharges. Nor was he sympathetic to proposals for more exhaustive government certification of contractors' cost-accounting systems—quite possibly at a cost not commensurate with the benefits.

Other contractors were aghast at government auditors' literal interpretation of inventory allocation. But where does the line fall between what the company manager sees as flexibility and efficiency in factory operations and what the government perceives as mischarging? Obviously, a lot depends on how carefully contractors and their employees keep their inventory accounting. Charging labor or material costs to an underbudget government program to hide an overrun on another, for example, strikes the government as illegal, an issue that figured in the Sundstrand case in 1988. But to the contractor's employee on the shop floor, who starts the basic paperwork that auditors fight about, it may look like the money is all coming out of the same pot. So what difference does it make?

The Aerospace Industries Association, one of several lobbying organizations that defense contractors use for jousting with the government, put together a position paper in support of Material

Requirements Planning systems and warning of contractor withdrawal from U.S. government business. The statement observes that any system can be manipulated if someone has the desire to do so. While withdrawal from government business would be a drastic step, the association claims that "the contractors feel their very survival in the marketplace demands successful use of these techniques. . . . Contractors cannot choose to apply them selectively only to non-U.S. government work while maintaining a less efficient system for government programs."

Still, prime defense contractors, those whose business is largely with the government, those bruised like Bell over its $22 million refund, do not have much choice. Defense companies cannot be converted easily to commercial manufacturing. Their organizations, their marketing staffs and skills, their engineering and technical competence are built around government work. An enormous part of their capability is locked up in just knowing the ropes of increasingly voluminous government acquisition regulations. Suppliers to the prime contractors are in a different position. Indeed, some with good commercial and industrial markets are increasingly disenchanted and are saying so to customers like Bell.

If it were not for the criminalization of the audit process, this inventory paperwork affair would be an esoteric little squabble of interest only to the few in contract management. Jousts over regulations, accounting conventions, contract management practices, and the like are typical of what has occupied government and defense contractors for a couple of decades. But criminalization catapults it into the policy realm, where it doesn't belong. There administrators typically decide to write more new regulations or congressmen decide more new acquisition statutes are absolutely necessary, adding more administrative burden.

Audits and More Audits

Of great concern from the policy standpoint is the proliferation of government auditors and the competition between them to see who can uncover the most—the kind of competition the country may well not need. Rooting out waste, fraud, and abuse is exactly the recipe that any good bureaucrat relishes to pad his own agency with funds and people. Industry's fears are of mushrooming government authorities to deal with—authorities, as in so many acquisition management situations, that have no responsibility for the technical outcome of the program. Industry can spend more time answering auditors' questions than manufacturing the stuff it is supposed to be making. Defense industry propaganda takes the line, "just get the auditors off our back and everything will be fine." But that is hardly the case, either, for proliferating audits are a symptom of the loss of public confidence, a symptom that there is trouble with the acquisition system itself.

In the aftermath of waste, fraud, and abuse, auditors were competing among themselves. Besides those from the individual services, there is the Defense Contract Audit Agency, an independent arm supervised by the Department of Defense comptroller. Then there is the Defense Contract Administration Service, part of the Defense Logistics Agency, which is in the plant representative game. The size of their staffs and those of the service auditors varies considerably with location, their effectiveness usually in inverse proportion to population. One or the other conceivably could become the nucleus for a Defense Department acquisition agency, if the task is taken away from the services. There is yet more competition: The Defense Department's inspector general also has audit authority.

A survey conducted for the Packard Commission by one of the Big Eight accounting firms, Arthur Andersen & Co., examined the respective authorities, functions, and, in the eyes of contractors, auditing competence of each. The survey made clear that there is duplication of effort, that the animosity between contractors and auditors has reached an unhealthy state, and that the government needs to take care that audits are properly planned, that its auditors are competent, and that inefficiency is minimized.

According to the Andersen survey, the current sorry state is, in part, the result of the eclipse of control by the contracting officer, whose ability to negotiate with and monitor contractor compliance has been debased as much as that of the program manager—in this case by competing auditors. The survey also blamed the situation on the increase in authority vested in the Defense Contract Audit Agency, which now acts as a decisionmaker, not an adviser—and one whom the contracting officer fears to contradict.

The Results and What to Do about It

While the auditors and the contractors argue about contract compliance, the effect on the shop-floor or office worker is dampening. It leaves an off-taste in the mouth, deflating and demeaning. Defense companies used to be distinguished by the esprit of their employees—their absorption with advanced technology, their sense of contribution to the national effort, their sense that they were doing something for the country that went beyond the boundaries of simply making a living. That spirit has begun to dissipate.

Relationships between government customers and industrial contractors have deteriorated as well, accelerated by the atmosphere of criminalization. Military and industry are grousing at each other rather than working together for the best interests of the nation. The gears of the military-industrial complex are not in mesh. Common cause in the name of patriotism is being lost in dog-eat-dog negotiation and cut-throat grasping for contracts.

Contractors sometimes create their own hardships. They seem to fluctuate between two behavioral modes with the regularity of a sine wave. One is deference to the customer to the point of obsequiousness—accepting things that are not good business practice or in a company's or the government's best interests. Then there is the other mode: arrogance, not-invented-here, ours is not only the best mousetrap but the only one. The customer is viewed as a supplicant at the throne. When the contractor is in an arrogant high, the government customer might understandably relish placing a program elsewhere—or the prospect of an indictment.

While seeking out criminals in the defense acquisition process may salve Congress and an outraged public, is this thrust going in the wrong direction—more the product of a long series of ill-fated decisions by top-level defense leadership than a solution to actual problems? Attention might better be focused on how well the centralized and increasingly dominant Defense Department has carried out its policymaking duties; on the kind of balance, or lack thereof, that exists between the Defense Department and the military commanders who do the fighting or the development, between the Defense Department and the industry that has to turn its requirements into producible and workable equipment.

A plausible brief could be written that the whole Defense Department ought to be flushed down the drain. Since its creation, it has been a failure in many respects: in the requirements process, in overstepping its role as a senior-policy-level decisionmaker into program management, and in usurping—for the worse—the traditional hegemony of combat-zone commanders.

Not that the Defense Department has not done good things. For one, it brought a measure of needed unification to the services—forcing joint development of equipment and joint operations in the field. (Though joint programs in the military-buying system also complicate the work and jack up the cost.) In addition, Defense Department oversight of research and development—in the golden days before the Office of the Director of Defense Research and Engineering was emasculated—furthered innovation, provided a check-and-balance over weapons development, and caught flaws in the services' weapons concepts. Defense Research and Engineering spoke with authority to Washington in an evenhanded voice, distinct from the individual interests of the services. Further, it had credibility with industry. But where is Defense Research and Engineering now? It was gutted in the name of defense reform.

Achievements do not erase the fact that the Defense Department has done as much to create layers of bureaucracy as it has to unify the services. Worse, it has set a precedent that creating more bureaucratic layers is the preferred way to manage the military. Combat is the acid test, of course, and the Defense Department, which presided over one lost war—in Vietnam—bears a significant share of the blame for that disaster for America. Its conduct of operations in the Middle East—from its centralized command authority in Washington, light-years away from the shooting—has not been anything to shout about either.

Elimination of the Defense Department is hardly likely. But trimming is not unthinkable. Former navy secretary John Lehman, for example, scrutinized various Defense Department organizations and raised questions about the usefulness of the Defense Logistics Agency. His conclusion was that this agency, among other things a source of the competing crowd of defense inspectors, a larger force in military buying than the public is aware, was unnecessary, even wasteful. The services did not need a centralized supply agency when they each have their own supply apparatus anyway—one that could just as well buy uniforms and canteens for their own troops. To avoid criticism of his own house bureaucracy while attacking that of the Defense Department, Lehman eliminated—as duplication—the navy's command that oversaw its systems buying organization. Not a great deal of real sacrifice ensued, for the few hundred people involved made their way to other federal billets. But John Lehman is gone now, as all political appointees are eventually. The Defense Department is still there, growing new auditors and inspectors, and so is the Defense Logistics Agency.

This is not meant to single out the Defense Logistics Agency, or any other, as incompetent. There is little evidence that the European System, for example, with a single civilian procurement agency separate from the uniformed services, has produced a product in the field that is any better or cheaper. The real villain is the proliferation of agencies and people that came with a powerful, centralized Defense Department. The Defense Logistics Agency is an archetype of what the Defense Department has often done in the name of commonality: created yet another layer of bureaucracy.

Criminalization may well be the final manifestation of the bankruptcy of Pentagon and congressional micromanagement of the military-buying process. The attitude is that if regulations, intensive oversight, and continual auditing cannot bring about successful programs, then throw the rascals in jail or cow them with a grand jury.

There are alternatives. While indictments get the contractors' attention and grand juries hasten compromises, these will not encourage industry to invent, produce, or control quality. It is essential that government policymakers define their targets and see that they are met. They are misconstruing their responsibilities by trying to do the jobs of the managers and then running to a grand jury when trouble sets in.

Further, it should be remembered that military acquisition can only be as good as its leadership. There is good reason to believe that that leadership has been transfixed with paper and regulation, and plagued with ineptness bred from inexperience. No solution for the ills of the acquisition system can come without an examination of the amount of clothing the Defense Department emperor is wearing.

Last but not least, something must be done about the fact that program managers and contracting officers, auditors and inspectors, military and civilians, all tend to work their own respective sides of the street. With this sort of do-it-yourself approach, with the adversarial relationships permeating the whole military-industrial complex, the teamwork essential to carrying out big programs is vanishing. Perhaps more than anything else, fragmentation of effort is devastating the military-buying system.

11

Where Do We Go from Here?

SPACE scientists talk about launch windows—those slits of minutes, hours, or days when a planet and the earth are lined up so that a satellite can hit its target. A political launch window for refurbishing the military-buying system opened the day after the 1988 presidential election, when the transition teams got down to work defining the administration's goals. Past experience suggests that for about eighteen months, the executive will have the will, popular support, and cooperation of Congress to tackle institutions. When the campaigning starts for midterm congressional elections, both Congress and the executive branch will shy off controversy and drastic measures. Then everyone starts running for the presidency again and the window will close for at least two more years.

The problems plaguing the acquisition system are clear. Paper, regulation, specification—the security blanket of bureaucracy—and micromanagement are stifling the day-to-day running of the acquisition process and producing unintentional disarray and extraordinarily long development cycles for weapons. The costs of the steady swelling of the development cycle, micromanagement, and excessive regulation are compounding daily, monthly, yearly. According to a 1987 report by the Center for Strategic and International Studies, as much as $6 billion (short term) and $10 billion (long term) could be saved annually (based on a $200 billion annual acquisition budget) if the oversight, auditing, and regulatory lard could be scraped off the acquisition system.

If the opportunity slips away, the outlook for the military-buying system is unequivocal. Both military managers and industry agree that the acquisition process is at its most frustrating, lowest ebb that veterans can remember. Rectification is dubious—even with solid recommendations like those of the Packard Commission or the Air Force's A³ study—without the weight of a powerful chief executive in the flush of his early presidency behind them. It is not just a matter of recommendations but of doing something with them.

Besides, no changes in regulations, no mere legislation is going to rescue the system from the swamp into which it is slowly sinking. No reorganization is going to fix those shortcomings that are not organizational or procedural to begin with. Reforms can and do improve procedures. But people run programs, not directives. When contract innovations, scientific-management methodology, or reorganizations overlook that elementary fact, their very sophistication, their fine intentions make the system ever more obdurate. So the most essential move the new chief executive can make is to set a climate, to create a state of mind to put performance first and paper somewhere after, to inject more Skunk Works- or Polaris-type project management into acquisition, to let the body try to heal itself of two decades of micromanagement and overregulation.

Much as its practitioners and its critics grouse about the acquisition system, the remarkable fact is that, burdened with bureaucracy as it is—like a supine Gulliver, bound by constraining threads—it has continued to work. Despite error, delay, and ballooning costs, the acquisition system has produced a broad range of extremely complex, technically advanced equipment for U.S. military forces. Things could, of course, be worse. Unfortunately, they are going to get worse if current trends remain unchecked. Sooner or later, if someone or something does not call a halt to, let alone reverse, the process, the system will not be able to produce at the standard the country expects or that national security demands.

Reducing Micromanagement

The erosion of the role of the program manager in defense acquisition has been stressed here because it directly relates to the detrimental swelling of voices in the Defense Department and Congress who can say no or raise issues that cause delay and the shrinking of those who can and will act. Both Congress and the Defense Department have to be shaken out of the micromanagement trance into which they have fallen. They are simply too far from the scene and too often lack the engineering and industrial management talent for the kind of detailed decisions they are making. Further, they are prone to enforce their decisions by statute or regulation—far too inflexible a way to run a development effort.

Solutions imposed by senior levels in the Defense Department or by Congress—in effect, by outsiders—have had a spotty record. As air force general Kenneth Meyer put it, "Bureaucracies have a great ability to chew up and digest reform movements without altering their form [i.e., the bureaucracy's] and they often turn simplifications into complexities or divert attention to the nonessential." Further, as General William Thurman stated, "If Congress is going to micromanage acquisition, then at least it ought to hire some good engineers." That is good advice. Congressional lack of understanding of the military-industrial process certainly eclipses that of Pentagon political appointees. But better yet, let those on the inside develop the next set of reforms. Listen to the shop floor, to the working stiff as well as the board chairman, for a change. After all, it is those on the shop floor who have to make the system work, who can best make the system work.

Senior Defense Department management must set cost, performance, and reliability goals for acquisition in line with strategic objectives, and see that they are met. The role of the Defense Department (and of Congress) should be that of a board of directors—that is policymakers not managers. This is a change of principle, not procedure. By dictating programs and detailed procedures, the Defense Department has become an advocate for weapons or technologies it favors, and has lost its objectivity as a reviewing authority. So has Congress. The roles of the Defense Department (and Congress) as micromanagers and operational commanders must be constrained. The Defense Department, and Congress, must return to policy decisionmaking and get out of program management.

The acquisition system must return to the straightforward principles of good, flexible, tight project management—that is, smaller, dedicated teams with responsibility and authority; expeditious decisionmaking; the replacement of layers of review and oversight with short, clear chains of command. Otherwise, little is in sight to reduce the length of the acquisition cycle—the time to develop and field new weapons—the best and final measure of how well the process is working.

What changes are needed in the Defense Department, and Congress, to roll back the spread in regulation and micromanagement? The director of the Bureau of Indian Affairs has proposed the unprecedented—that his own department be phased out of existence. Attractive a target as the Defense Department bureaucracy may be for like treatment, reduction for the sake of reduction should not be a primary goal. Besides, reducing a bureaucracy is seldom practical. Once the government hires a civil servant, it is next to impossible to lay him off the way private business does with its employees when business goes sour. The problem with the expansion of the Defense Department auditing corps and the Defense Inspector General's staff is that these people will be around, digging for something to justify their paychecks, long after the crisis that brought them on board has passed. The nits will get pickier and the taxpayer will support the growing government roster until these civil servants hit retirement age twenty-five years down the road.

Report after report has stated that there are too many people in military acquisition. That is not completely true, especially in light of the detailed tracking and recordkeeping that must be done—not to mention the useless regulatory and paperwork tasks imposed on the troops. People are not the burden so much as paper. If the paperwork and the useless duties created by legislation and regulation were reduced, then so could the ranks be reduced.

What the taxpayer should think about, though, is at least the phasing out of a centralized Defense Department bureaucracy. It has become too large and too immersed in operating detail to do its policy and oversight jobs. Caspar Weinberger has been attacked in the aftermath of the Pentagon payoff scandals for turning over too much control to the services, but he had the right idea: Tell the services broadly what their jobs are but not how to do them. He simply failed to find enough capable, defense-experienced deputies to carry out this policy.

The Defense Department should function the way the National

Security Council does. The secretary of defense should become a presidential adviser, not a bureaucrat supervising a bureaucratic army. George Shultz's idea is a good one: move the secretaries of state and defense to the White House annex where they would concentrate on broad strategic policy and budget levels, leaving the day-to-day operations and acquisition chores to the professionals in the departments. The Office of the Secretary of Defense should be reduced and streamlined into a lean project-management type of staff.

A Hoover Commission-style broad policy group might be established to study the usefulness of the Office of the Secretary of Defense, its relations with the services, the wisdom of defense centralization, and the impact of Congress on national security and its policymaking. Similarly it could examine the functions of the divisions and offices in the services.

The roles of Defense Department agencies, like the Defense Logistics Agency, the Defense Advanced Research Projects Agency, the Defense Communications Agency, and the Defense Intelligence Agency should be reappraised—specifically in terms of whether their functions lie with the services or with the Joint Chiefs of Staff. Consolidation or even privatization of portions of some defense agencies might be feasible. An independent accounting firm, for example, could handle some of the government's routine audit functions less antagonistically than competing auditors from various agencies.

Further, the Defense Department ought to do away with the Packard Commission's concept of an acquisition executive in the Pentagon and return to the organization in which Packard himself shone. That is, the number two man in the Defense Department— the deputy secretary of defense—should be the formally designated chief Pentagon acquisition executive.

The deputy secretary of defense, usually a tested manager with a breadth of industrial know-how, generally has assumed that task (informally). But William H. Taft IV, who held that post in the Reagan administration, is a lawyer with no discernible understanding of manufacturing, development, or technology. Difficult as it is to attract them to government service, tough, heavy-industry-seasoned managers might be arm twisted into accepting senior Pentagon jobs—especially the deputy secretaryship. It is up to the new administration to go after them, as George Bush seemed to be doing post-election, and Congress to remove the legislative barriers. Cutting away micromanagement and paperwork to give the deputy secretary of defense sharper visibility from the top and faster response from the field would help.

So many layers of management have been built up in the Pentagon that the secretary of defense himself can hardly cope with them, let alone deal with the broad policy questions he faces, without a strong deputy to handle the day-to-day routine. It has become next to impossible for one man to deal with a monster acquisition system, global tensions, forces scattered over the globe, politics and the congressional hearing mill, and, not the least, the capital's omnipresent, unavoidable social scene.

Not that the Defense Department is alone in creating layers. A good question exists over whether the services need big acquisition-command headquarters staffs with monitors to keep tabs on the same programs managed by project offices in field centers. But the Defense Department sets the tone. If it micromanages, so will the services. A new administration, if it wants to streamline, needs to open the top of the can first before it can get at the beans on the bottom.

Restoring Confidence in the Military Program Manager

Even if the new president wants to eliminate the layers of authority and bureaucracy and congressional oversight, that is not enough to make them go away. None of the Skunk Works-type streamlining, none of the program manager's original authority will return until the electorate and its representatives regain confidence in the acquisition system and its managers. Total-package procurement in the C-5A program was designed to restore this confidence. Prototyping in the lightweight fighter competition was designed to do this. Ben Bellis's stringent management of the F-15 was designed to do this. Former navy secretary Lehman's emphasis on competition and second sourcing was designed to do this. Most of the Packard Commission's recommendations were designed to do this.

Despite all these efforts, confidence has eroded further. No magic elixir, no study recommendations, no new sets of regulations, no indictments, no new scientific management systems—by themselves—are going to restore what has been lost. Only government and industry managers can restore confidence through better performance. Unfortunately, the dice are loaded against them, for they will not get an opportunity to demonstrate their ability without a remarkable transmutation in the restrictive legislation and regulation generated by the critics of waste, fraud, and abuse.

Restoration of public confidence in the system is going to come hard, especially with the latest scandals. But lost confidence must be superseded by comprehension that all failures in weapons development are not scandalous; that the industry and government people who make and buy weapons are far more competent than given credit for, but not infallible; that with innovation, with reaching beyond the technology that is firmly in hand, comes risk. Some projects will fall short, but not because of venality. If nothing is ventured, nothing is gained. And inhibition threatens to make military acquisition so risk averse it will atrophy. Congress and the public must recognize that the right way to manage is not by legislation, overregulation, and threats of prosecution.

Acquisition needs its fair share of the best and the brightest if confidence in program managers is to be restored. But despite the efforts of the services to make acquisition management an attractive career path, it is rare, if ever, that any top-ranking generals or admirals who have specialized in acquisition are chosen as chief of staff for their respective service. The service chiefs are combat commanders. Perhaps that is the way it should be. Still, it sends a message to junior officers as to where rank and honor lie. Discouragement of acquisition as a career path narrows the talent pool from which future program managers are drawn. A graveyard spiral starts. Top people avoid acquisition. Second-rate performance brings further opprobrium to the system. More top talent is turned off acquisition as a career. Further, while acquisition does have some high-rank and high-visibility jobs, budgeters are too stingy with grade levels to allow acquisition to attract all the good people needed.

Acquisition also suffers from the drawbacks of the service system of rotation. Commonly, the acquisition program manager will be a military officer. Just as commonly, he will be rotated into the program manager's job without any prior experience with the project. He may be assigned to smaller projects without any acquistion experience at all. Too often, the program manager will just be getting up to speed when his orders come to move on—possibly to another acquisition program or perhaps back to the operating forces. Rotation is not all bad; it does bring experience from other areas. But when the program manager moves on, his experience will be lost to the program he was assigned to, and possibly to the development command as a whole.

Training could be improved for career acquisition officers—not formal schooling but what universities call work-study or on-the-job types of training. Young military officers headed for permanent careers in acquisition should serve more often as interns in industry—not in the front office but in the design rooms and, most important, on the shop floor. Unlike in Japan, too many design engineers in American industry never get this kind of exposure, which is essential to product economy and quality. Letting future military managers get their hands dirty in the factory would reduce the gap between what they—let alone political appointees in the Pentagon or staffers in Congress—think industry does and how things really get done.

Civil service employees make up an experienced cadre in acquisition now, and there are problems in this area as well. The old timers in acquisition—the corps that came in with the explosive expansion of the military in World War II—have been retiring in a cresting wave that began back in the 1970s, when cutbacks in funding encouraged bailouts. Without the money to bring in replacements, civil service ranks were thinned. Since then, the waste, fraud, and abuse furor has torpedoed morale and encouraged further bailouts by fed-up civilians. Moreover the custom of a military officer serving as program director, rather than a civil service employee, has left the civilians with too little responsibility. The sad fact is that they might have better qualifications, in terms of experience, to manage programs than the officers to whom they report. It is time to attack the second-class-civilian mentality, to expose the drones, and to give first-class civilians opportunity.

The Center for Strategic and International Studies report proposes upgrading civil service billets in acquisition, as Congress did in creating the senior executive service, to improve the caliber of the people involved. The Center for Strategic and International Studies report points out that "many reforms tend to focus too much on the process and too little on the processors. The outcome of this tendency is that the more cumbersome and convoluted the acquisition process becomes, the more difficult it will be to attract and retain able people."

Perhaps the answer lies in a combination of steps. Rotate acquisition officers into and out of combat commands as is done now, but increase the civilians' management role in military buying. Better yet, award program management to well-qualified civilians. Lieutenant General William E. Thurman, when he commanded the Aeronautical Systems Division for the Air Force Systems Command, did just that at Wright Field, for the Maverick missile specifically. Or charge the military program director with meeting—or challenging—the user's requirements and those of the civilian top deputy, and with managing the technical and manufacturing aspects of the job.

To restore confidence in the program manager, the services should, for one, enhance the career status of acquisition officers and bite the bullet on rotation of officers to recognize that expertise in acquisition is not a talent one is born with, but acquired the hard way—through years of experience. In addition, the services should broaden existing opportunities for capable and experienced civil service career people to have a shot at the top job in program offices.

In the broadest policy sense, wages and working conditions have to be made more attractive for the government's talented technology managers. Their departure for private industry or consulting has compounded the Pentagon's difficulties in managing its acquisition system.

Restoring Confidence in Military Contractors

Restoring confidence in the military program manager is half the challenge. The other is restoring confidence in industry and the military program manager's counterpart, the contractor's project manager. Industry has taken an unfair drubbing in some instances, but it has made its own troubles as well, in ways that range from crawling into a hole when challenged, to sloppy accounting on military contracts, to quality and manufacturing lapses. Industry also has taken on the color of big government. But where government's security blanket is paper, industry's is the meeting. Meetings not only substitute for useful work, but also spread responsibility around enough to obfuscate what went wrong. Industry is not innocent of bureaucracy.

Paperwork and auditing in military contract compliance has burgeoned beyond comprehension, but if a contractor wants to stay in the game he must play by the rules. The stress on contract compliance stems not only from the horror stories and the subsequent Packard Commission recommendations, but also from a deeper industrial problem—one that extends beyond the defense industry. Its main symptom is the increasing difficulty American industry has had in staying competitive in world markets—in matching the quality, reliability, and cost of the best from overseas, from automobiles and consumer electronic equipment to heavy forgings.

Military contractors also have a particular demon of their own: the transition from development to production. Congress and the media, which, in a sort of unholy alliance, feed each other acquisition scandal and wrongdoing stories, have ignored this aspect of government acquisition by haring off after perpetrators of $5,000 coffeepots. The Defense Department is concerned enough to have produced a thick manual of guidelines for contractors on this transition process, and it has sent teams to meet with contractors around the country to exhort them to do the kind of innovative job in manufacturing that they have done in engineering and design. Clearly, when the government has to get out a manual to tell contractors how to manufacture new technology—a skill at which industry should excel—there is something amiss.

According to the navy's Will Willoughby, who headed the Pentagon team that analyzed the transition from development to production, the solution lies in allowing industry to fix—in fact, forcing it to fix—its own leaky plumbing. There is no mystery about how to do this. For years, acquisition managers have asked the customer to give industry a performance specification, to tell industry in broad terms what it wants, and then to let competitors vie to see who can do the best design and manufacturing job. But instead, government exerts more and more control over more and more detail of how industry does a technical job, through incessant reviews, regulations, and paperwork. The army's contract with the Wright brothers for the first U.S. military flying machine could serve as a useful model. It is short enough to fit in a picture frame; a model of simple, clear specification of what the customer wanted; with no appendices, no boilerplate standards. And delivery was in months, not years. Documentation in defense has been all downhill since.

Government cannot have it both ways. It cannot have an independent and innovative private industry if it turns private enterprises into government arsenals. It cannot have more open competition, fixed-price contracting, and contractor investment in facilities while demanding its money back if it doesn't like the way the deal turns out. It makes no sense to haggle over a 1 percent profit margin while ignoring what low production rates and excessive paperwork are doing to the other 99 percent. It cannot have a streamlined acquisition process while adding new layers of authority, regulation, and specification. It cannot be surprised at competitive intelligence-gathering run amok if it goes overboard on competition itself.

Nor can industry have it both ways. It cannot complain about tougher rules of the game and low profit margins while bidding on every defense job in sight. It cannot accept a fixed-price contract and then finagle to have the terms changed if they seem too onerous, or slough off on quality or manufacturing responsibilities. It cannot bemoan the paper blizzard while slopping through accounting chores.

Further, industry cannot continue to hire consultants, to pay "commissions" to overseas customers, and to throw money around Washington for everything from fancy offices to influence peddlers and then wonder where public confidence has gone. It cannot put coins into every outstretched hand on the assumption that the customer wants it this way, or that it has to do so to win new business. Most of all, it cannot become so engrossed in winning new contracts that it forgets the public service aspects of its role—that defense companies should be held to a higher standard than just making money like their commercial counterparts.

Contractors will give the customer what they think he wants, perhaps mistaking what he wants. But it is not clear whether that is high technology or low cost—or perhaps a mutually exclusive both. An air force general worries that the Advanced Tactical

Fighter, now starting development, will become so cost directed that it will be short on technology—matching what the Soviets can do now, but obsolete in ten years. Congress and the public fret about defense budgets and about waste, fraud, and abuse. The cost-performance message that industry is receiving is a mixed one.

Returning to industry the job that is industry's—innovative design and quality manufacturing—and returning to the program manager the job that is the program manager's—sound decision-making and accountability—are complementary sides of the same structure. These are matters of style rather than regulation. It takes an administration that wants to operate this way—for it is the administration that sets the policy for its appointees. The opportunity to make these changes is now here.

Revamping the Congressional Role

Ronald Reagan took advantage of his mandate to start to rebuild U.S. defenses. His troops did start to tackle at least some of the ills of the acquisition system, but neither he nor his senior deputies detected the looming waste, fraud, and abuse crisis or understood the size of the procurement burden they were about to toss onto the backs of a shrunken acquisition organization.

In the fading days of his administration, as a lame duck facing a hostile Congress, Reagan could not strike out in new directions in defense acquisition. Congress must acquiesce in changes in policy of this magnitude, formally or otherwise. Reagan's era is over. It is up to the new president to take the initiative, to set the tone. The executive branch cannot force Congress to clean up its act, but the executive can furnish the example. Unfortunately, there is no public or political pressure on Congress to straighten out the mismanagement of its part of the acquisition process; in fact, the public is cheering it on.

The new administration can make the case with the new congressional leadership that statutory regulation of military buying has gotten out of hand—that program managers and industry must have the freedom and authority to fix their own problems. It also should attempt to convince Congress to appoint a Hoover-style commission or, failing that, its own Packard Commission, or even just one of its own committees to study its own procedures, the defense budget-approval process, the extent of new legislation and proliferation of committees and subcommittees strangling the acquisition process, and what might be done to simplify defense buying.

Early in 1988, after nearly a decade of reform legislation, Congress indeed began to wonder what it had wrought. Specifically, it became concerned about pullbacks by companies in bidding for defense contracts. A study then by three trade associations, entitled "The Impact on Defense Industrial Capability of Changes in Procurement and Tax Policy," warned of pullbacks, citing Hughes Aircraft's balking at the terms of the competition a year before to develop the radar for the air force's Advanced Tactical Fighter.

The Pentagon, where Frank Carlucci had replaced Weinberger, echoed congressional hesitation. It backed away from fixed-price contracting for research and development, which forced the sort of risk, in a nebulous market, that turned Hughes away from the advanced fighter radar program. As a compliance officer for a contractor told me, the defense industry initiatives that followed the Packard Commission report were beginning to work. Negotiations between industry and the Pentagon on standards for using the Material Requirements Planning System were nearing fruition. After skirmishing over progress payments, a government-industry peace treaty was in sight.

Then the corruption investigation erupted in mid-1988. "Two years of wound healing went down the drain," the compliance expert said. "We're faced with spending millions on our own internal investigation and on outside counsel. And a whole spate of new legislation is ready to hit the fan."

One of the first reactions from Congress was to threaten to cut off progress payments to any company mentioned in the FBI wiretaps. Cooler heads prevailed. Not only would such a step penalize a company without a trial, or even an indictment, but it also would disrupt weapons production at the waste of millions of dollars.

Still, such is a foretaste of what is to come. No resurrection from burial in paper is in sight for the nation's military acquisition system. With the new taint of scandal, there appears to be little hope for restraint of contradictory legislation, of regulation and (especially) oversight, of review and investigation. Worse, the scandals—as noisome as they are going to be—will deflect attention from the real ills of the system: the lack of confidence in, and restraint on, managers at the scene to move programs along faster.

This is not to say that program managers don't need regulation or control, that they are smarter or more capable than secretaries of defense, congressmen, commanding generals, auditors, or prosecutors. Nor is it an attempt to say that the services are always right and the Department of Defense or Congress is always wrong; that industry is always clean and government always the bumbler. But too much distance—in paper, in layers of management, in outside interference—lies between the responsible manager at the project level and the responsible senior commander. Day-to-day accountability and flexibility must be restored at the end of the chain, with a quicker and less oppressive policy response from the top.

Defense Department and congressional micromanagement, volumes of regulatory minutiae, buildings full of bureaucrats all have achieved one end: the obscuration of responsibility for results. Everybody is to blame and consequently nobody is to blame. Few in the upper echelons in the chain of command can readily put a finger on the causes of failure, or even identify failure with certainty. If the contractor has filled in all the squares in the paperwork, if the regulations have all been observed, if the auditor has certified all the accounting, if the program manager has cleared all the decisions with higher authority, if the secretary of defense has told Congress, if Congress has authorized the program, who can say how, why, or whether the development went wrong?

Escalating costs flourish in such an environment. But rather than attempting to change the environment, attention has focused on waste, fraud, and abuse, and, most recently, corruption. The military-buying horror stories all insinuate that military budgets are eminently cuttable. But while military spending is a comparatively easy target for Congress (cutting entitlements like Social Security or Medicare is political poison), the critical question is whether military spending will be cut wisely. It can, of course, but history suggests that it will not be. Consider, for example, Louis Johnson, a now forgotten and discredited defense secretary under Harry S. Truman, who went after fat and instead emasculated U.S. forces on the eve of the Korean War.

Last minute, legislatively mandated cuts are usually shortsighted and risky. The bulk of the military acquisition budget is for the thousands of items (expensive or not) required to keep forces in the field operating—not for the billion-dollar controversies aired in the media. In fact, since obligations for contracts extend over several fiscal years, only the largest weapons programs account for as much as a couple of billion dollars in any one year—and usually much less. Thus the immediate savings from cancellation of a single, highly visible weapons-development program are relatively small in relation to what the quick budget-cutter needs. Further, the risk of such a cut is high, because of the long lead times for developing weapons. Midstream cancellation of weapons projects is also uneconomic, because of termination costs and loss of defense jobs.

The elimination of waste is everyone's favorite way to cut the military budget—or any other governmental tab. It would be nice if there were a precise budget item labeled "Waste—$10 billion." But few program managers would admit, even to themselves, that they are wasting money. Few senior Pentagon secretaries would admit to themselves that they had not already excised the fat from their budgets. Congressmen see waste everywhere—except in their home districts. Waste is always somebody else's program.

Congress tends to look toward military operations and maintenance as the way to get quick, easy budget reductions. That means fewer steaming hours for ships; fewer field exercises; fewer flying hours; slower maintenance, repair, and overhaul. All this adds up to less military readiness. But long-term reductions could be made with less risk, long-term military buying costs could be cut without any loss of equipment, if only commitments could be prudently scaled back, if politicians knew what they wanted, and if the paper-encrusted acquisition system is allowed to move faster.

The Choices Ahead

Long-term efficiency in weapons buying is one way to make long-term savings. The number of weapons programs should be kept under control, so that those with priority have the funding they need for efficient production. Competition, valuable as it is, becomes meaningless if quantities are too low to support initial sources, let alone second sources. And front-end investment should be provided to buy out programs quickly. A good start would be to attack the paper, regulation, and bureaucracy that breed inefficiency in acquisition. Good ideas like multiyear contracting to avoid funding instability or joint government-industry funding of factory modernization seem to fade into paperwork or political blind alleys. Maligned as it was, cost-plus contracting had a shining virtue—it produced stuff faster. It will be a Herculean chore to deal with almost four decades of paper accumulation—an Augean stable to cleanse—but it is a no-risk course for holding down defense costs, albeit a slow one.

Control must begin at the strategic policy and requirements level. Difficult strategic policy decisions must be made: Will the United States rely predominately on relatively cheap nuclear forces or does arms control mean buying more costly conventional forces? Should the United States maintain costly conventional weapons and personnel in Europe? What is the right balance between air, ground, and sea forces?

Administrations have been criticized for teeter-totter strategic policy, but they need more than sharpshooting from Congress—they need constancy in support. Congressional degeneration into budgetary whim—one force level or one weapons program this year, another the next—bodes for stagnation and eventually chaos. If U.S. military policy is to remain effective, it needs the kind of bipartisanship in Congress that underwrote the Marshall Plan, saving Europe after World War II.

In the wake of the new round of scandals in 1988, it is not clear how much sober reflection will be given to the real problems of the acquisition system. What the system needs is less micromanagement and the freedom to move faster. What the investigations into corruption are bound to bring are cries for new laws, new regulations, more control. In fact, though, more regulation may mean less control, for the job becomes too burdensome to manage effectively. Caspar Weinberger found that out. He was unfairly criticized for failing to root out corruption when that should not even remotely have been considered the job of the secretary of defense. The secretary of defense is not a cop. His task is strategic policy direction.

As much of a sideshow as they may become, the 1988 scandals also have the potential to produce improvement. They might, for example, focus sorely needed attention on the people problem.

This would include consideration of what kind of background clearance is being done on, or what short-sighted political litmus test is being applied to, Pentagon appointees. Though clearly there were exceptions in the Reagan era, in general the Pentagon sank into a miasma of incompetence or into obsession with how decisions played in Congress rather than with their technical soundness. Consideration also should be given to well-intentioned congressional ethics legislation that, combined with continual roasting from both Congress and the media, has turned away industry technical stars and production whizzes from senior Pentagon jobs. The result is that, under Reagan, technical posts often went to those in industry who were ready to retire, or whose companies wanted to see the last of them. Chastened, Reagan vetoed a new ethics bill in the waning days of his presidency. Equally important is consideration of the difficulties of attracting and retaining smart military and civil service people in acquisition.

Consulting is another part of the people problem. And it is not a simple case of damning all Pentagon retirees, who weigh heavily in the consultant ranks. The military pastures out officers in the prime of life—officers who are not ready or willing to retire. They revel in the challenges and pine for the action. Should they be denied the right to stay in the game and earn their keep in the process? Some retired officers or civilians sell their expertise and their access circumspectly—and access to what is going on in the Pentagon is what companies will buy. Others blatantly solicit their former colleagues. Some indulge in high living, in wheeling and dealing. Some big consulting firms provide the manpower the federal government cannot hire directly under congressional budget ceilings, contracting for them instead under procurement or research accounts in winked-at subterfuge. Others are an old-boy network that does esoteric studies to give decisionmakers justification for doing what they want to do anyway—or for doing nothing. Then some are ready to do for industry the kind of seamy jobs it cannot ask its own employees to do. Or some sell their services to a contractor one day, the government the next, all the while dealing with the same program, in an obvious conflict-of-interest situation.

Still another type of consultant opens a sticky kind of Venus flytrap. This is the specialist in the hot technology of the moment, who leaves the government to sell expertise. Government offers stability, but not much these days in the way of public esteem to offset the lure of a lucrative foray into consulting. The first contractor he approaches has little choice but to accept his offer, because whether it is insight on the contract up for bid at the moment or on a blueprint for which door to open in the Pentagon labyrinth, rejection would mean that the information would go to the contractor's closest competitor.

James H. Falk, a Washington lawyer who specializes in contractor protests over the way the Pentagon awards its programs, maintains there are adequate checks and balances in the system and enough fraud law to restrain both government employee and contractor. Not so for consultants. He has proposed an idea that David Packard once broached, that consultants be required to register as lobbyists do, and also disclose who their clients are as a safeguard against conflict of interest. The idea has merit, for if consultants had certificates, like stockbrokers or lawyers, that the government could revoke in cases of misconduct, it would bring some order into a wild and free-swinging game. Congress thought so, too, for Senator David Pryor included the idea as an amendment in the bill funding the Pentagon's 1989 fiscal year, and it passed. Should the 1988 investigations turn over the consulting rock for a good look at what the busy ants underneath are up to, it will benefit the whole defense apparatus as well as the taxpayer.

Reaction to the 1988 investigations reflects a worrisome misunderstanding. Both the public and their elected representatives increasingly conceive of the acquisition system as a method for catching crooks, for detecting fraud. That misconception has deflected the acquisition system from its basic objective—equipping the troops—into a "gotcha" system, with myriad rules aimed at tripping up transgressors. Further, it reflects a lack of understanding of the shift in military acquisition from technical to price competition. When the government began to buy weapons more as commodities than as scientific and engineering breakthroughs, it changed the pressures of the game. Ultimately, it created the potential for the kind of fixing and chiseling that can go on in competition concentrated solely on price.

Corruption, waste, fraud, abuse, all are side shows to the central problem of the acquisition system. In a word, this is speed. Micromanagement, regulation, legislation on top of legislation, even paperwork, are not in themselves fatal. Given time to adjust, the system can produce weapons for the combat forces under almost any rules. It cannot do so quickly, however, under the rules that exist today. It will be slower under the rules likely to exist tomorrow. That is where the costs pile up.

Two basic choices confront the nation in dealing with its military buying system. It can opt for more regulation, more supervision, more review—for a "gotcha" system. Or it can opt for simplicity along the lines of Skunk Works management. It could be a $15 billion or a $25 billion or even a $50 billion-a-year difference in defense budgets. If the country decides its military acquisition managers and its defense industry cannot be trusted to function without intense scrutiny, it must pay the billions of dollars for paperwork, people, and time to try to keep them rigidly in line. It must run the risk of seeing the defense industry slide into nationalization and a weapons development cycle that capitalizes ever more slowly on fast-moving and difficult-to-develop technology that is the crux of survival.

Selected Bibliography

MOST of this book is distilled from nearly thirty years of formal interviews, informal conversations, briefings, presentations, and speeches and such at factories, military bases, airfields, and the Pentagon. Some also comes from remembered reports and articles discarded long before the prospect of writing this book came along—their names and authors now faded from memory.

Besides those quoted in the text, there is a long list of field and flag rank military officers whose views are represented, as well as the views of those (military and civil service) in project management or supervisory grades, corporate chief executive officers, vice presidents, project engineers, marketing troops, Washington representatives, bankers, and investment analysts. Most were primarily concerned with defense but many as well with space and commercial aviation. Hence there are views from both sides of the fence.

Primarily, I spoke with Americans, but the list encompasses those from Canada's often overlooked defense industry, from South America, Great Britain, France, West Germany, Italy, Spain, Japan, Singapore, Australia, Indonesia, India, Pakistan, Israel, Saudi Arabia, Czechoslovakia, and the Soviet Union. The last named has an unusual defense establishment, in which designers and researchers are grouped in bureaus separate from manufacturing plants, run by a government ministry.

Books and reports, cited in the text or otherwise, that contributed include:

Aerospace Industries Assn. *Position Paper on MRP Systems*, Washington, D.C., undated.

Art, Robert J. *The TFX Decision: McNamara and the Military*. Boston: Little, Brown, 1968.

Augustine, Norman, R. *Augustine's Laws* (revised and enlarged edition). Washington, D.C.: American Institute of Aeronautics and Astronautics, 1983.

Barron, John. *MiG Pilot, The Final Escape of Lieutenant Belenko*. New York: Reader's Digest Press and McGraw-Hill, 1980.

Burrows, William E. *Deep Black: Space Espionage and National Security.* New York: Random House, 1986.

Center for Strategic and International Studies. *U.S. Defense Acquisition: A Process in Trouble.* Washington, D.C., 1987.

Edwards, John. *Super Weapon:. The Making of MX.* New York: Norton, 1982.

Gansler, Jacques S. *The Defense Industry.* Cambridge, Mass.: MIT Press, 1980.

Gorn, Michael H. *Vulcan's Forge: The Making of an Air Force Command for Weapons Acquisition (1950–1985).* Office of History, Headquarters, Air Force Systems Command, Andrews AFB, Md. 1985.

Hallion, Richard P. *The Commonality Chimera: Joint Service Development of Fighter and Attack Aircraft and Its Implications for the Advanced Tactical Fighter.* Paper published by the U.S. Air Force Systems Command, 1986.

Halloran, Richard. *To Arm a Nation: Rebuilding America's Endangered Defenses.* New York: Macmillan, 1986.

Hitch, Charles J., and Roland N. McKean. *The Economics of Defense in the Nuclear Age.* Cambridge, Mass.: Harvard University Press, 1960.

Johnson, Clarence L. (Kelly), and Maggie Smith. *Kelly, More Than My Share of It All.* Washington, D.C.: Smithsonian Institution Press, 1985.

Kelley, Albert J., Robert C. Fraser, and Donald Koretz. *Changes in Defense Business Practices.* Cambridge, Mass.: Arthur D. Little Program Systems Management Co., 1985.

McDonnell, Sanford N. *Covering Letter to Notes on Procurement Policy,* submitted to the Packard Commission. St. Louis, Mo.: McDonnell Douglas Corp., 1985.

Newhouse, John. *The Sporty Game: The High-Risk Competitive Business of Making and Selling Commercial Airliners.* New York: Knopf, 1982.

Peck, Merton J., and Frederic M. Scherer. *The Weapons Acquisition Process: An Economic Analysis.* Cambridge, Mass.: Harvard University Press, 1962.

President's Blue Ribbon Commission on Defense Management (the Packard Commission). *Interim Report to the President* and *Final Report, A Quest for Excellence.* Washington, D.C.: U.S. Government Printing Office, 1986.

Rickey, John. *The Free Enterprise Patriot.* St. Louis, Mo.: Book Tree, 1963.

Scherer, Frederic M. *The Weapons Acquisition Process: Economic Incentives.* Cambridge, Mass.: Harvard University Press, 1964.

Schilling, Warner R., Paul Y. Hammond, and Glenn H. Snyder. *Strategy, Politics and Defense Budgets.* New York: Columbia University Press, 1962.

Stubbing, Richard A., with Richard A. Mendel. *The Defense Game: An Insider Explores the Astonishing Realities of America's Defense Establishment.* New York: Harper & Row, 1986.

Index

A³. *See* Affordable Acquisition Approach (A³) study
AH-64 Apache, 44
Accountability, 56, 163, 204
Accounting, 95, 97, 180–183, 195, 201
Acquisition executive, 8–9, 28, 165, 195
Acquisition policy, 16–17
Acquisition system. *See* Procurement system
Advanced Tactical Aircraft, 106, 119
Advanced Tactical Fighter (ATF), 119, 141, 201–202, 203
Advanced Technology Bomber. *See* Stealth bomber
Adversarial relationship: between Pentagon and contractors, 3–4, 13, 15–16, 50, 189
Aeronautical Systems Division (air force), 24–25, 199
Aerospace companies, 10, 13, 17. *See also* specific companies, e.g. Hughes Aircraft Company
Aerospace Industries Association, 183–184
Affordable Acquisition Approach (A³) study, 143–144, 146, 147, 192
Air force, 11–12; procurement system, 9, 22, 23, 24–25, 81, 83, 84, 141, 150, 166, 174, 178–180; support equipment contracts, 57, 90–91, 94, 95–96, 99–100, 102–103; weapons programs, 42, 61–62, 65, 71–72, 109–117, 118–119, 132, 135, 137–138, 156–162, 167–168
Aircraft companies, 13, 72, 125, 137
Airplane crashes, 158–159, 164
Airplanes, 111–112, 117–118, 119–120, 123, 130–133, 178; capabilities, 23, 35, 71, 111, 132, 134, 137–139, 140, 141; components, 57, 94–103; costs, 85, 88–89, 99, 100, 110–111, 131–135, 138, 139–142, 152, 167–168. *See also* specific planes, e.g. F-16 (fighter)
Andrews, Mark, 57
Appropriations. *See* Budget
Appropriations committees, 54, 56, 178

Armed Services Board of Contract Appeals, 173
Armed Services Procurement Regulations, 78
Arms control, 20
Army, 11, 83; mission, 50; weapons programs, 44, 61–62, 106, 173, 180
Arthur Andersen & Co., 185
Arthur D. Little, Inc., 16
Aspin, Les, 146, 179–180
Auditing of contractors, 55, 84, 114, 173, 178, 180–185, 200
Auditors, 76–77, 82, 167, 173, 179
Augustine, Norman R., 7, 43, 46
Auxiliary equipment. *See* Support equipment

B-1 bomber, 25, 148, 155–162, 164, 165, 168, 169, 178
B-52 bomber, 6, 159, 160, 161
Ballistic Missile Early Warning System (BMEWS), 6, 7
Battista, Anthony, 62
Beggs, James M., 172–173, 178
Bell Helicopter Textron Inc., 181–182, 183, 184
Bellis Ben, 142–143, 196
Blackbird. *See* SR-71 reconnaissance aircraft
Black programs, 8, 56, 155, 161, 163–165, 166–167, 168
Boeing Company, 9, 96, 102, 108, 111, 112, 157, 165
Boeing 707 (plane), 62
Bradley Fighting Vehicle program, 106
Breakout (in equipment buying), 91, 92, 93
Bribes, 10, 102, 172, 174
Budget, 25, 33–35, 54, 115–116, 129, 145, 146, 152, 204–205. *See also* Funding instability
Budget cuts, 14, 46, 56, 87, 204, 205
Budget (fiscal 1985), 38, 54
Budget (fiscal 1986), 56, 159
Budget (fiscal 1987), 35–37, 38–39, 41–42
Budget (fiscal 1989), 208

Index

Budget planning, long-range, 3, 39–40, 60, 125–126, 147–149
Bureaucracy, 5–6, 7, 12, 15–16, 53, 79, 176, 184–185, 191; congressional, 53–54, 57; in Defense Department, 9, 15, 187, 194. *See also* Micromanagement
Burrow, William F., 167
Buying of equipment, 78–79, 93–98, 100–102, 105, 106–107, 113, 199. *See also* Fly-before-buy approach; Prices of equipment

C-5 (cargo transport), 94, 107–117, 141, 142, 143, 196
C-17 (cargo transport), 85, 114
CIA. *See* Central Intelligence Agency
Capabilities of equipment, 19, 21–23, 157, 192. *See also* Airplanes, capabilities; Cost-performance tradeoffs
Carlucci, Frank, 60, 61, 203
Carter, Jimmy, 71, 146, 155, 159, 161
Carter administration, 40, 121, 122, 160
Center for Strategic and International Studies, 19, 20, 55, 191, 198–199
Central Intelligence Agency (CIA), 166, 167
Channellock, Inc., 96
Commonality in weapons, 105, 117–121, 123, 126, 128
Competition for contracts, 14, 66–68, 77, 91–92, 136–140, 173–174, 205; and costs, 14, 34, 105–106, 107, 108, 124–125, 151
Competition for funds, 33, 135
Competition in Contracting Act, 67, 77
Compliance with contracts, 3, 4, 69, 109–110, 176–177, 186; problems with, 83, 85, 110–111, 150, 178–184
Component programs, 28, 57, 127, 143, 151–52, 156–157
Computers, 131, 165
Concept definition, 23–24, 26, 131–132, 140, 156
Concurrency, 127, 157–158
Configuration control, 143
Congress, 15, 206; role of, 1–2, 49, 58–59, 63, 202–205. *See also* Bureaucracy, congressional; Decision making, by Congress; Defense Department, and Congress
Congressional power, 38, 49. *See also* Oversight
Consulting, 207–208. *See also* Experts, government
Contract disputes, 171–172, 173, 179–180

Contract negotiation, 45, 57, 75, 171, 173
Contract termination, 178, 180, 203, 205
Contractor Operations Review (COR), 179, 180
Contractors, 4, 10, 65, 72–73, 102, 174–176, 183–184; internal oversight of, 176–178; role of, 29–30, 90–92, 93
Contracts, 4, 29, 80, 143, 145, 205–206; winning of, 66–68, 151. *See also* Compliance with contracts; Cost-plus contracts; Fixed-price contracts; Underbidding of contracts
Cost, 17, 42, 66, 74, 131, 152. *See also* Airplanes, costs; Budget; Buying of equipment; Mischarging on contracts; Prices of equipment; specific costs, e.g. Labor costs
Cost-benefit analysis, 21–22, 58, 183
Cost-effectiveness, 43, 91, 92, 93, 121, 123–124, 131
Cost estimates, 4, 34, 43–47, 67, 70, 74, 90, 141, 165
Cost overruns, 4, 7–8, 34, 45, 46, 75, 107, 110–111, 125
Cost-performance tradeoffs, 41, 121, 134, 149, 202, 208
Cost-plus contracts, 68, 69, 72, 73, 77, 124, 206
Cost recovery, 14, 141
Cost savings, 93, 106, 120, 122, 134, 145, 151, 166, 181, 184, 191
Cost sharing, 29–30, 68, 70, 75, 136–137, 206
Costello, Robert N., 165, 183
Criminal investigation, 83, 172–174, 178, 183, 184, 188, 203, 204
Curtiss-Wright Corporation, 137

Data rights, 91–92, 174, 180
Decision coordinating paper, 27
Decision making, 5, 7, 9, 27, 47, 67–68, 120, 127, 193; by Congress, 3, 62–63, 112, 115–116, 119, 128, 160, 179–180; by military 53, 121, 127–128, 185
Deep Black (Burrow), 167
Defective pricing, 75, 114–115
Defense acquisition. *See* Procurement system
Defense Acquisition Board 27, 28
Defense Contract Administration Service, 81–82, 185
Defense Contract Audit Agency, 55, 114, 185
Defense Department, 15, 127–128, 180, 193–196; and Congress, 29, 54–55, 59–60, 179–180; criticism of, 138,

186–188. *See also* Bureaucracy, in Defense Department; Decision making, by military; Secretary of defense
Defense Federal Acquisition Regulations, 78
Defense industry, 1, 13–15, 55, 56–57, 122. *See also* Aerospace companies; Contractors; Military-industrial complex
Defense Logistics Agency, 81, 179, 185, 187–188, 195
Defense policy, 20, 22, 30, 50, 52, 121–123, 206
Defense Research and Engineering, 187
Defense Science Board, 147
Defense System Acquisition Review Council (DSARC), 29, 30–31
Delivery schedule, 39, 136, 141, 149, 166, 169; problems with, 46, 73, 146, 150, 157, 158, 162, 176, 180
Demler, Marvin, 113
Design phase. *See* Concept definition
Dickinson, William L., 8
Dingell, John D., 56, 99, 100, 114, 115, 163
Downey, Thomas J., 180

E-Systems Inc., 83
E2C Hawkeye, 100
Eaton Corporation, 157, 158, 178
Efficiency: of bureaucracy, 6, 12, 79; in procurement system, 2, 4, 8, 51, 85, 113, 172, 205–206; in production, 42, 84
Eisenhower, Dwight D., 5, 126
Eisenhower administration, 34–35
Electronic systems Division (air force), 25
Ellis, Richard, 160
Employee attrition, 44, 52
Employees, 180, 186. *See also* Government employees; Program managers
Evans, Lew, 116
Evans, William J., 165–166
Experts, government, 51–54, 60–61, 120, 121, 207–208

F-4 (fighter), 119, 128, 132, 133–134, 137, 139
F-5 (fighter), 71
F-14 (fighter), 82, 124, 132, 134; costs, 116, 133, 135, 138, 152, 167–168
F-15 (fighter), 103, 132, 134–135, 136, 142–146, 196; capabilities, 139, 140; costs, 88, 133, 135, 138, 140, 152, 167–168

F-16 (fighter), 25, 29, 72, 121, 122, 128, 135–137, 168; capabilities, 71, 132, 137–139; costs, 88, 99, 100, 139–140, 145
F-18 (fighter), 71, 122, 132, 135, 138–139, 140
F-19 (fighter), 164
F-20 (fighter), 71–72
F-111 (fighter), 119, 124, 128, 158, 178
Failures in programs, 26–27, 82–83, 180, 197. *See also* Delivery schedule, problems with
Fairchild Republic Company, 178–180
Falk, James H., 208
Federal Acquisition Regulations, 78
Federal Aviation Administration, 94
Federal Bureau of Investigation (FBI), 83
Fitzgerald, Ernest, 115
5000 (directive series), 27, 79
Fixed-price contracts, 73 74, 75, 76, 77, 201, 203
Fly-before-buy approach, 129–130, 133, 140–142. *See also* Prototypes
Ford Aerospace and Communications Corporation, 106
Forrest, Bedford, 133
Fraud, 83, 171, 182–175, 208. *See also* Bribes; Mischarging on contracts
Funding. *See* Budget
Funding instability, 19, 39, 40–41, 129, 142, 144, 146–148, 150, 152, 159

Gansler, Jacques, 2
General Accounting Office, 55, 76–77
General Dynamics Corporation, 99, 118, 124, 136, 173
General Electric Company, 95, 102, 112–113, 136, 137, 139, 174
General Services Administration, 11, 80
Godwin, Richard, 28
Goldplating, 21–22, 30, 76, 94, 153
Goldwater, Barry, 54, 59, 60
Government employees, 11–12, 15, 54, 67, 198–199. *See also* Auditors; Bureaucracy; Experts, government
Government Systems Corporation, 173–174
Gramm-Rudman-Hollings budget-ceiling amendment, 151
Gregory, William H., 82, 88, 101, 103, 142, 160, 175
Grumman Aerospace Corporation, 100–101, 103, 116, 124

Hallion, Richard P., 118
Hayward, J. T., 133

Helicopters, 44
Henry, Charles R., 77, 106
Heritage Foundation, 87–88
Hitch, Charles, 125
Holmes, D. Brainerd, 6, 7
House Armed Services Committee, 8, 54, 56, 146, 178, 180
House Oversight and Investigations Subcommittee, 56, 99, 100, 114, 115, 163
Hughes Aircraft Company, 82–83, 149–150, 151–152, 203

"Impact on Defense Industry Capability of Changes in Procurement and Tax Policy, The," 203
Incentive-type contract, 73–74
Industrial espionage, 173–174
Inflation, 93, 109, 116; and weapons costs, 13, 77–78, 114, 133, 145–146, 149, 152
Inman, Bobby R., 8
Inspection of programs, 83–84, 92, 157
Inspector general, 55, 88–89, 177, 185
Inventory, 182–183. See also Spare parts

Johnson, Kelly, 166–168
Johnson, Louis, 204
Johnson, Lyndon, 120
Joint Chiefs of Staff, 40, 195
Joint Requirements and Management Board, 29, 30–31
Joint Surveillance Targeting Attack Radar system (Joint STARS), 61–62
Justice Department, 173–174, 175, 177–178

Kelly: More Than My Share of It All (Johnson), 166
Kennedy, John F., 120
Kennedy administration, 5, 126
Kissinger, Henry, 20
Korean War, 132, 204

Labor costs, 9, 39, 79, 96, 97, 98, 100
Leadership, 15, 26, 61, 188, 202. See also Experts, government
Learning-curve economics, 43–44, 74, 106, 144, 146, 159
Legislation, 1, 55, 75, 114, 151, 207
Lehman, John, Jr., 55, 100–101, 106, 120, 175, 187–188, 196
Lobbying, 15, 103, 115, 183–184
Lockheed Corporation, 41, 107, 108, 109–115, 117, 139, 164, 166–168

Logistics Command (air force), 90, 91
Loh, John M., 55

MX missile, 146, 160
Mahler, Thomas W., Jr., 97
Maintenance costs, 39, 95–97
Maintenance of equipment, 58, 90, 99–100, 140, 167
Management, 12, 17, 34, 88, 196. See also Bureaucracy; Micromanagement; Program management
Marine Corps, 118, 128
Market size, 70, 144, 145–146, 150, 151, 152, 159, 162
Material Requirements Planning system, 180–182, 183–184, 203
Material substitution, 85, 93
Maverick missile, 116, 149–152, 153, 199
McDonnell, Sanford N., 9
McDonnell Douglas Corporation, 44, 111, 114, 115, 116, 138, 168
McMillin, Thomas M., 149, 151
McNamara, Robert Strange, 5–6, 9, 108, 113, 118, 120, 123–124, 126–127, 128; and Congress, 49, 59
Media, 1, 87, 88–89, 102, 161, 169
Meese, Edwin, 173
Meyer, Kenneth V., 17, 193
Micromanagement, 49, 54–57, 58–59, 116, 121, 128, 133, 168–169, 192–196, 208–209; criticism of, 1–2, 3, 8, 13, 79–84, 143–144, 167, 191, 200–201. See also Decision making
Midgetman (missile), 42
Milestones (program stages), 26–27, 29, 33, 147
Military Airlift Command (air force), 22, 109
Military-industrial complex, 2, 13–17, 186, 193
Mischarging on contracts, 10, 114–115, 173, 176, 181, 183
Missile Command (army), 106
Missiles, 35, 41–42, 106, 131, 134–135. See also specific missiles, e.g. Maverick missile
Mission need statement, 26
Mission of military, 50, 121–122, 124, 127
Modernization of equipment, 40, 42, 59, 63, 160, 161, 206
Modification of equipment, 36, 139; costs, 92, 94–97, 98, 100–101, 120, 153
Monahan, George L., Jr., 99
Mott, Stewart, 88

Mullins, James P., 14

NATO. *See* North Atlantic Treaty Organization
National Aeronautics and Space Administration (NASA), 45, 172–173
National security, 56, 160, 162, 177, 178, 192, 193. *See also* Defense policy
National Security Council, 53, 194–195
National Security Division Directives, 51
Navy, 30, 76, 90; mission, 50; procurement system, 75, 83, 84, 106, 122–123, 150, 188; support equipment contracts, 100–101; weapons programs, 41, 61, 82–83, 118–120, 126, 132, 138, 166
Neumann, Gerhard, 112–113
Nixon administration, 59
North, Ollie, 53
North Atlantic Treaty Organization (NATO), 121–123
Northrop Corporation, 71–72, 136, 137, 138, 146, 155, 164, 165, 177
Nuclear weapons, 12, 34, 119, 146
Nunn, Sam, 115

Office of Defense Research and Engineering, 6–7, 24
Office of Management and Budget, 47, 51
Operational systems development. *See* Modification of equipment
Operations costs, 35, 39, 42–43, 90–91, 96, 144–145, 158, 162
Overhead costs, 36, 79, 92, 95, 96, 100, 152
Overmanagement. *See* Micromanagement
Oversight: of military, 15, 28, 54; of programs, 56–57, 81–82, 167, 169, 176–178, 187
Owens, Wayne, 115–116

P-80 (fighter), 166
Packard, David, 8, 26, 133, 208
Packard Commission, 19–20, 21, 50–51, 54, 56–57, 87, 172, 185; criticism of, 129, 192, 195; recommendations by, 8–9, 30, 105, 106, 129, 147–148, 176–177, 196; results of, 27, 29, 79, 130, 141, 203
Paisley, Melvyn, 175
Paperwork, 4, 12, 16, 184, 194, 196, 200–201; costs of, 3, 85, 95
Peacekeeper. *See* MX missile
Pelehach, Mike, 135
Pentagon. *See* Defense Department

Perception: of contractors, 12–13, 87, 199–202, 204; of defense, 10, 12, 20; of procurement system, 1–2, 3, 61, 77, 107–108, 185, 196–199, 208
Performance of equipment. *See* Capabilities of equipment
Perry, William, 121
Phases (program stages), 26
Phoenix missile, 82–83, 134
Polaris missile, 166
Prather, Gerald L., 5
Pratt & Whitney Aircraft Group, 88–89, 101, 102, 112, 136, 174
Pre-Planned Product Improvement (P3I), 139
President's Commission on Defense Management. *See* Packard Commission
Prices of equipment, 42, 75, 88–89, 92, 95–98, 105–106, 114–115, 151
Procurement: costs of, 36–37, 39, 41–42, 43–44, 78–79. *See also* Budget
Procurement system, 1, 60; problems with, 3–4, 191–192, 200–201, 208–209
Production, 26, 35, 144, 150. *See also* Delivery schedule; Market size
Production stability, 144, 145–146, 147, 151, 152
Productivity, 84
Profit 13, 44, 55, 92, 96, 139, 180; regulation of, 73–74, 75–77, 181, 201
Program element monitor, 41
Program management, 25–29, 128, 141, 149, 156, 165–167, 179, 192, 193–194; external control of, 5, 49, 143–144, 185, 188
Program managers, 2–3, 4, 17, 121, 129, 189, 204; control by, 142, 166, 188; responsibilities of, 6, 25, 29, 59, 128, 167–168, 169
Program Objectives Memorandum (POM), 39–40
Project for Military Procurement, 87, 88
Propulsion Laboratory (air force), 25
Prototypes, 26, 128, 130–133, 135–140, 141, 153, 166, 178, 196
Pryor, David, 208
Provisioning, 87. *See also* Maintenance of equipment; Spare parts; Support equipment

Quality control, 80–81, 83–84, 140, 188; problems with, 82–83, 85, 146, 165, 176; responsibility for, 65, 92, 93, 165, 201

RCA American Communications, Inc., 6
Radar systems, 25, 61–62, 158, 203
Rand Corporation, 147
Rasor, Dina, 87
Raytheon Company, 150, 151, 175
Reagan, Ronald, 8, 59, 145, 155–156, 162; defense policy, 88, 146, 155–156, 159–160, 202
Reagan administration, 91, 122, 124, 126, 127, 171, 174, 195, 207; and Congress, 52, 202–203; criticism of, 2, 175, 177
Realism: about costs, 34, 46, 47, 74, 125, 147, 148; in requirements, 20, 30–31, 162
Red tape. See Paperwork
Reform proposals, 4, 5–7, 8, 205–209. See also Packard Commission
Regulations, 75–76, 78, 102, 168, 181, 204, 206; problems with, 1, 4, 17, 78–84, 184
Reprogramming, 41, 45
Requirements, 19–21, 22, 23, 109, 180–182; of weapons systems, 109–110, 124, 127, 133, 144, 152, 167
Research and development, 29–30, 34–35, 42, 124; costs, 35–36, 68, 203; funding for, 126–127, 136–137. See also Technology development
Review of programs, 27, 28, 29, 41, 51, 83, 144, 176, 179. See also Auditing of contractors
Rich, Ben R., 167
Risk: in contracts, 55, 70, 71–72, 74, 108–109, 111, 114, 116, 152; in technology development, 132, 147, 150, 157, 160, 197
Rockwell International Corporation, 156
Russ, Robert, 94
Russell, Richard, 112, 115

SR-71 reconnaissance aircraft, 164, 166, 167
SRAM 2 (missile), 9
Second sourcing, 150–152
Secrecy, 162–164. See also Black programs
Secretary of defense, 23–24, 26, 27, 28, 79, 114, 119, 195–196, 206
Senate Armed Services Committee, 54, 56, 112
Senate Committee on Government Operations, 121
Senate committees, 2, 10
Sergeant York antiaircraft gun, 173
Sherick, Joseph, 88, 89
Shultz, George P., 53, 195

Skantze, Lawrence A., 157–158, 159, 160, 169, 177
Skurla, George, 101
Smith, Harry, 99–100
Sole source (contractor), 67, 105, 108, 116. See also Competition for contracts
Soviet Union: defenses, 156, 161, 163–164; military threat by, 6, 34, 59, 133, 146, 162, 168, 202
Spangenberg, George, 137
Spare parts, 9, 87, 89, 90–92, 100–103, 162, 167
Specifications, 80, 84–85, 110–111, 112–113, 157, 200
Standardization, 106, 118, 121–123, 151
Standards, 80, 83–84, 95, 97, 123, 181
Star Wars. See Strategic Defense Initiative
State Department, 128
Stealth bomber, 155–156, 160, 161, 162, 164–165, 168, 169, 177
Strategic Air Command (air force), 22, 119, 160–162
Strategic Defense Initiative, 25, 53
Stretch-outs (in production), 145–146, 147, 158
Sundstrand Corporation, 183
Support equipment, 87, 89, 90, 93, 94–101, 102–103
Symington, Stuart, 168
System concept, 127
System Program Office (SPO), 25, 142
Systems Command (air force), 24–25, 90–91, 143, 176, 179, 199

T-33 (trainer), 166
T-38 (trainer), 71–72, 136
T-46 (trainer), 178–180
TFX (fighter), 5, 118–121, 126, 127, 128, 175
TRW Inc., 176
Tactical Air Command (air force), 22, 118–119
Taft, William H., IV, 61, 177–178, 195
Tankers, 95–96
Technical innovation, 29–30, 127, 165–166
Technical uncertainty, 39, 45–46, 109, 129–130, 144, 146–147, 153, 169
Technology development, 26–27, 108, 124, 130–133, 146, 147–148, 160, 197; costs of, 30–31, 33, 35–36, 39; time involved, 7, 8, 157. See also Prototypes
Thayer, Paul, 60–61
Thurman, William E., 193, 199
Tigershark. See F-20 (fighter)
Titan 3 space-launch vehicle, 65

Tomcat. *See* F-14 (fighter)
Tooling, 35, 42, 130, 142
Total-package procurement, 107–117, 124, 141, 149–152, 196
Trade, 101, 137, 140, 144
Tradeoff studies, 42–43, 51. *See also* Cost-effectiveness; Cost-performance tradeoffs
Trident II (missile), 41, 61
Truman administration, 204

U-2 (airplane), 62, 164, 166–167
Underbidding of contracts, 14, 34, 107, 108, 125
Unit costs, 42, 43, 139–140, 144, 145, 159, 165
United Technologies Corporation, 175

VanderSchaaf, Derek J., 89
Vietnam War, 40, 44, 49, 132

Warranties, 57–59, 112
Waste in procurement, 88, 90, 94–101, 102–103, 205
Weapons Acquisition Process, The, 142
Weinberger, Caspar, 28, 59–60, 61, 88, 100, 160, 162, 163, 194, 206
Westinghouse (corporation), 99–100
Whistle-blowing, 177
Willoughby, Willis J., 59, 80–81, 82–83, 200
Woodward, Harper, 125
World War II, 10–11, 117, 150
Wright-Patterson Air Force Base, 11–12, 24–25, 103, 199

YF-17 (fighter), 136–137, 138, 140

Zussman, Arthur L., 149

About the Author

As a Navy fighter-bomber pilot in World War II Bill Gregory first encountered the quirks of the military acquisition system. The supply office always seemed to be closed when he tried to draw or turn in personal flight gear. Later as a newspaperman at the *Kansas City Star* in his home town and during thirty subsequent years as an editor and writer with *Aviation Week & Space Technology* magazine, he watched reforms complicate military buying to the point of disarray. Now he and his wife, Virginia, live near Tucson, Arizona, where he contributes to newspapers and magazines and dabbles in arid lands mineralogy and plant life.